the
Doubtful
Gift

Strategies for Educating Gifted Children
in the Regular Classroom

the
Doubtful
Gift

Strategies for Educating Gifted Children in the Regular Classroom

Ken W. McCluskey
and Keith D. Walker

Ronald P. Frye & Company, Publishers
Kingston, Canada

ISBN 0 919741 64 9

Cover by June Ricklefs

Printed and bound in Canada

To Our Families

Acknowledgements

Any project that takes more than eleven years to complete will, almost by definition, have a lot of changes occurring in and around it. Certainly, since so much time has flown by from inception to completion, we are indebted to a number of people from different "eras" for their help and support. The writing of this book has gone through the administration of three superintendents to whom we would like to express our thanks: Arnold Minish, Bill Regehr, and Ken Halldorson. All have provided very real encouragement and tangible resources to back it up.

We also feel the need to mention our own Lord Selkirk School Division #11 (Selkirk, Manitoba, Canada) — a place where a lot of good people are making a lot of good things happen. Lord Selkirk has a reputation for care and excellence with good reason; a succession of supportive teachers, principals, superintendents, and board members have allowed us the freedom to try new things and the time to document the results. Our co-workers at the Human Resource Centre — now virtually a family — have been an inspiration over the years. They have made the H.R.C. a wonderful place to work.

Without doubt, we must acknowledge the contributions of three "secretaries", who became more like co-authors as time went by. Back in 1975–76, Judy Desmet helped us prepare our first manuscript, and her positive attitude and enthusiasm made our vision of "The Doubtful Gift" seem possible, even in those long past "germ-of-idea" days. Later, Marilyn Souter took over work on the manuscript, and her happy efficiency really got us moving. Most recently, we have become tremendously indebted to our own Secretary/Librarian, Nadine Jenkins, who has done all kinds of work and suffered through years of changing ideas and revisions. It is a blessing to have an innovative educator as secretary, for Nadine was able to input with suggestions, criticisms (plenty of those), and creative ideas.

One change that occurred before the book went to press should not have happened. We started out writing together, but last summer Keith Walker lost a short but courageous battle with cancer, leaving me — with a great sense of personal loss — to finish up alone. With Keith's passing, the province of Manitoba, Canada, has been deprived of a dynamic and powerful educator. The last conversation he and I had was about "The Doubtful Gift". Fighting off the effects of morphine, Keith asked me to put in the acknowledgements that — as always — his work on the book had been done for Marge and "the boys", Duane and Scott. He wanted them to know his last thoughts were of them. So, to you Marge, Duane and Scott, with love from Keith.

I would personally like to acknowledge my parents, the major factor in my learning. I am what I am because of them (I can almost see them cringe with embarrassment). Sister Jill and I were given absolutely gifted childhoods: encouragement, not pressure; support, not demands; and happiness, not problems. Be it school, sports, work, or whatever, Mom and Dad were (and still are) there. I know if I try to be just like them, I can't go too far wrong.

In addition, I have to thank the ones who make it all worthwhile, Andrea, Christopher, and Amber. Andy has made me terribly happy; it is nice having someone who works along with you day after day. At this very moment, she is upstairs finishing up the indices as I struggle to meet the last deadline for this book. We are a good team. The first book off the presses goes to Andy, the person who is first in my heart.

Christopher is at the betwixt and between stage, somewhere between noticing girls and secretly still wanting parental "huggie-wuggies". Amber-Lee — a going concern — will always be a "daddy's girl". Andy and the kids have been so supportive through this final period of suffering. Now the book is all done, and we can get back to bike rides, picnics, soccer, squash, travel, and pancake breakfasts. Starting tomorrow!

Ken McCluskey

Contents

1. **Giftedness: What is it?**   *1*
   A Definition   *1*
   Characteristics of the Gifted   *4*
   Why Are They Gifted?   *8*
   Problems of the Gifted   *11*
   School and the Gifted Child   *13*
   Summation   *17*

2. **The Gifted: Who are they?**   *19*
   Two Paths of Giftedness   *19*
   A Poor Track Record   *21*
   Intelligence Testing   *24*
   Creativity Tests   *28*
   Measures of Achievement   *29*
   Do We Really Need All These Tests?   *30*
   In-School Testing   *34*
   More Subjective Measures   *36*
   Other Forms of Nomination   *44*
   Summation   *46*

3. **The Gifted: Once you've found them, what do you do with them?** *49*
   A Brief History of Gifted Education   *49*
   Unequal Education for the Gifted   *52*
   Acceleration   *54*
   Ability Grouping   *57*
   Segregation   *59*
   Integrated Approach   *67*
   Partial Pullout   *71*
   Summation   *72*

4. **Teachers and Parents of the Gifted**   *75*
   Who Should Teach the Gifted?   *75*
   Characteristics of Successful Teachers of
      the Gifted   *78*
   What Can Parents Do?   *86*
   Summation   *91*

5. **Establishing a School-Based Program**   *93*
   Getting Things Going   *93*
   Factors in Setting Up a School-Based Program   *95*
   Summation   *103*

6. **Programming for the Gifted**   *105*
   A Schematic Working Model   *105*
   Alternative Learning Environments   *110*
   Productive Thought and Problem Solving   *121*
   Creativity   *139*
   Questioning   *151*
   Classroom Organization   *157*
   Positive Self-Image   *169*
   Summation   *173*

   References   *175*

   Name Index   *189*

   Subject Index   *193*

1

Giftedness: what is it?

A Definition

All too frequently, articles and books on "the gifted child" begin with a one sentence definition attempting to specify just what exactly giftedness is. While they may have their value, it is singularly unfortunate that such oversimplified definitions are carelessly bandied about by laymen and educators alike. A description of giftedness simply cannot be reduced to one sentence; there is a certain uniqueness about the phenomenon that defies analysis and renders any short definition somewhat sterile.

In order to get an overall picture of the area, then, it is perhaps most realistic to take a broad (and in some senses, an untidy and unsatisfying) look at giftedness in general. Rather than imposing a single arbitrary definition of the concept, we will offer up some of the more common ones for discussion and evaluation, along with a few off-the-cuff remarks of our own. While this approach may not arm the reader with neat catch phrases with which to describe giftedness in children, it should serve to communicate a feeling for and an awareness of the complexity of the issues at hand.

Let us say at the outset that we are decidedly out of sympathy with definitions which state that a gifted child is one who scores "at the 98th percentile or above on a full scale individual intelligence test" or who falls in "the top five (or whatever) percent of the school population" (cf.

Hersom, 1962). Such definitions are clearly narrow, limiting, and dogmatic, in that they do not allow for: 1) exceptional performance outside of school and testing situations; 2) error in IQ results due to cultural, environmental, and experiential variables; 3) underachieving gifted students who, for one reason or another, perform below potential on tests and in school; and 4) other important factors such as maturation, motivation, drive, and interest (Whipple, 1958).

Witty (1959) has come up with a much more viable, albeit nonspecific, definition of giftedness. He sees the gifted as those "whose performance in any valuable line of human activity is consistently or repeatedly remarkable". This definition is worthwhile precisely because it is loose and nonspecific enough to encompass various types of giftedness in various types of human endeavour. Many other investigators, as well, emphasize the broad nature of the concept. While insisting that we all possess certain natural gifts and creativity, they acknowledge an elite higher order of giftedness in individuals with truly unique intellectual, vocational, athletic, artistic, or social leadership capabilities.

Another solid definition of giftedness, which attempts to summarize major conclusions and generalizations emerging from the literature, has been proposed by Renzulli (1978). In his words:

"Giftedness consists of an interaction among three basic clusters of human traits — these clusters being above average general abilities, high levels of task commitment, and high levels of creativity. Gifted and talented children are those possessing or capable of developing this composite set of traits and applying them to any potentially valuable area of human performance. Children who manifest or are capable of developing an interaction among the three clusters require a wide variety of educational opportunities and services that are not ordinarily provided through regular instructional programs."

Adapting from the work of Rice (1970) and Gold (1965), Irv Sato — Director of the National Leadership Training Institute for the Gifted and the Talented — stresses that individuals can have extraordinary talent in one or more areas while not possessing it in others. He speaks of various talent areas, including:

1 kinesthetic: athletic, ballet, and other activities requiring fine or gross motor skill;
2 psychosocial: leadership ability, social or political acumen, and the like;
3 creativity: originality and vitality of thought in almost any field (music, art, science, etc.);

4 academic: the ability to acquire and apply knowledge in the more traditional, academic sense.

Sato emphasizes his point by way of anecdotal example. To illustrate, if you were about to undergo open heart surgery, you would undoubtedly appreciate having a doctor well-versed (preferably gifted) in the academic ins-and-outs of the working of the heart muscle. However, academic knowledge alone would not be enough — you would like your surgeon to demonstrate highly developed kinesthetic abilities during the actual operation. No doubt, you would find yourself less concerned with psychosocial and creative abilities in this case. As a matter of fact, you would probably choose a staid, conservative surgeon over a creative one who had come up with the brilliantly original notion of moving your heart valves to and fro to see if they would continue to operate in different positions.

The point is, of course, that there are many kinds of giftedness. As Taylor (1968, 1985) highlights via his Multiple Talent Approach and Talent Totem Poles, people can be gifted in a variety of ways. In any school system, there are many differently "constructed" students. Who is the more gifted: the exceptional athlete or the oddball mathematician who continually trips over beams of light shining in through the classroom window? (Believe it or not, this is a real-life example — we have seen a "light tripper" in action in our own district.)

Another "disabled" grade one youngster we know couldn't even begin to print his name on his own. The teacher knew the youngster couldn't handle this particular task, yet the boy always managed to have it done perfectly whenever papers were collected for marking. It was clear the boy was copying, yet neither the teacher nor anybody else could catch him . . . he was an absolutely gifted copier! (We finally nabbed the little guy when he inadvertently copied a classmate's name on the top of his own paper.) Despite his problems, the boy in question possessed a valuable skill.

Essentially, what we are saying is that people are not all the same; they have different kinds of abilities. That is, there are many forms of "giftedness". No person — not even a gifted one — can have equal abilities in all areas. Keeping this fact in mind, the United States Office of Education has proposed a useful working definition, wherein a gifted child is considered to be one:

"(1) possessing demonstrated or potential intellectual, creative, or specific academic abilities, or leadership capability, or talent in the performing or visual arts, and (2) needing differentiated education or services beyond those being provided by the regular school system to the average student in order to realize these potentialities" (National Archives, 1976).

An important aspect of this definition is that it recognizes that the gifted require special help. The feeling has existed, especially in education, that it is a waste of time and effort to help gifted children who have tremendous natural advantages over others in the system and who, supposedly, can manage well enough on their own. This type of laissez-faire — or, as we term it, "lazy-unfair" — attitude is far from being a healthy one (Walker & McCluskey, 1981a). Gifted children do not necessarily possess a set of cut-and-dried academic abilities that grow of their own accord, but rather a highly complex, vague, and idiosyncratic assortment of skills and attitudes that must be well-nurtured and judiciously developed (cf. Burroughs, 1977).

As others have noted, a young plant will wither and die if left unattended, and a human limb will atrophy and become useless if kept permanently immobile. A gifted individual must work to maintain his gift at peak levels; a première ballerina, for example, does not remain première for very long if she stops practicing. In the same fashion, a talented child must be challenged and stimulated if he is to make the best use of his gift and develop to his fullest potential. In essence, gifted children are unique and "abnormal" (in the sense of being away from the norm) and, as such, need considerable specialized attention at home and at school.

Also, however, there is a danger of glorifying things too much and seeing the "gifted" as mythical, god-like creatures. This sort of view can be counterproductive in some ways, and cause us to forget that people are people. Those in education have a responsibility to work with — not stand in awe of — gifted students. Further, there is no reason why either the super-gifted or the mentally handicapped should receive all the attention at the expense of the more numerous bright, solid, students who could also use a bit of extra help. We prefer to view "gifted" children not as "far-out" geniuses, but simply as "sharp" individuals who have the potential to benefit from enrichment, stimulation, and something "more" to their school experiences.

Characteristics of the Gifted

Some of the pioneers in the area studied and made inferences about giftedness by using the somewhat questionable technique of estimating the IQs of great men of the past. For example, an attempt was made to discover at what ages in their childhoods prominent historical figures had begun to read, use certain words, solve arithmetic problems, compose tunes, and so on. Where such biographical data were available, it was possible to match this information against Stanford-Binet standards and derive a rough IQ score. Using this procedure, the IQs of various eminent men have been estimated as follows: Charles Dickens, 145; Benjamin Franklin, 145; George Frederick Handel, 145; Thomas Jefferson, 145; Rene Descartes, 150; Wolfgang Amadeus Mozart, 150; Alfred Tennyson, 155; John Quincy Adams, 165; Johann Wolfgang von Goethe, 185; Francis Galton, 200 (cf. Cox, 1926).

While this type of estimation is of limited value and no doubt inaccurate in many respects, it is nevertheless interesting in that it highlights one important point. Basically, it seems that if gifted individuals channel their abilities appropriately, they are capable of making a tremendous contribution to society and, in effect, even changing the course of history.

A more meaningful study of the problem, and one that has guided techniques for identifying gifted children over the years, was undertaken by Louis M. Terman, the originator of the Stanford-Binet Intelligence Scale (Terman, 1925; Terman & Oden, 1947, 1959). After testing literally thousands of subjects, Terman and his co-workers identified approximately 1500 gifted children. (The children were selected solely on the basis of individual intelligence test scores, such that any child with an IQ of 140 or higher was considered to be gifted.)

Terman's detailed longitudinal studies followed the progress of these gifted individuals right into adulthood. Perhaps the major contribution of his work is that he showed that giftedness tends to perseverate. To illustrate, of the 700 or so subjects who could be contacted after 25 years, "about 150 were very successful judged by such criteria as (1) being listed in *Who's Who* or *American Men of Science,* (2) holding responsible managerial positions, or (3) receiving recognition for outstanding intellectual or professional achievement" (cf. Morgan & King, 1971).

The majority of the others in the gifted group, while not reaching the heights attained by the most outstanding individuals, were still much more successful than the average person of "normal" intelligence. For the most part, the gifted children in Terman's sample went on to make significant social and intellectual contributions once they reached adulthood.

Terman's (1925) work went a long way towards dispelling the myth that the gifted are unhealthy and socially maladjusted; the popular notion that gifted individuals were all lanky, absent-minded, briefcase-carrying misfits with horn-rimmed glasses, who could accomplish any number of amazing things (except function "normally"), was put to rest. On the contrary, gifted children in his sample were found to be above average in height, weight, and general appearance, and to possess a strong capacity for leadership.

Carroll and Laming (1974), in a review of the work carried out in the United States from 1962–1971, have outlined the characteristics ascribed to gifted children in more detail. Another list summarizing the characteristics of the gifted was offered by Miriam Goldberg at the 1975 Kentucky State Conference on Gifted and Talented Children and Youth. Really, there are all sorts of these lists around, and often they contain arbitrary, dogmatic generalizations that should not be taken at face value. In many ways, it is almost pointless to try to delineate a list of characteristics that gifted individuals supposedly possess. Obviously, the gifted come in all shapes and sizes: they can be thin, fat, distinguished, nondescript, rich, or poor. Still, many researchers in the area have gone to a great deal of trouble to develop lists of identifying characteristics. In deference to their work, and since such lists at least serve to give a perspective and an "introduction" to giftedness as it were, we felt it might be helpful to borrow from Carroll and Laming, Goldberg, and others in an attempt to put together a down-to-earth list of our own. Modifying, adapting, and extending earlier work to meet our specific needs, then, we came up with the following list.

1 The gifted tend to walk and talk earlier than other children.
2 They develop their cognitive and basic learning skills early; they possess good memories.
3 They have special talents in one or more areas, such as reading, writing, mathematics, science, mechanics, art, music, etc.
4 Gifted children are frequently curious; they have a variety of interests and hobbies.
5 They have a creative "style" and come up with work that has freshness and vitality about it — often creating unique products.
6 They tend to deal at a high level of abstraction, and have the ability to see relationships, evaluate ideas, and think critically.
7 The gifted are often interested in philosophical questions (e.g.: "Is there a God?", "Is the universe infinite?", "What is the meaning of life?").
8 Gifted children are not always satisfied with rules and regulations; they want to know "why".

9 They frequently have a unique sense of humour, often with a sarcastic bite to it.

10 They sometimes show well-developed leadership skills.

11 They tend to seek challenges.

12 The gifted can be quite anxious about peer relations. Since they are "different", it is not unusual for extra-bright children to run into various "social" problems.

13 They are frequently single-minded in pursuit of that which captures their interest and are sometimes difficult to redirect into other activities.

There is no doubt, as Terman emphasizes, that giftedness can be something very positive. However, many writers — ourselves included — feel that an overly optimistic view of giftedness may cause us to ignore the other side of the coin. Things are often not quite as rosy for the gifted as Terman and others make them out to be. In any case, this issue will be raised again, with a vengeance, somewhat later in this chapter.

Terman found — and at first this aspect of his research engendered little argument — that the greatest number of gifted children came from the upper socioeconomic classes. That is, while approximately half of the children in his gifted sample were from upper business-class homes and a third from homes of professional people, only about seven percent came from lower-class families. Another massive longitudinal study lends support to this finding. Brown, Nichols, and Kennedy (1975) followed more than 26,000 children from the prenatal period to the age of four. When, at this point in time, the children were given the Stanford-Binet Scale, it was found that socioeconomic status (along with the related variable of maternal education) was the factor affecting IQ scores to the greatest extent.

On the other hand, Hauck and Freehill (1972) point out that many gifted children have been found in unlikely and disadvantaged environments. Lyon (1973), going a step further, insists that there are as many gifted children in the ghettos as there are in upper middle-class suburbs. Whatever the actual statistical breakdown may be, it is important not to lose sight of Lyon's humanistic belief that: "Intelligence knows no income levels, it knows no race, it knows no socioeconomic level".

Other aspects of family life, aside from socioeconomic status, have been researched extensively. It has been found, for example, that a disproportionately large number of gifted children are first born, and that they often have unusually intense (though not necessarily positive) relationships with other family members (cf. Hauck & Freehill, 1972). As well, the family has been shown to exert a strong influence in directing the work and careers of gifted individuals (Goertzel & Goertzel, 1962).

For the purposes of the present discussion, it is unnecessary to pour out this type of qualitative and quantitative information (regarding socio-economic status, birth order, family background, etc.) ad infinitum. A number of sources are available that go into various aspects of giftedness in more detail (Barbe & Renzulli, 1975; Burt, 1975; Dennis & Dennis, 1976; Freeman, 1979; Gallagher, 1975; Gowan & Torrance, 1971; Keating, 1976; Khatena, 1978; Maker, 1982; Newland, 1976; Passow, 1979; Stanley, George, & Solano, 1977, 1978; Tannenbaum, 1983; Taylor & Getzels, 1975; Torrance, 1962; Vernon, 1970; Vernon, Adamson, & Vernon, 1977; Whitmore, 1980). Once again, the point is that giftedness is an involved and multi-faceted phenomenon, and that many factors play a part in its development. Incidentally, we should note here that we have no desire to turn this work into a "scholarly" opus or tome. In the interests of parsimony, many important references do not appear. For those who may be interested, an updated, annotated bibliography of most of the works on giftedness with which we are familiar is available elsewhere (Walker & McCluskey, 1985).

Why Are They Gifted?

Researchers in the area of giftedness cannot help but find themselves caught up in the throes of the nature-nurture controversy which pervades academic psychology and related fields (cf. Hollingworth, 1929; Tobias, 1974). On the one hand, certain investigators insist that mental ability is due solely to genetic factors (heredity). In contrast, however, other theorists hold that mental capacity is purely the result of learning (environment). In their view, parents can raise their children's intelligence simply by providing a more stimulating environment for them.

The Nature Position

Galton (1870) was among the first to emphasize the hereditary nature of genius. Since his time, innumerable others have subscribed to the belief that genetic factors are everything and that heredity is the overpowering force in the creation of intellect (cf. Kennedy, 1971; Horowitz & Paden, 1973).

Some of the best support for the heredity position has come from studies involving identical and fraternal twins living together in a similar environment or living apart under totally different environmental conditions. The basic rationale underlying these twin studies is that if heredity is a major factor in the "creation" of intelligence, people's mental ability should be more similar the greater the degree of genetic relationship. And indeed, numerous studies have shown that identical twins, regardless of whether they were reared apart or together, possessed more similar IQs than fraternal (nonidentical) twins brought up together (cf. Burt, 1958; Nichols, 1965; Shields, 1962). Erlenmeyer-Kimling and Jarvik (1963), in a comprehensive review of the literature, note that twin studies in general support the nature position, in that "a marked trend is seen toward an increasing degree of intellectual resemblance in direct proportion to an increasing degree of genetic relationship, regardless of environmental communality".

As Syphers (1972) has noted, the feeling of adherents of the genetic viewpoint is summed up quite nicely by the renowned Spanish University of Salamanca. The motto of this venerable institution reads: "What nature does not give, Salamanca cannot supply".

The Nurture Position

At the other extreme, we have the environmentalist stance that experience is the central factor in the development of intelligence and giftedness. Strang's (1955) argument represents this position well: she feels that most children placed in the gifted category in schools are favoured with fortunate childhoods, exceptional family backgrounds, and good community environments which foster their intellectual growth. The combination of these factors supposedly makes possible the development of their intellectual talents and abilities.

Support for the environmentalist view can be drawn from the Iowa studies of the 1940s (Skodak & Skeels, 1949; Skeels & Harms, 1948; Wellman, 1939), which demonstrate convincingly that mental ability can be modified through manipulation of environmental variables. For example, Asbell, in the "Case of the Wandering IQ's", describes how Skodak and Skeels raised the intellectual ability of children by moving them from deprived to enriched environments (cf. Kennedy, 1971). In their initial investigation, Skodak and Skeels observed two infant girls (aged thirteen and sixteen months) who had been transferred from an orphanage to a hospital for the mentally retarded. In the orphanage (where they were more or less ignored), the children's IQs were 46 and 35 respectively (that is, in the defective range). In the mental institution, however, retarded women more or less "adopted" the children and lavished attention and affection upon them. Within six months, the girls' emotional health had improved markedly, and their IQs had risen to 77 and 87. In another year, the IQs rose yet again to 100 and 88.

Intrigued by the powerful effects of simple TLC (tender-loving-care), Skodak and Skeels undertook a more comprehensive longitudinal study (cf. Skeels, 1966). They sent thirteen additional children from the orphanage to live with adult retardates, and left a control group of twelve children behind. After three years, the children in the orphanage control group had IQs which had, on the average, fallen into the deficient range, while the mean IQ of the transferred children had risen from 64.3 to 91.8 (into the normal range). Even after a period of twenty years had elapsed, the individuals who had been in the orphanage control group were still functioning at the defective level, while the ones who had been given retarded foster mothers continued to function normally.

The Middle-of-the-Road Position

One of the reasons that the heredity-environment dispute is so intense is that advocates of both the nature and the nurture positions can make very strong cases for their respective viewpoints. Yet, to us, it is a pointless argument in many ways. Heredity and environment are both inextricably involved in the creation of intelligence, for even in the womb, you cannot have one without the other. As Jersild (1968) puts it: "Genetic and environmental factors that shape the course of a child's development start to work the moment he is conceived".

Rather than going to extremes, many contemporary researchers tend to take a more sensible middle-of-the-road approach to the situation. While they feel that we are born with certain inherited potentials, they have faith in change through enriched experience. In other words, since the two cannot possibly be separated, heredity and environment are considered to be of equal importance. In Roberts' (1967) words: "The child, and finally the adult, is what he is at any given time because of the hereditary constitution which he originally received and the nature of the environment in which he has lived up to that time". In a sense, then, what we are is 100 percent the result of heredity and 100 percent the result of environment; the two are inseparable.

As educators, however, we much prefer that teachers — if they must choose one camp or the other — take the environmentalist position. There is really not much teachers can do about heredity — genes are genes! However, regardless of what we have to work with at the start, we can intervene and enrich a student's environment in many ways. In short, we cannot do anything about heredity, but we can, and should, modify and improve environmental conditions as much as possible.

Problems of the Gifted

As mentioned previously, Terman (Terman & Oden, 1947, 1959) held a positive view of giftedness and demonstrated that it perseverates over time. However, not all investigators share Terman's optimism. Strang (1951) felt that lack of opportunity, financial difficulties, parental pressure or neglect, and poor instruction in study and work habits are frequently causes of maladjustment in gifted children. She went on to point out that many gifted youths fail to develop to their full potentials merely because, in an effort to be like their peers, they hesitate to use their true capabilities. Carlson (1947) believed that a large number of gifted children grow up to become emotionally immature, ineffectual, and socially useless members of society. And Terman himself found that a certain proportion of gifted individuals were far from making their mark in the world, with some even developing emotional problems and ending up as vocational misfits or criminals. In one case study, Hauck and Freehill analyzed the behaviour of a gifted youth who — like so many others — turned to delinquency and crime. The individual in question is now confined to a maximum security prison, his "potential unfulfilled . . . his loss, our loss" (Hauck & Freehill, 1972).

It is essential to recognize that gifted people are not perfect, and that they often have more than their share of problems. Syphers (1972) offers a list — originally drawn up by May V. Seagoe — of characteristics of gifted children, in which a positive trait is always coupled with a negative one. While such a list might be overly generalized and arbitrary in many ways, it certainly illustrates how giftedness can be a double-edged sword. Therefore, we decided to follow Seagoe's lead and adapted a list to our own setting.

The Two Sides of Giftedness: Common Characteristics of the Gifted

Positive	*Negative*
1 Learning comes easy;	develops a tendency to become careless, lazy, and to omit detail; resists guidance and direction.

2 Abstract reasoning abilities; philosophical outlook;	tendency to pseudo-intellectualize and make excuses; can lose contact with reality.
3 Questioning attitude; critical thinking skills;	impatient and critical of others; being "different" creates problems in peer relationships.
4 Ability to work independently; formulates unique ideas;	can become an elitist, nonconformist; a misfit.
5 Possesses a sense of humour;	can be mischievous or a "pain"; sometimes sarcastic to the point of cruelty.
6 Good memory; strengths in analyzing and synthesizing information;	dislike for routine and drills; unwillingness to get down to task; can easily become bored.
7 Solid task commitment; goal directed;	recalcitrant, stubborn; often refuses to change direction.
8 Has a variety of interests;	sometimes interests take a single, narrow, and inflexible path.
9 Eager, alert; a high energy level;	frustration when things do not go one's own way; gets "turned off" easily.
10 Sensitive, empathic;	fragile ego; extreme sensitivity to criticism.

The positive aspects of giftedness carry with them the threat of the negative; indeed, one of the major conclusions to arise from the 1975 First World Conference on Gifted Children in London was that gifted individuals who are mishandled can become more severe social problems than the mentally deficient. The "lazy-unfair" attitude mentioned in passing earlier — that a gifted child will somehow "make it on his own" — was shot down with a resounding thud. Researchers concluded that the potential of gifted children is in large part wasted, and that, deplorably, the gifted tend on the average to fulfill only fifteen percent of their true capabilities. It was even remarked that a gifted child gone bad may indeed succeed, but at great cost to others. For example, some of the major unsolved crimes throughout history have very likely been committed by gifted individuals; they made it on their own alright, but not precisely in a socially desirable fashion. Certainly, misdirected giftedness can be a very real problem; a normal person who turns to crime may simply be an annoyance, but a gifted criminal can become a major threat to society.

As Rowlands (1974) and Burroughs (1977) both point out, gifted children often face all sorts of problems that people commonly overlook; giftedness can at times be something of a "doubtful gift". By way of example, some parents of gifted children are overprotective (or deferential and afraid of their children's abilities), while others are often overly demanding in that they push their offspring unmercifully (Thom & Newell, 1945). As well, since his peers lack his vocabulary and his insightful way of looking at things, a gifted child often has a difficult time forming meaningful relationships with others (Hersom, 1962; Janos, Fung, & Robinson, 1985). We have found some talented youngsters who go to almost absurd lengths to hide their giftedness in a pathetic attempt not to appear different from their peers. If these children do not receive the affection and stimulation they require, they may react by seeking attention through clowning around and misbehaving, or by becoming apathetic and disinterested. Clearly, the gifted do not always have as easy a time as one might expect; giftedness can sometimes be a curse instead of a blessing. Underachievement is common among the gifted (Whitmore, 1980), loneliness can be a problem (Kaiser & Berndt, 1985), and some gifted students are culturally disadvantaged and discouraged (Fitzgerald, Sato, Wilson, & Weaver, 1975). Interestingly, certain gifted individuals have even been diagnosed as learning disabled (Wolf & Gygi, 1981). The fact that gifted children have special abilities does not make them "untouchable" or unapproachable. They may be bright, but they need warmth, attention, and friendship just as much as other children. Waxing philosophical for a moment, we must remember that a gifted child should always be looked upon as a child first, and as gifted only second.

School and the Gifted Child

Testing gifted children can be quite an experience, to say the least. Not long ago, while assessing an extremely bright kindergarten child, we asked what the alphabet was. If the average kindergarten pupil can tell you that the alphabet is the "ABCs", he is doing not too badly. This little guy, however, proceeded to inform us in no uncertain terms that the alphabet was a series of letters used in combination to form syllables, words, and sentences, and thereby convey meaning. He went on to add that there were 26 letters in all. When praised for his answer he replied, "Thank you very much" in a very matter-of-fact tone, as if his performance was the most natural thing in the world. After the session, we wondered who had tested whom!

We have also had occasion to see another five-year-old kindergarten boy who was referred to us for "disability" and "major behaviour problems" (essentially as a candidate for a "special ed" class). During our testing it did appear initially that the child was having difficulty — he seemed unable to answer any question appropriately. Something in his contemptuous manner, however, caught our attention and encouraged us

to keep on with the session. At times, it was as if the youngster were making mistakes on purpose and, as it turned out, that was precisely what he was doing.

Eventually, the boy began to respond to the odd question correctly, albeit in a slightly off-colour fashion. For example, after "bombing out" on several simple items on the WPPSI (Wechsler Preschool and Primary Scale of Intelligence), he quite unexpectedly took us aback with one of his answers. Specifically, when asked, "Why do we wear clothes?", he responded crudely but succinctly by noting that "We'd freeze our asses off if we didn't!"

Even when we decided to bring out the heavy artillery and switch to the more challenging WISC-R (Wechsler Intelligence Scale for Children – Revised), our foul-mouthed little fellow continued to swear away indiscriminately and make deliberate, diabolically clever errors. Frequently, he would go out of his way insidiously to reverse cause and effect. For example, he responded to the question, "What must you do to make water boil?" by recommending that we "Put hot dogs in it!"

In the end, the boy became less disdainful, even enthused, when the WISC-R items finally began to challenge him. This child, whose reading ability was later found to be at the grade six level, exhibited remarkable knowledge for a pupil his age; he knew that Edison invented the light bulb, that Canada and Mexico border the United States, that silica is the main component used to make glass, that hieroglyphics is a type of ancient Egyptian picture writing, and that Darwin proposed the theory of evolution. He was even able to tell us that turpentine is made from the sap of fir trees (something we had not known — we had never gotten that far on the test before)! When all was said and done, our "disabled" and "emotionally disturbed" child had turned out to be "gifted". At first glance, all this seemed marvellous. After some reflection, however, it became clear that the young fellow might not be all that well off. Obviously, he was not getting along well with his peers, and his parents didn't know quite what to do with him. Understandably enough, he was becoming a behaviour problem because he was extremely bored by kindergarten work designed for the average child. Incidentally, as Hymes and Bullock (1975) note, this problem of boredom comes up repeatedly and is one of the major difficulties teachers of the gifted have to contend with.

In addition to his other problems, this boy's teachers and teachers-to-be were not exactly enthused about having him in their classes. Showing regrettable perspicacity, they most certainly did not think that his presence was going to make their job any easier. One cannot precisely blame them either, for it can be extremely threatening and ego-deflating to try to teach a child whose potential is much greater than your own (Syphers, 1972). No matter which way you looked at it, for a young child about to enter grade one, this boy had quite a few problems ahead of him.

Although it is the responsibility of the school to provide for gifted children of this type, their needs often go unmet. Many districts pour literally millions of dollars into special facilities, materials, and teacher training programs for E.M.H. and T.M.H. (Educable and Trainable Mentally Handicapped) children. And there is often questionable payoff here; you can work for years just trying to get a mentally handicapped youngster to tie his shoelaces. Also, many researchers virtually make their livings by studying mentally deficient youngsters (who are readily accessible, captive subjects who do not know enough to complain). Admittedly, we have to be careful here; we are certainly not advocating taking away from the below-average child. Still, it seems a pity that, while low functioning individuals get all sorts of attention from the school system, so little is done for the many children at the other end of the spectrum who have so much to offer. The bell-shaped, normal curve (that statisticians are so fond of) tells us that there are just as many gifted students in our schools as there are handicapped pupils. By ignoring the needs of these bright children, we are wasting a vast reservoir of human potential.

In education today, there is a clear dearth of information about the problems of being gifted. Where concrete information does exist concerning school and the gifted child, it is often negative. Certain writers have raised questions as to why schools destroy initiative and repress spontaneity (Weir, 1956), fail to distinguish between children with different talents (cf. Hersom, 1962), and, in effect, train exceptional children not to be exceptional (Weir, 1956).

These are very poignant questions indeed. Schools and teachers should be obligated to have something meaningful to offer their gifted pupils. For one thing, teachers interact with their students for about five hours a day, and thus play a central part in their young lives (McCluskey, 1976). Since teachers spend so much time with their charges (putting them, after the parents, in a position to effect the most change in behaviour), they should be obliged to know what to do with a gifted child should they get one.

Yet, within education, interest in giftedness appears to be impermanent and cyclic; hot one moment and cold the next (Adler, 1967). The Russian launching of Sputnik in 1957 was one event that stimulated a search for creative and gifted individuals in America; it was unthinkable that we should fall behind the Soviets. The early programs were pragmatic in the extreme, focusing on identifying the gifted for the benefit of management, industry, and the military. The thrust gradually shifted to the setting up of special school programs for the gifted, but — despite periods of revived interest — overall support has been inconsistent at best.

It is not easy to accommodate a gifted child in today's school system. Nonetheless, it behooves school authorities to face any problems (and there are a multiplicity of them) vis-à-vis. A gifted child with a less than ideal home life needs all the help he can get from the school. In fact, according to Witty and Bloom (1955), even an exceptional child who is fortunate enough to have a stimulating home environment "needs the help of the school in exploring and enriching his interests in developing skills and aptitudes". We need to motivate our gifted students, for if talented children are challenged appropriately in school, their latent abilities are likely to emerge to their fullest potential (Goldberg, 1958).

Summation

Giftedness is, beyond a doubt, a vague and intangible concept. Extrabright children certainly cannot be lumped together into one category and arbitrarily labelled "gifted". Indeed, there are many and varied types of giftedness and, in a very real sense, each gifted child is unique. Be that as it may, certain children — due to an interaction of inherited and environmental factors — have special abilities in various areas of human endeavour. Such abilities do not just appear in full-blown form — they must be carefully nurtured if they are to develop to their fullest potential. If gifted children receive the understanding, encouragement, stimulation, and individualized attention that they need, they are capable of making a tremendous contribution to society once they reach adulthood.

All too frequently, however, gifted children are virtually ignored. While millions of dollars are being poured into programs for the mentally handicapped, very often nothing is done for the large numbers of bright children at the other end of the spectrum. The First World Conference on Gifted Children in London made it abundantly clear how much human potential is being wasted by our neglect of the gifted.

Handling the extra-bright in the classroom is not always an easy matter — it can be tantamount to walking a tightrope for the beleaguered educator. Gifted children often have manifold school difficulties revolving around teacher alienation, poor peer relations, and boredom. Nonetheless, facing the problems and trying to provide a healthy educational environment can go a long way towards changing a child's life for the better. Much needs to be done, and school is the logical place to begin to meet the challenge of providing for the gifted.

2

The Gifted:
who are they?

Two Paths of Giftedness

Case histories of gifted individuals should not, of course, be applied too
globally. Since every individual is unique, it is often inappropriate to
generalize from one case to another. Still, a couple of case studies we are
familiar with illustrate the two-sided nature of giftedness so well that we
feel it is appropriate to outline them briefly here.

Happily Ever After

John M. was born of upper middle-class parents in a large North American city. His mother and father felt he was a fairly clever boy (no more)
and reacted by providing him with a stimulating home environment.
Early in grade three, John was identified as gifted on a group intelligence
test (certainly not the best, or even a good method of identification) and
placed in a special class for extra-bright children (to our minds, not the
best method of intervention either).

The point is, however, that something was done. John responded
positively to the changes in his school life. It seemed that most of his
intellectual and emotional needs were met, and he went on to become a
high-achiever and a top student.

From the time he was identified as gifted, there was never any doubt
that John would go to college. He entered the faculty of medicine, where

he excelled in extra-curricular athletic activities, became popular with his classmates, and finally graduated at the top of his class.

Throughout his academic career, John was able to dedicate himself to the task at hand and postpone rushing into things others around him were enjoying. After graduation, he set about establishing himself and laying the foundation for his practice. John waited until the age of 24 before he bought his first car, until 26 to get married, and until 29 to start a family.

Currently, John is making a significant contribution to society through his flourishing practice. In addition to his professional success, he has a "lovely home and a beautiful wife and family". In short, his is a full, happy, and productive life.

Gifted Gone Bad

George S. was also from an upper middle-class family in a large North American city. His parents felt that he was an unusual child who needed special attention. Although they were concerned and trying to help, they did not know quite what to do for George or how to reach him.

George always seemed to need a lot of attention in elementary school. By grade four, his attention-getting behaviours were becoming pronounced, and by grade five, they were a serious problem. Chiefly as a result of these behavioural problems, George was placed in a special class for slow learners for the first few months of his grade six year.

Although he was unpopular with his teachers and peers, George managed to work his way back into the mainstream and to get through junior and senior high. His academic life was a struggle, however, and he was always downright unhappy in the school setting. Due to parental pressure, George enrolled in commerce at university, where he immediately proceeded to fail miserably in his first year.

At this point in time, George's parents and girlfriend (who had newly appeared on the scene) insisted that he go for a psychological assessment. After intensive interviews and testing, the psychological report — much to everyone's surprise — indicated that George was gifted. After getting the news, George, to put it in colloquial terms, "got his head together" for a while. He rallied academically and did well in repeating his first year. He then completed years two and three in brilliant fashion.

Unfortunately, George could not maintain this level of performance. In his fourth year of commerce, he began having run-ins with the law (repeated reckless driving charges, for the most part). He broke up with his girlfriend who was genuinely devoted to him and cut off communications with his parents. Further, becoming bored and dissatisfied with the intellectual climate at college, George dropped out not two months before graduation.

As you might expect, things went from bad to worse. George got involved in the drug scene, and was finally picked up for trafficking. At present, he is serving time in a penitentiary, where prison officials label him as a "bad one" and prophecize that he will be in trouble all his life. It goes without saying that it is a tragedy (both on the personal level and with respect to the wasted potential for society) for a gifted child to end up as George has done.

Poor Track Record

While it may not really be fair to compare these two case histories, it is probably safe to say that identification (or lack thereof) played a major part in their respective outcomes. In one instance, a gifted child was identified early and provided for; in the other, the child was not spotted soon enough and nothing was done until it was too late.

It appears self-evident that the first step towards helping some gifted children is to recognize their needs and provide for them as early as possible. We are told, however, that the track record with respect to identification is not a very impressive one. Many parents who have gifted children do not know it, and many teachers fail to recognize the gifted in their classrooms. In one study, Walton (1961) found that only one in five gifted individuals was identified by his teachers. Along the same lines, a study in Pittsburg schools showed that teachers selected as gifted less than half of those who met the intellectual criterion (Pegnato, 1955; Pegnato & Birch, 1959). In fact, more than half (57 percent) of the educational administrators sampled by the U.S. Office of Education in the early 1970s felt that there were no gifted children in their schools. Many gifted students receive no special attention whatever, and it has been reported that the neglect of this group is more than double that of any handicapped population. It would appear that the gifted are sometimes discovered late — or not at all (Hauck & Freehill, 1972) — and, as a result, often end up bored, ignored, and alienated from the school system.

When society is in trouble, interest in giftedness increases; people seem to be looking for somebody to save them. As mentioned earlier, America started getting heavily behind gifted programs shortly after the launching of Sputnik. Once this Soviet threat subsided, however, the interest in the gifted diminished rapidly. Now, with our current energy and economic crises, the United States and Canada are suddenly interested again (Lyon, 1980). In any case, despite genuine concern from many sources, the unpalatable fact remains that well thought out programs for gifted children are few and far between (Martinson, 1974). In the province of Manitoba, for example, a 1978 Department of Education survey indicated that only 354 of an estimated 4,345 gifted children were being

served at that time. Although things have been improving of late (Lyon, 1980), we still have a long way to go in meeting the needs of the gifted. Given the current state of the union, one can again see how it may well be a "doubtful gift" for a child to possess a special talent, only to have it misdirected, ignored, or even remain unnoticed by certain school personnel.

It is only natural to assume that the first step in any gifted program would be identification; we have to find them before we can do something for them. To be perfectly frank, however, we do not really believe this. Indeed, in practice we de-emphasize traditional identification and do not care all that much about it. Specifically, although we feel it is important to realize when a child has special needs and talents, we do not think it is necessary to waste time playing the "identification game" for years on end. Identification can be informal, relaxed, and relatively simple — not as rigourous and time-consuming as it has been in the past. In fairness, however, we will not only present our biases in this regard; we will spend some time reviewing the more traditional approaches to identification.

People tell us that if we wish to make meaningful changes in the school lives of the gifted and really do something for them, the first thing that is needed is an improvement in our methods of identification. Bearing in mind that giftedness is an abstract concept that is difficult to pin down, it seems limiting to rely solely (as schools so often do) on one identification technique. Sato, at a 1977 conference in Fargo, North Dakota, noted that schools could learn a great deal about identifying candidates for gifted programs from professional and college football coaches. These coaches, you see, use more than one criterion to select their players (they look at height, weight, age, strength, speed, ability, performance, attitude, etc.). Also, after identifying their players, coaches have a pretty fair idea of how to bring out the best in the athletes and improve their skills (through specific drills, studying films, designing and practicing plays, and so on).

To be more blunt, to select gifted students on the basis of an IQ test alone is so ridiculous that we will not even discuss it. Though we blush to confess it, there have been many gifted programs that have accepted only students with a tested IQ of 130 or more . . . those with 129 did not make it! Along with many other professionals, we are seriously displeased by such an approach (which we ended up talking about after all). Today, most educators have come to realize that giftedness is much too complex to be reduced to a single IQ score.

Partly as a reaction to people using only one test score to "identify" the gifted, the "multiple criteria" movement came into being. As a matter of fact, much of the "enlightened" literature of the day now tells us that the "multiple criteria" approach is the only way to go in identification. To put it simply, the "multiple criteria" people seem to think it is almost obligatory to look at a multiplicity of identification procedures. That is, they suggest that we use group intelligence tests, individual intelligence tests, tests of creativity, tests of achievement, teacher nomination, parent nomination, peer and even self-nomination, etc., to identify our gifted. And at first sight, this position seems unassailable — there is something to be said for taking a thorough look at a child by using a variety of tests.

Since there are varied and idiosyncratic types of giftedness, serious educators must obviously consider a number of factors when making any attempt at identification. Ruth Martinson (1974) in California has compiled an extensive set of multiple criteria for use in the identification of gifted children in the schools. While it is really not possible to put together a definitive set of procedures, the multiple identification criteria she proposes represent an honest attempt to deal with the task of identification in a concrete and practical manner; some of her selection criteria will pop up frequently throughout the remainder of this chapter (starting now).

Intelligence Testing

Certain tests of intelligence can be administered to several people simultaneously (group intelligence tests), while others are designed specifically to be given to only one person at a time (individual intelligence tests). *Group* tests (mostly of the paper-and-pencil variety) are popular tools in the primary, intermediate, and secondary grades, chiefly because they are fairly inexpensive, easy to administer, and easy to score (often by machine). They make possible en masse testing of large numbers of students (which may or may not be a good thing). Some of the more popular group tests on the education scene today include the Otis-Lennon Mental Ability Test, the Lorge-Thorndike Intelligence Test, the California Test of Mental Maturity, the Test of Cognitive Skills, the SRA Short Test of Educational Ability (STEA), and the Cooperative School and College Ability Tests (SCAT). At a higher level, we have the Graduate Record Examinations (GREs) required for entrance into graduate schools throughout Canada and the United States.

If employed in combination with other methods, group intelligence tests are sometimes thought to be useful for the initial screening of potentially gifted students. On the other hand, group tests should never be used as the only indicator of giftedness. They are neither valid nor reliable enough for final identification purposes (and, being designed for the "normal" population, they simply contain too few items aimed at identifying the gifted with any degree of accuracy). For example, in a study in which all students in a large junior high were given the Otis Group Test, only about 40 percent of the gifted pupils were identified (Pegnato, 1955).

Although the costs are far greater in terms of time and money, *individual* intelligence tests naturally tell us more about a child than an impersonal group test. Since they are administered on a one-to-one basis, individual tests give the tester more of an opportunity to establish rapport with the child, motivate him, and pick out some of his strengths, weaknesses, and idiosyncracies.

Certain individual tests have become popular in our schools due to their relative simplicity. They are quick and fairly easy to run, such that testers (usually resource teachers) do not require an extraordinary amount of training to administer them. Some of the more commonly used simple individual tests are the Peabody Picture Vocabulary Test — Revised (PPVT-R), the Full Range Picture Vocabulary Test, the Quick Test (QT), and the Slosson Intelligence Test. While these tests certainly have their place, they are a bit too simplistic to have definitive value in providing an in-depth analysis of any particular child, especially one who possesses unique, hard-to-tap abilities. And unfortunately, many of these tests yield a global IQ score, when they best might be viewed merely as measures of language development.

According to some investigators, perhaps the best indicators of giftedness are the Stanford-Binet Intelligence Scale and the Wechsler Intelligence Scales (i.e., the WPPSI — Wechsler Preschool and Primary Scale of Intelligence; the WISC-R — Wechsler Intelligence Scale for Children – Revised; and the WAIS-R — Wechsler Adult Intelligence Scale – Revised). These tests, by far the most intensive and well-known of the individual measures of intelligence, take somewhere around an hour to administer (and, supposedly, should only be given by highly trained testers, psychologists, and other demi-gods). While we have no wish to enter into the "what is intelligence?" controversy, it appears that both the Stanford-Binet and the Wechsler Intelligence Scales measure far greater numbers of verbal and nonverbal intellectual abilities than group tests or simple individual tests could hope to measure. Even though they may still only tap relatively few of the vast multitude of abilities that comprise intelligence, individual tests are sometimes useful for identification purposes due to the fact that children with marked superiority in one area are usually above average in others as well (Liddle, 1958; Wilson, 1953).

Since the Stanford-Binet encompasses a higher IQ range and measures more separate abilities than the Wechsler Scales (Gowan & Bruch, 1971), some feel it is the better indicator of giftedness. We prefer the WISC-R, however, because it provides quite a nice comparison between verbal and nonverbal abilities. The Verbal tests take a look at such things as general knowledge, reasoning ability, arithmetic, comprehension and vocabulary; the more "nonverbal" Performance tests include finding fine detail in pictures, pictorial sequencing, block design, object assembly, and visual memory. By looking at these various subtests, it is possible to get a pretty fair notion of where a student's strengths and weaknesses lie (and one can do this without ever calculating the IQ). Certainly, the WISC-R is more fair than many other tests to students who are weak verbally, but who have solid nonverbal abilities (which rarely surface in the school setting).

To digress a bit, Madeline Hunter's (1976) intriguing article, "Right-Brained Kids in Left-Brained Schools", shows how the school system often works against "right-hemisphere-type" children. Whether the schools are fair or not is almost beside the point here, but it is nice to have a test that gives equal weight to nonverbal abilities. While the WISC-R has this advantage, however, there is no need to overdo it and test continually without even thinking about possible alternatives.

Whatever test is used, it is important to remember that IQ scores are not the be-all and end-all in the identification of giftedness. Despite the fact that they may be helpful in alerting attention to certain cases of giftedness which might otherwise be overlooked, scathing criticisms can be levelled at individual tests in general (Feuerstein, 1979; Gardner, 1983, 1984; McCluskey, 1976; McCluskey & Baker, 1982; Perone, 1977; Salvia & Ysseldyke, 1985; Vernon, 1965). For example, they 1) tell us little about such variables as creativity, values, habits, perseverance, and so on; 2) are able to give information about only a few of the abilities that make up human intellect; and 3) can label children inappropriately (sometimes with disastrous consequences). In any case, the first chapter of Feuerstein's (1979) book eloquently summarizes many of the problems with contemporary testing and outlines reasons for the growing anti-test movement.

Many people, including certain psychologists who should know better, do not seem to realize that there are definite limitations to intelligence testing. A test is only as good as the tester, and all testers should make it a priority to guard against potential mistakes, misinterpretations, and abuses. Kaufman's (1979) call for "intelligent intelligence testing" should not go unheeded.

Another criticism of traditional American intelligence tests is that they emphasize verbal and culture-related skills, thereby discriminating against children with language handicaps and from deprived or culturally different backgrounds. In a reaction to the outcry that these tests discriminated against Blacks, Indians, and other minority groups and cultures, psychologists went to some pains to develop the so-called "culture-fair tests" of intellectual ability. Cattell came up with a group paper-and-pencil test of this nature (the Culture Fair Intelligence Test). Also, the Goodenough-Harris Drawing Test has often (and erroneously) been considered to be culture-fair. Certain individual tests, such as the Kahn Intelligence Test: A Culture-Minimized Experience, try to be culturally fair by focusing on nonverbal tasks rather than on supposedly biased verbal tests. For example, instead of asking a child questions, they may require him to manipulate objects. Indeed, on the Nonverbal Test of Cognitive Skills, pantomimed directions take the place of verbal instructions. And on the Leiter International Performance Scale, both spoken and pantomimed instructions are virtually eliminated — figuring out what you are supposed to do on each task is treated as part of the test.

Unfortunately, the nonverbal tasks that permeate the culture-fair tests may be as culturally loaded as the verbal items of the more traditional intelligence inventories. As a consequence, it has been argued — with good reason — that there can be no such thing as a test free from cultural biases. Overall, then, while culture-fair tests represent a novel and sometimes useful alternative for testing children from different cultural backgrounds, it would be a mistake to put too much faith in them.

Certain culture-fair tests have been named in a tongue-in-cheek fashion. For example, the BITCH test (Black Intelligence Test of Cultural Homogeneity) — designed to give black students a fair "break" — is comprised solely of black-biased items. For testers with a facetious turn of mind, however, BITCH is also an acronym for "Black Intelligence Test Counterbalanced for Honkies".

The problem with intelligence testing as we see it is that it is impossible even to define, let alone test, intelligence. Just what is intelligence anyway? Can it be described by Guilford's Structure of the Intellect Model as a 4x5x6 cube (Guilford, 1967) or measured by Reuven Feuerstein's Learning Potential Assessment Device (Feuerstein, 1979, 1980)? Of course it can't — not really. We realize we are doing an injustice to various theorists in the area, but they are well aware of the complexities involved. Certainly, one of the things theories of intelligence have done is to highlight the fact that people can be intelligent in many different ways. This is precisely the point — intelligence is simply too complicated to measure. In a manner of speaking, it might be suggested that there is no such thing as "intelligence" — so why worry about it. Any attempt to measure the unmeasureable is apt to fall short; any time one test is given by one tester to one child in one place at one time to yield one score, there is all sorts of room for more than one error.

Creativity Tests

Creativity, like giftedness and intelligence itself, is one of those concepts that is virtually impossible to define. To some people, creativity (whatever that may be) is almost synonomous with giftedness (another whatever that may be). Partially because of the fact that they are relatively new and untried instruments, the educational community has not as yet evinced an overwhelming interest in tests of creativity. Still, it is worthwhile to take a look at such tests, for they seem to have some potential for identifying the divergent, gifted thinker (Martinson, 1974).

Tests of creativity involve verbal and nonverbal production and elaboration of ideas, expression of emotion, taking a variety of perspectives in problem solving, and synthesizing ideas and details. Guilford (1967), in his Southern California Tests of Divergent Production, has made an effort to analyze and measure divergent thinking by having subjects respond to various stimuli (each designed to measure one of the 120 abilities outlined in his Structure of the Intellect Model). Torrance (1959, 1962, 1966), on the other hand, tries to get at the phenomenon by presenting complex tasks designed to trigger the release of creative abilities. To illustrate, Torrance's Tests of Creative Thinking involve things like giving a child a toy and asking him how he would improve it, or asking him to list the uses of a cardboard box (to see if he views it only as a container, or if he goes one step further and sees other possibilities for it as well).

The designers of creativity tests usually criticize the individual intelligence tests for being narrow and limited. And they are right; neither the Stanford-Binet nor the WISC-R measure enough facets of intelligence. As a consequence, Torrance has devised his innovative Tests of Creativity, looking at both the Verbal and Figural realms (which ties in well with the WISC-R); Guilford has created his tests based on the Structure of the

Intellect Model; and Meeker and Meeker have devised their SOI Screening Form for Gifted based on Structure of the Intellect. In certain respects, tests of creativity have filled a void, in that they have forced us to look at some hitherto untapped or unmeasured variables; their open-endedness sometimes gives the opportunity for creative thoughts to emerge. However, the same criticisms that creativity test constructors aim at individual intelligence tests can be levelled at creativity tests themselves. It is the same problem. No test can measure all facets of "intelligence" or "creativity". Who is to say tests of creativity measure what tests of intelligence do not? Incidentally, another problem with tests of creativity involves the administration and scoring; they can take quite a long time to run, and — since one has to consider such elements as originality, elaboration, and flexibility of the responses (and other finely detailed criteria) — they can be the very devil to score.

Measures of Achievement

Some people rely heavily on measures of achievement to identify their gifted, and certainly, achievement can tell you a great deal. Essentially, exam results, honour roll listings, group and individual achievement test scores, and the like are all indicators of performance. However, there is a danger here: while many gifted children show exceptional achievement in school, many do not. Achievement tests are geared for pupils within a specific age and grade range, and as such are unsuitable for both the higher performing and underachieving gifted child. Some children who are not all that bright do very well on achievement tests; they are just overachievers (if there can be such a thing). And very bright children often work below potential for a variety of reasons and simply do not show up on achievement tests. Still, while some gifted children do poorly on tests of achievement, others do exceptionally well. In other words, tests of this nature are useful for identifying some of the bright students some of the time. What we are trying to say, then, is that measures of achievement can be helpful in identifying the gifted, but they should be used in conjunction with other criteria; they cannot stand on their own.

Some of the better known group achievement tests are the California Achievement Tests, the Canadian Achievement Tests, the Canadian Test of Basic Skills (based on the Iowa), the Metropolitan Achievement Test, the SRA Achievement Series, the Sequential Tests of Educational Progress (STEP), and the Stanford Achievement Test. One of the more established tests, the Wide Range Achievement Test (WRAT), is in part individually administered. Another attractively packaged, highly motivating individual test that has been well-received in the schools is the Peabody Individual Achievement Test (PIAT). The PIAT measures five distinct areas of functioning (General Information, Spelling, Mathematics, Reading Recognition, and Reading Comprehension). It can test from very low to very high levels. For example, on the Reading Comprehension subtest, the student is asked to read the first passage, "A man jumps out of an open car", and is then required to choose the correct alternative from one of four pictures. The material becomes more difficult, and, at the end of the test, top readers are given passages such as: "The pundit who was exorbitantly pedantic and obviously erudite in his didactic activities was the subject of unanimous adulation from those who had matriculated as a result of his elucidating discourse".

One advantage of the individual achievement tests is that, since you are working with a child on a one-to-one basis, you can really watch what he is doing. In other words, you can "see" how a child is thinking and determine when he makes creative mistakes (which, of course, a group test would miss). In any case, it has been suggested that the PIAT is an appropriate instrument to use with bright kindergarten and grade one students (Shorr, Jackson, & Robinson, 1980), as well as with older pupils. The feeling is that the information obtained from the PIAT can be helpful in making decisions about placement of students in enriched math, spelling, or reading groups. Personal observations pertaining to the students' maturity level, persistence on task, artistic and physical abilities, and the like should also be taken into account.

IQ tests, tests of creativity, and achievement tests comprise the more objective portion of the "multiple criteria" approach (other less formal measures — such as assessment of work products and teacher, parent, peer, and self-nomination — will be discussed momentarily). First, however, we would like to change gears and pose a question for consideration.

Do We Really Need All These Tests?

At this point, we are going to risk offending all sorts of pioneers in the area and set down some of our own feelings concerning testing and identification. In the first place, the "multiple criteria" approach is certainly too impractical for use in most districts. With only a few psychologists typically serving a multitude of students, people are going to be in for a long wait if they want to have all the potentially gifted children screened on individual IQ tests, to say nothing of all the other tests they might want. It would simply take too long. It seems to us that we in education are much too concerned with testing, and often spend so much time searching for the perfect test battery or method of identification that nothing really gets done. We might do better to ask ourselves just what we are trying to identify anyway. In some senses, "gifted" is a misnomer. We use it for simplicity's sake and to communicate, but it is a gross over-simplification and *impossible to test for*!

All too often, psychologists run through an intelligence test in an effort to determine a child's learning potential. Sadly, however, most of these tests do not look at "potential" at all. In contrast rather, as Feuerstein (1979) has noted, they tend largely to examine past experience. That is, many traditional test items measure prior learning experiences — not learning potential. To truly examine potential, we would have to set up the T-T-T (Test-Teach-Test) paradigm Feuerstein recommends. In other words, first give the youngster the test items and see how he makes out, then endeavour to teach the concepts involved in any way you can, and finally retest in an attempt to measure the amount of learning that has taken place. By adopting this more flexible, oftentimes more humane, approach to testing, one can at least feel justified in beginning to make some inferences about growth and potential.

No doubt it is becoming obvious that the two of us tend to treat all tests — and individual IQ tests in particular — somewhat irreverently. We really quarrel with the whole concept of IQ, and do not believe that intelligence is a physical thing that can be measured like height and weight. Intelligence is too complicated; we do not know — and probably never will know — what it is. We feel, then, that IQ is often socially constructed by the test situation. For example, in any testing session the examiner is obviously in the position of power; it is much better to be the tester than the testee. The tester gets to control the materials, sit in the more powerful position, and show authority by pulling out a stopwatch (a vile tool at the best of times). It is surprising how many testers even lean back in their chairs and make "elephant ears" (take a high-status position with hands clasped behind the head) while a child struggles with the various problems presented. Many kids do not respond well to this sort of arrangement, and tests conducted in this manner very often do not really tell you what the child is capable of.

If it were psychologists and educators who were being tested so indiscriminately, tests would be a lot less popular; it is extremely anxiety-arousing and ego-threatening to be tested. In our society, it is terribly important to be "intelligent" — just like it was to be of "good family" in Regency England. Intelligence is a highly valued commodity, and there is no surer way to insult somebody than to tell them they are stupid. Most of us seem to have a need to think (and have others think) that we are smart. Certainly, the majority of the people attending the various gifted conferences which we have frequented all appeared to feel that they themselves were gifted (while, in reality, only a couple of us truly were).

To repeat, it is threatening to be tested. This was brought home to us not long ago when the first author closeted himself away in his office and attempted to work through a test of creativity. (We often experiment and run tests on ourselves before we try them with the youngsters.)

"Even though I was all alone in the office and no one else knew what was happening, such is the threat of having one's mental ability examined that I started to get nervous. Soon I found I wasn't doing at all well . . . in fact, I started to bomb! I grew fidgety, my palms started sweating, and I couldn't think "properly". Here I was having trouble with a kid's test — and I'm supposed to be smart! It was traumatic. I finally decided I had had enough and that I should go home and try again the next day (when, incidentally, I did much better). However, if I had been a child, there would have been no next day!"

It always amazes us, with all the psychologists running around testing in the schools, that more of them do not feel sorry for the kids and stop it. Of course, there is a time to test; it can be helpful to discover where a child's strengths and weaknesses lie. Even in our infrequent testing sessions, however, we find we often learn more by the subjective things the child does than by the test scores. In one case, for example, we ran into a determined grade one student who insisted on attempting each and every question; he refused to give up even when the items became too difficult for him. When asked, "What does the stomach do?" he replied: "If we didn't have stomachs, our heads would be on our bums". While he may not have perfectly understood the workings of the digestive system, there was no doubt at all that this boy was thinking. And he did know a great deal about many unusual subjects. A short time later when another person on our team asked him to define the word "donkey", the child did not respond. The tester — in the hope of getting a reply — repeated the word, putting a high-toned inflection on the last syllable ("don key") and gesturing for the child to say something. The boy did; he said "hoté". It turned out he knew all about Cervantes' Don Quixote, windmills, and the like.

Using items from the WISC-R, we have also asked a junior high student: "What would you do if you found someone's wallet on the floor of a supermarket?" His reply gave us pause. Paraphrasing as closely as possible, the response we got was: "If the truth be told, there is an inverse relationship to this type of problem; the inverse relationship being, the greater the amount of money in the wallet, the less the likelihood of anyone ever seeing it again!" He answered another question by noting it was better to give money to a well-known charity than to a beggar on the street because "It is more advantageous for income tax purposes". And perhaps it would be best for us not even to discuss his sarcastic response to the question: "What are the advantages of having senators and congressmen?" The point is, of course, that this fellow was telling us something about himself. Even though, technically, his responses might be considered incorrect (if one scored according to the "rules"), it was obvious that he was extremely bright. And we could have found this out simply by talking to the youngster; it is usually unnecessary to go through an intensive battery of tests. Although traditional testing can give us certain "data", there are often other informal ways of getting as much (or more) information.

When we do test, we take certain liberties to make things more enjoyable (and, we think, more meaningful). When using the WISC-R, for example, we run the Picture Completion subtest (a pleasant rapport builder which does not force failure) before the Information subtest (which is less fun and does force failure) — even though the latter test is supposed to be run first. We also throw away the stopwatch. Simply doing these two things seems to raise the IQs of children we test more than ten points on the average. Traditionalists have told us that we cannot do this sort of thing because we are "screwing up the test norms". However, we want to see what the child is capable of at his best. Since most of us perform best when we are relaxed and happy, we consider any test session a failure if the student did not have fun. We do not care about (and do not even calculate) the IQ score; we would rather screw up the norms than screw up the kids. If programming — not labelling or categorizing — is the goal, the norms are not all that important anyway.

You might say that we are questioning the very validity of IQ itself; we are not comfortable playing God and trying to measure "intelligence". To us, there is an artificiality to the testing situation and, basically, the tests simply do not measure what they are supposed to measure. Besides, it seems odd that we can easily raise IQs simply by showing children how to do the things they could not do at first. In any case, there is absolutely no doubt that tests are often abused, and that kids sometimes end up being labelled, pigeon-holed, "WISC-ed" away, and segregated on the basis of very questionable test scores. Even though some people seem to think that the WISC-R can identify everything from learning disability to giftedness, we do not. Indeed, the only thing we believe the WISC-R identifies accurately 100 percent of the time are the school psychologists, because they always trot into the building carrying the damn thing!

In-School Testing

What we are saying, simply, is that perfect identification of the gifted is not possible; one has to live with the fact that we cannot find them all. We are going to miss some youngsters who should be given the advantage of "enrichment", and we are going to "enrich" some who perhaps will not be able to cope. But we are going to make these mistakes whether we test or not! Setting up programs for bright youngsters should be obligatory, but getting involved in gifted education need not involve massive division or district-wide testing. As pointed out in the paper, "EDUCATIONAL psychologist or educational PSYCHOLOGIST" (McCluskey & Baker, 1982), the loyalties of professionals in the educational community should be to education and programming, not to "psychological testing". Some members of the educational community are even beginning to ask whether any identification procedures are necessary at all (Birch, 1984).

While it is easy to criticize and say that testing is not that big of an issue, some school districts setting up gifted programs are not going to have any choice; many principals, superintendents, and board members want and expect testing. "Gifted" educators may have to give them something. For a more complete review of specific tests that can be given, we refer you to Buros (1978), Salvia and Ysseldyke (1985), or to many of the catalogues available in most schools. Still, we feel educators would be ill-advised to base their identification of candidates solely on test results that can miss so much.

If one must test, it seems logical not to wait forever for the experts; testing can be done in your own school! Some data on most children should already be on hand in the cumulative files (group IQ tests, individual IQ tests, and achievement results are often on file). After checking to see whether or not relevant information is already on record, a teacher can proceed on her own. If more information is required, the teacher can run — or have the resource teacher run — a Quick Test, the Peabody Picture Vocabulary Test, a Slosson, or some other quick screening instrument. As mentioned earlier, while we do not subscribe to the fact that some of these tests yield IQ scores, they can give some information

— especially with respect to language development. If one wants to, however, it is possible to go further and have a resource teacher run a Woodcock-Johnson Psycho-Educational Battery (cf. Hessler, 1982), which, in many ways, is every bit as informative as the WISC-R or Stanford-Binet. This test can be used by school personnel — you do not have to be an "expert" — and it examines a variety of skills (including cognitive ability, spatial relations, visual-auditory learning, analysis, synthesis, concept formation, analogies, etc.). It even looks at achievement and interest. While we still see certain problems with it, this sort of in-school test is quite handy; it yields a lot of information in a short amount of time.

It is even possible for teachers to look at "creativity" on their own without calling in psychologists. Although we have noted that creativity tests can be difficult and time-consuming to score, we do not see any reason why people cannot run them without scoring. (Not everyone will agree with us here.) If you simply look at the responses on Torrance's Tests of Creativity, for example, you can tell what is creative; after perusing several tests, you get a "feeling" for what is "good" and "special". Easier yet, you might just modify things a bit. (For example, put several circles on a page and ask your students to draw something in or around each circle. This is basically a technique used in many creativity tests. Simply by looking at the responses, you can see which students are showing something extra and unusual.) Also, in terms of achievement tests, you can do your own — exams are, after all, nothing more than tests of achievement; as well, other group and individual achievement tests are easy to obtain and score.

We can anticipate the screams and howling criticism from die-hard psychologists of the old school, who feel that only highly-trained experts can identify gifted children (that is, special students must be identified by specialists using special tests). It goes without saying that this view leaves us singularly unmoved; every reader is going to have to make his own decision, but we feel that specialists are not always needed in identification of the gifted. In fact, we have often felt like consigning testers and their tests to a place of great heat. Besides, we like to think that teachers, in general, are capable of making decisions. There are some bad teachers, of course, but there are also some bad consultants, psychologists, and other specialists who have very little to offer. We prefer to view teachers as professionals who are responsible for the children in their classrooms. We help and support them when we can, but have neither the time nor inclination to make decisions for them.

Unfortunately, many teachers think that they cannot make important decisions like identification of the gifted without specialists, tests, and "data". We, however, feel that as professionals most of them can. Perhaps we can illustrate this anecdotally. Just suppose a fellow meets a young woman; they hit it off, date for five or six months, and he decides to pop the question. This is, if not the most important, certainly one of the most important decisions of his life. What does he do? Does he give her an IQ test or a questionnaire to see if she is acceptable? (Some of us wish we had!) No, of course not! He just makes the decision. We can do the same with the gifted. Life is full of decisions; we do not always have to wait for in-depth test results.

More Subjective Measures

Teachers in the regular classroom who have no quick access to specialists — or teachers who have quick access to incompetent specialists — have to take things into their own hands. Since giftedness is such an intangible concept, there is certainly room for subjectivity and flexibility in terms of identification procedures. As Martinson (1974) and others have pointed out, there is a very real need to look at less objective (and sometimes more useful) methods of identification. There are a number of informal criteria which should be considered.

Teacher Nomination

As previously suggested, many researchers feel that teacher nomination is one of the most unreliable methods of identification (Pegnato & Birch, 1959; Walton, 1961) and contend that teachers somehow miss noticing from 50–80 percent of the gifted children in their rooms. And we have all heard the horror stories concerning how educators have shortchanged the gifted: Isaac Newton did poorly in grade school; Caruso's teacher told him he had "no voice at all"; Einstein was thought to be "slow"; Churchill failed grade six; a young Beethoven was termed a "hopeless" composer; and Tolstoy failed college. (We must remember, however, that not necessarily all famous people have been intellectually gifted — "normals" can do great things too. That is why we emphasize over and over again that a good curriculum should be good for all kids; it should motivate the "lowest" individuals in class, provide content and stimulation for the "normals", and be challenging and flexible enough that the "gifted" — or others — can move beyond to a higher level of thinking.)

Rather than merely lamenting the lack of teacher sensitivity in picking out the gifted, it might be more beneficial to try to train teachers in what to look for. That is, although teachers have a poor track record with regard to identification, it does not have to stay this way — they can get better with training and practice! In other words, by becoming aware that these types of kids exist, being alert, and simply looking out for the bright, teachers can become much more accurate in their identification. In many ways, it is a matter of attitude. Sensitive teachers have always been excellent judges of creativity and talent. Other teachers too will be able to identify the gifted if they create situations designed to allow talent to emerge and then look for it. What we are saying, then, is that we are willing to rely heavily on teacher empathy and sensitivity; a sensitive teacher is usually better than any test. In an effort to add some "objective subjectivity" — as paradoxical as that sounds — to the whole process, we have come up with a checklist to help teachers learn what to look for in identification of their bright students. While we do not regard this simple list — adapted and extended from the work of Martinson (1974) and others — as an infallible, magic cookbook for identification, we have found it helpful in getting teachers to look more carefully at the children in their classrooms. (See pages 38–39.)

Checklists of this sort abound in the literature. Another such instrument to help teachers with the identification of gifted and talented children has been designed by Renzulli and Hartman (1971). In their Scale For Rating Behavioral Characteristics Of Superior Students, they ask teachers to rate a child in terms of his learning, motivational, creative, leadership, artistic, musical, and communication (precision and expressive) characteristics. To illustrate, one of the items to assess learning characteristics reads: "Is a keen and alert observer; usually 'sees more' or 'gets more' out of a story, film, etc., than others". The teacher simply rates the student on a four-point scale, in terms of whether she has seldom or never observed this characteristic in the child in question, has occasionally observed it, has observed it to a considerable degree, or has observed this characteristic almost all of the time. Through addition and a weighting procedure, a definite and sometimes illuminating score is obtained for each of the foregoing characteristics.

Work Products

Another thing teachers can do is look at and evaluate samples of the students' work. This is, after all, part and parcel of a teacher's job. Kids are different, and one has to be on the lookout for a whole range of

Identification Checklist and Referral Form
(To aid elementary teachers in the identification of gifted children)

Do any children in your class clearly possess several of the following characteristics? If so, circle the appropriate numbers for each child in question. In making your assessment, take a good look at all the children, including those who may be behaviour problems, culturally or socially different, or have speech defects.

1 Has a very good memory (e.g., able to remember important dates and events).
2 Has an unusually long attention span.
3 Has a good vocabulary and/or uses long sentences for his age.
4 Is reading well above grade level.
5 Is curious, observant, and alert.
6 Is responsive to challenging situations (e.g., perseveres and shows a willingness to attack difficult work).
7 Is quick to appreciate humourous situations (i.e., is "sharp" in the sense of being able to play on words or understand a clever pun).
8 Has special abilities in one or more areas (e.g., math, reading, creative writing, music, art, etc.).
9 Produces highly original, creative work with vitality to it.
10 Has the ability to think things through critically (i.e., can recognize, organize, integrate, and evaluate ideas and relationships).
11 Has exceptional athletic ability.
12 Has hobbies and interests out of school that have caught your attention (e.g., stamp or coin collecting, building models, etc.).
13 Exhibits leadership in group activities (can influence others).

If any of your pupils show several of these characteristics, you may wish to pursue things further. Feel free to refer in this regard: please include the following information.

Student's name: _____   Birthdate: _____

Home phone: _____   Sex: _____

School: _____   Grade: _____

Teacher: _____

Additional information that may help in the assessment of the child (e.g., school performance, peer relationships, and classroom behaviour to date):

_____

_____

_____

If you wish to meet concerning this referral, specify a convenient appointment time:

_____	_____
Time	Principal's Signature
_____	_____
Date	Teacher's Signature

things, including subjective work products. If teachers take the time to look and listen, kids will tell a lot about themselves through their words, behaviour, and the work they turn out. The opportunity to identify a gifted pupil increases if you stay on the lookout for him to produce an unusual and unique piece of work in one or more subject areas (for example, music, art, writing, etc.). If in and out-of-school activities are observed closely, it is often possible to pick the children who stand out from the rest (cf. Martinson, 1968, 1974).

We, ourselves, have come across some almost unbelievable work samples. Take this poem written by an eleven-year-old boy:

"I think of the earth and the *lands* afar
And long so much to travel there,
Taking different views of the same star,
Becoming fulfilled and more aware.
　　So easy to say, so hard to do.

Standing alone gazing up at the *sky*
Heavenly expanse that can't be owned,
One wonders how, one wonders why,
You want to know what can't be known.
　　So easy to look, so hard to touch.

The waves of the *sea* caress the shore
And you think to yourself it's an impossible sin,
To dream of descent and of reaching more,
Of probing the secrets that lie deep within.
    You can probe a bit, but not that far.

Running along, the *wind* in your face
It rushes ahead with incredible ease,
It conquers time and it conquers space,
And you just can't grab the intangible breeze.
    You feel its touch, yet it slips through your hands.

It seems so hopeless, there's just no time
To strive, to learn, to heed the call,
I want the knowledge of life to be mine,
Yet I feel so terribly pale and small.
    It's hopeless for sure, there's just no way.

But back from the depths of abysmal despair
I call forth the strength to see it through,
To explore the earth, the sea, the air,
To work, to strive, and attempt to do . . .
    The impossible, which may not be.

    For we can travel the land
    And sail the sea
    And pierce the cumulus,
    We can ride on the wind
    And touch the sky
    So much depends on us."

Also remarkable (almost mind-boggling) is the following paragraph by a little girl not yet turned ten:

"What is life? Does it end at death or begin anew for eternity? Eternal life is a tantalizing thought, but maybe an unrealistic one. Is death to be feared or welcomed? I think and think and think about this eternal puzzle, yet seem to resolve nothing for all my thought. It's a hopeless feeling, this not knowing. My mother says I'm not to worry my pretty little head about such things. She's probably right, but these ever intruding thoughts cannot be willed away."

If you get this sort of thing from a nine-year-old girl, you must realize something special is going on! Most adults would be proud to write half as well. Although we do not mean to imply that all bright students produce work of this calibre, they often do come up with something out of the common way. If we are not "dull of soul", we can often "pick up on" what they have produced. It is a matter of giving them the opportunity to produce it in the first place.

Even with "low" kids, one can often spot something through their writing. In one instance, we put a grade four student — who was reading and working far below grade level — on "HITS PAK", a cassette-worksheet reading program based on the lyrics of popular songs. For one of his assignments, the boy in question wrote a few lines concerning how he felt about Paul Simon's first big hit, "I Am a Rock". He summed up his feelings about the selection somewhat inarticulately by saying: "It was good it has 2 Fs and 3 Ss". At first sight, this appeared absurd; we did not know what he was talking about. However, upon looking over the lyrics again, we found the line, "On a freshly fallen silent shroud of snow". Now things made sense! While it was incredibly poorly stated, the student had noticed something and had, in fact, picked out the alliteration. As we continued working with him (with renewed vigour in a way, since we had begun to look at him differently), we realized that — despite his decidedly limited academic skills — the boy had ability. Now, some years later, he has clearly demonstrated the fact — he has caught up and is reading well above grade level.

It is interesting to see how strongly the questioning nature (the need to know, as it were) comes through in the work of the gifted. The philosophical probing of their writings is often profound. Again, while not all gifted children turn out incredible work, many do occasionally come up with "something special". In many, one sign of the depth of their thoughts is their sense of humour; the gifted often have a biting, sarcastic, subtly clever way of looking at the world around them. In fact, various researchers suggest that it is about time we start taking a "serious look at humour" as an indicator of giftedness (cf. Bleedorn & Ferris, 1980; de Bono, 1985).

Some individuals show giftedness in other ways. Certain students demonstrate it in a social sense by taking leadership roles, and others by their athletic abilities on the playground. Other pupils show it through their music. For example, many gifted children become accomplished musicians — some even compose first-rate pieces — long before they reach their teens. Teachers should take note of the fact that the more a child is encouraged to engage in unstructured and relaxing activities such as poetry, prose, and music, the more chance there is for unusual abilities to come to light.

As might be expected, a lot of information can surface through a child's artwork as well. Recently, a little four-year-old girl being assessed for early entrance into kindergarten produced the excellent self-portrait which follows. For a youngster her age, she included a remarkable amount of well-drawn detail (witness the hair, eyebrows, ears, fingers, buttons, shoes, etc.). Reacting to this drawing, we took a closer look at

this girl — a look which convinced us that she did indeed have special talents in several areas.

We are familiar with another intriguing case wherein a gifted grade one boy got himself into all kinds of trouble through his artwork. Being an observant little fellow, he had somehow noticed that "real" artists tend, seemingly as often as not, to paint female nudes. Evincing wisdom far beyond his years, this boy decided to try his hand at it. The end result was that he managed to paint an extremely realistic female nude of his own in his grade one art class.

No nudes is good nudes!

The reaction of the teacher was startling, to say the least. She ran (quite literally shrieking) to the principal, the parents were called in, and our diminutive hero was tongue-lashed and threatened with expulsion. It was not until the mother pointed it out that the teacher slowed down long enough to realize that this boy had shown exceptional ability through his drawing. After things settled down, the teacher very efficiently set about encouraging — and redirecting — the boy's artistic talents.

To reiterate, *the crucial thing is to provide the opportunity for creativity to emerge*. This is not to say that one wants a totally unstructured or chaotic classroom. Structure and organization are important and, if there is too much noise, effective learning cannot take place; a reasonable level of discipline must be maintained. However, there are times when it pays to "loosen up" and just let things happen. For example, in art classes, we usually have students do their work on regular 8½" x 11" sheets of paper. If one occasionally lets them do whatever they want — whether it be a mural on the blackboard or a fine line drawing on a match box cover — it is surprising the sorts of creative products the kids can come up with. At times, the "art" in teaching may simply be in allowing something original to emerge.

If you take the time to look, it is amazing what "signals of giftedness" you can pick up. One thing that we have noticed, for example, is that gifted children sometimes exhibit remarkably adult-like behaviour on the telephone. Often a bright child on the phone sounds absurdly like an efficient mini-secretary, asking who is calling, taking messages, and generally oozing politeness and good manners. Other gifted children take a more assertive, uppity tone whenever they get the chance to intercept a call intended for mother. One little devil we know delights in subjecting callers to a virtual "telephone inquisition", demanding in an arrogant and highhanded fashion to be told the caller's name, occupation, and reason for calling before finally condescending to put his mother on the line.

Other Forms of Nomination

Techniques other than testing and teacher nomination can also be used in an attempt to identify bright students. Instead of relying on specialists and teachers to determine which children are gifted, some educators recommend asking parents, classmates, and the children themselves.

Peer Nomination

One oft-neglected selection technique in identifying gifted children is peer nomination. A great amount of information can be gleaned by having the teacher ask young students to list their classmates who: 1) have special abilities in certain areas; 2) have original ideas; or 3) are likely to be asked to help others with their homework. Most often, kids know who in the class is "different" or smart. As mentioned earlier, however, it is important to remember that gifted children may effectively conceal their abilities from their teachers and friends so as to conform to peer expectations (Martinson, 1974; Strang, 1951). Also, some children will nominate others for a variety of inappropriate reasons (misperception, for example, or social approval, etc.).

Self-nomination

Self-nomination is also a realistic possibility. Even though no one else may notice, many gifted children are well aware that they are different and possess special abilities. They know they are smart, and precisely that fact can cause no end of difficulty. If you take the time to ask them (verbally or in written form), they might well be able to tell you just what their particular skills are.

Parent Nomination

A better technique for teachers is to listen to what parents have to say about their children. Not surprisingly, almost all parents feel they have gifted children. Teachers hear so many proud (and unrealistic) parents describing the abilities of their offspring that it is difficult to take any of them seriously. Nonetheless, it is a mistake to dismiss all information from parents as stemming from pride or wishful thinking. Sometimes they are right, and their children are gifted. Many parents spend far more time with their child than does the teacher and, even though certain parents notice nothing, others do in fact realize when their child's behaviour is somehow out of the ordinary. Some researchers suggest that parents are clearly better at identifying giftedness in their children than are teachers (Jacobs, 1971), so their opinions definitely should not be ignored. Indeed, opening channels of communication between the school and the home (and getting together with parents) can alert teachers to any number of intriguing facts about a child.

As Martinson (1974) notes, teachers can obtain a lot of information about a child by asking parents various pertinent questions. Lists of sample questions that might be helpful in gathering information from parents of potentially gifted children have been drawn up by Martinson, ourselves, and others. Some typical queries include:

1 At what age did your child start to talk?
2 When did he begin to walk?
3 Does your child learn new things quickly?
4 When did he begin reading and taking an interest in books?
5 When did he begin writing?
6 What types of things does he like to read?
7 Does he have a high level of task commitment (on complicated assignments, models, etc.)?
8 Does your child have any special interests or hobbies (and show classifying skills in collecting stamps, coins, etc.)?
9 Does he have a unique sense of humour?
10 What does your child want to be when he grows up?
11 How does he get along with others?
12 Do other children follow his lead at home or at school?
13 What special opportunities has he had (lessons, trips, etc.)?
14 What does your child prefer to do when he is alone?
15 Does he have any special abilities or talents (in music, math, computer games, chess, etc.)?
16 Does he have any problems or special needs?

Summation

One would hope that the message reverberating throughout this chapter has come across loud and clear. We believe that if educators wish to improve their distressingly low batting average with respect to identifying the gifted child, testing is not the only alternative. When used judiciously, of course, there is a place for testing in some cases. Achievement tests, group intelligence tests, and the simple, quick individual intelligence tests can sometimes be used for initial screening. And oftentimes, the heavy artillery (creativity tests or high-powered individual intelligence tests, such as the Stanford-Binet or Wechsler) can provide useful information about students. However, testing should never be regarded as a panacea; too much testing is as impractical as it is unnecessary. Clearly, testing is done far too often with far too much importance placed on IQ results. By taking a subjective look at a student's special abilities in virtually any area (mathematics, science, literature, music, art, etc.), it is possible to come up with all sorts of information that tests simply cannot supply. Peer and self-nomination, parent nomination, and teacher nomination should all be considered in identifying the gifted. In terms of the latter nominating technique, the various checklists that are available are useful tools to help make teachers more aware of what to look for. And since teachers do have a lot to be on the lookout for, they should feel free to use every scrap of information they can get their hands on — test results or something else — in an attempt to identify and meet the needs of bright children. It helps if teachers make a point of giving youngsters the opportunity to produce something "special".

Since we feel so strongly about the matter, we will conclude this chapter in rather dogmatic fashion by stating unequivocally that, since they are the ones who have to work with gifted children in the schools, teachers should be the ones doing the identifying. Naturally, they should get some support from principals, resource teachers, and outside specialists, but the classroom is really the centre of the action, so to speak. If the teacher is convinced in her own mind that she has spotted a child with potential, she is halfway there in terms of meeting his needs. Also, we can get self-fulfilling prophecy (Rosenthal & Jacobson, 1968) working for us. Once somebody feels a particular child is "gifted", he automatically receives some measure of special attention simply as a result of being "identified".

Essentially, then, we take a much more informal view of identification than do many other investigators. As we have said earlier, we think it is a mistake to get too obsessed with identification; we prefer to move quickly through this step to where the real work lies — actual programming. Programming is always the thing that takes the most planning in education, and programming for the gifted can be amazingly involved and time-consuming (cf. Kaplan, 1974; Ward, 1961; Williams, 1958). Keeping things in perspectivie, identification is not the priority — doing something for children is! Assuming the aim is to come up with programs and techniques that are good for all students — including the gifted — identification becomes less important; the majority of time should be spent finding and designing alternatives that will challenge and stimulate all students. In any good educational setting, however, programs should be available that teach process as well as content, and offer bright students a chance to take things further.

3

*Whether or not a creative child
will become a creative adult will
depend in a large measure upon
how the school and society treat
his curiosity need.*
— Torrance

The Gifted:
once you've found them,
what do you do with them?

A Brief History of Gifted Education

Special education for the gifted is far from being a child of the twentieth century. As a matter of fact, as early as 350 B.C., Plato was advocating that gifted youth be identified, segregated, and provided with specialized curricula in philosophy, science, and metaphysics (Henson II, 1976; Kirk, 1972). In his *Republic*, Plato (cf. Grube, 1974) even went so far as to suggest that the very survival of the sacrosanct Greek democracy depended upon the state's ability to educate the gifted for leadership positions (that is, to create "philosopher kings"). Following the lead of the Greeks, educators of the Roman Empire also took pains to isolate and make special provision for gifted children — especially in terms of their military training.

Several centuries later, Charlemagne (742-814) recommended that "bright" children of the working class (as well as those from more elite backgrounds) be singled out and placed in special schools funded by the state. Charlemagne made a sincere effort to extend education in western Europe, and his work on behalf of the bright and talented is sometimes regarded as the first attempt at public education for the gifted (Henson II, 1976).

During the sixteenth century, the mighty Turkish Empire also provided for gifted individuals. Under the guiding hand of Suleiman the

Magnificent, the Turks endeavoured to seek out the gifted Christian youths scattered throughout their territory (Sumption & Luecking, 1960). Talent scouts of sorts were ordered to scour the countryside for gifted youngsters. Once identified, these extra-bright children were immersed in Turkish philosophy and schooled in art, science, religion, and war, ending up as virtual "pawns" or "weapons" of the state. From the Turkish perspective, the success of this policy was obvious; a generation after Suleiman had initiated his "gifted program", the Ottoman Empire became so powerful that it threatened to overrun the whole of Europe.

If one stops to think about it, the undercurrent running through all these ancient programs for the gifted is that they were designed almost exclusively for the good of the state. In a manner of speaking, such programs were almost blatant attempts to exploit the gifted for society's gain. The state was paramount, while the individual mattered very little. Even in this century, we have tended to emphasize the needs of society and to underplay the needs of the individual. For example, in the U.S.S.R. — where great importance is placed on developing the intellectual potential of superior citizenry — special programs in math and science have clearly been directed towards meeting the ends of the state. And, as mentioned before, the event triggering the initiation of gifted programs in the U.S. was the launching of Sputnik by the Soviets in 1957. In an effort to keep pace with the Russians, educators on this side of the ocean started looking to our gifted youth (and emphasizing math and science as well).

Fortunately, however, the current educational climate is shifting towards a more humanistic bent. Although there is no denying that the benefits to be derived by the state remain a major concern in any gifted program, they are by no means the only consideration. Gradually, educators are adopting the philosophy that all children — those with special needs included — have a right to a good education. And more specifically, many teachers are beginning to realize that we are obligated to provide challenging, stimulating school environments for our gifted students in order to help them develop to their fullest potential. One of the most significant moves directed towards this end was the establishment — after extensive professional and parental lobbying — of the Association for the Gifted (as part of the Council for Exceptional Children) in 1958. The creation of this Association served as a springboard for program development designed to meet the special needs of gifted children throughout North America.

We have already noted that interest in giftedness has been cyclic and inconsistent. Some locales, it is true, have had gifted programs for quite some time now. In certain areas, for example, segregation of gifted students into major work classes goes back many decades. And, as Hildreth (1952) pointed out, Hunter Elementary School in New York took a different direction, becoming one of the first institutions to provide for the gifted by deformalizing curriculum, removing subject matter boundaries, and supplying more study time. In contrast, early in the 1950s, Scheifele (1953) was advocating meeting the needs of the gifted in the regular class.

The fact remains, however, that interest in the gifted in America was really spurred on by Sputnik and the creation of the Association for the Gifted. In the late 1950s and early 1960s, then, things really started to boom, and gifted programs sprang up all over the place. Just one example was the intensive Cullowhee program in North Carolina which worked successfully with gifted children assembled at a college campus for several summers in succession (Bixler, 1962; Bixler, Carter, & Killian, 1959; Morrill, 1959).

Unhappily, due to poor follow-up and lack of systematic program evaluation, it proved impossible to maintain the momentum of the gifted movement. Indeed, the notion of making special provision for gifted children fell into disfavour throughout much of the 1960s. In the 1970s — thank goodness — we started to come full circle once more, and new life was infused into gifted education per se. Many mistakes were made, but at least the interest was there. The widely disseminated Report to Congress on the Education of the Gifted and Talented in 1972 was a major step in the right direction; in fact, this report was in large measure responsible for the spirited rebirth and revitalization of interest in the gifted.

Other developments followed thick and fast (including the rather dramatic revival of the *Gifted Child Quarterly*). Perhaps the most notable of these was the passage of Public Law 93.380 in the U.S. in 1974, which legislated the Office of the Gifted and Talented and authorized the first categorical national funding of gifted programs. Although Congress appropriated only 2.56 million dollars of the 12.5 million authorized, a definite beginning had been made. For those interested in looking further at the national scene, historical reviews of the gifted movement are available elsewhere (Bish, 1975; Kirk, 1972; Trezise, 1973). More recently, Lyon (1980) talks about the tremendous growth of gifted programs over the last few years.

At the moment, almost all states are contemplating or have already initiated some type of gifted program. The State of Michigan, for example, has recently funded twelve pilot projects and — apparently subscribing to the philosophy that there is really no substitute for putting the gifted "with other students of similar interests and abilities at least some of the time" — seems to be moving towards total or partial segregation (Trezise, 1976). As Lazzaro and others make clear, segregated models have operated — apparently successfully — in Cleveland for very many years. Taking a different perspective, other areas (such as California, North Dakota, and various centres in Canada, etc.) appear intent on trying to handle the gifted in the mainstream.

Through the use of extensive state funding (to the tune of many millions of dollars annually), California has implemented perhaps some of the finest education for the gifted in America. San Diego and Oakland have comprehensive programs. Further, Ventura County project personnel have delved into almost all aspects of giftedness, producing top-notch work in the areas of identification, curriculum programming, mainstreaming, and evaluation (Delp & Martinson, 1975; Kaplan, 1974; Martinson, 1974, 1976; Olivero & Sato, 1974; Renzulli, 1975). New York, too, has a number of solid programs, including the Astor Program for Gifted Children. Other programs we are familiar with and indebted to are being carried out in Colorado, Connecticut, Georgia, Illinois, Kentucky (cf. Trammell, 1975), Pennsylvania, and Virginia. In Canada, we know of programs in most of the provinces. However, these programs usually exist in isolation; there are pockets of interest (Calgary, Coquitlam, Vancouver, Ottawa-Carlton, Selkirk, etc.) rather than province-wide delivery systems (which may not necessarily be a bad thing).

Unequal Education for the Gifted

Although there is currently a great deal of hustle and bustle about special education for the gifted, we have only just been initiated into it in many respects. Decided progress has been made, of course, but there is a long way to go before we can expect programs to come anywhere near fruition. For it must be remembered, after all, that we have many years of neglect to make up for.

It is a sad fact of life that "teachers" still exist who cannot see the need for making any kind of provision for the gifted (and it is a certainty that several of these absurd creatures lie in wait in every school district in the U.S. and Canada). Perhaps the first task of the more enlightened educator who cares about the gifted is to get others to subscribe to his philosophy.

Gallagher (1975) — an intuitive and entertaining pioneer in the area — tells a relevant little story about Mr. Palcuzzi, an elementary principal trying to convince his local PTA to support a gifted program. Exhibiting devious subterfuge, Palcuzzi advanced several proposals for meeting the needs of gifted students. Among other things, he suggested: 1) advancing children on the basis of ability rather than age; 2) grouping by ability; 3) providing specially trained, highly salaried instructors for children with special abilities; 4) setting aside some part of the school day for special instruction; and 5) meeting transportation costs to enable gifted and talented children to share their skills with students in other schools.

As Palcuzzi had anticipated, his proposals were met with groans, sighs, and shrieks of outrage. PTA members began to clamour that such a program would be elitist, discriminatory, ego-deflating for those students who failed to qualify, too expensive, etc. Apparently, Mr. Palcuzzi sat sedately through this scathing criticism, waiting until the ranting and raving had subsided before revealing that he had been speaking not of a new gifted project, but of the popular program for gifted basketball players that had been enthusiastically supported for years! Although he went on to rub it in a bit, nothing more need have been said; the point was made in cunning and effective fashion.

Although we do not feel that the specific recommendations laid out in the "Palcuzzi Program" are necessarily required for gifted students, something certainly is. Let's face it, all men are *not* created equal. Eyebrows are rarely raised when we implement special programs for the physically handicapped or mentally retarded. By the same token, it should not be taken as elitism when we suggest special help for the gifted (cf. Gardner, 1961).

As Gowan and Torrance (1971) point out, Lincoln himself had something to say about the statement of "equality" made in the Declaration of Independence. He felt that the authors of the Declaration "did not intend to declare that all men were equal in all respects. They did not mean to say that all were equal in colour, size, intellect, moral development, or social capacity." Moving this type of argument into the realm of education, the Rockefeller Report of 1958 stated: "By insisting that equality means an exactly similar exposure to education, regardless of the variations in interest and capacity of the student, we are in fact inflicting a sublte but serious form of inequality upon our young people" (cf. Syphers, 1972). Consciously belabouring the point with impunity, we cannot resist including yet another popular quotation that sums up our feelings quite nicely: "Gifted programs are not undemocratic. The absence of them is."

Even if we go so far as to make the questionable assumption that the majority of today's educators are favourably disposed towards special provision for the gifted, the problem still remains as to what kind of action to take. It is easy to scurry hither and yon prattling that we must meet the needs of the gifted, but it is tough getting down to brass tacks and designing something that actually works (hence our emphasis on pragmatics throughout this book and the inclusion of Chapter 6). At this point, then, it would seem logical for us to discuss and evaluate some of the alternatives open to those considering initiating a gifted program.

Acceleration

One school of thought maintains that since gifted children are supposed to be particularly bright, they should move through school more quickly than the average student. Traditionally, the most common method of speeding a gifted child's progress through school has been by "skipping". Actually, acceleration seems to us to be an unusually simple-minded way of handling things. All too often, the "accelertors" (people recommending acceleration) forget that a gifted child is still a child; he may be gifted intellectually but still have the social and emotional needs of a "normal" youngster. In many respects, acceleration is the easy way out — a child can be skipped a grade and forgotten. Very often nothing is done for the gifted child in the receiving classroom; he is still different, still out of place, and — unless a special program is designed — still not having his "academic" needs met. Besides, schools cannot accelerate indefinitely. What do you do with a grade three student who is reading five years above grade level? Obviously, putting him in grade eight is not the solution. In other words, it seems to us that acceleration is frequently inappropriate and simply an admission that people cannot deal with the child where he is.

It is necessary to temper our criticism and admit that acceleration may be beneficial in some instances. In some cases it works; particularly in the math and science areas (Stanley, 1975; Stanley, Keating, & Fox, 1974). For example, the excellent math program at Johns Hopkins has shown it is possible to teach very advanced mathematical concepts to young gifted children. Further, in practical terms, it is sometimes necessary for principals to "skip" children. Parental pressure is often brought to bear, and occasionally it is best for the child if the school gives in rather than fight. If you make a placement decision about a child, but everything you do is opposed and sabotaged at home, you might be wisest to reassess the situation. It also sometimes happens that a bright child is stuck in a room with an insensitive old "battle-axe", while a humane "gifted" teacher waits in the next grade. In this sort of situation, a certain amount of flexibility may be called for. Still, any move to accelerate a student should be well thought out. We tend to look more favourably at acceleration in the junior and senior highs, where "gifted" students have maintained an "edge" over time and are usually old enough to take care of themselves. Before we accelerate any student, however, we take a long hard look at the situation. Age, size, teachers, and the type of class to which the student will be going are all variables to be considered.

While acceleration frequently seems to go very well at first, negative things often start to show up later. To illustrate, one often sees a young girl that has been accelerated still playing with Barbie Dolls, while her peers are developing physically and starting to chase the boys. Also, while their classmates are all out getting their drivers' licenses, accelerated students may still be walking all on their own. Again, it appears to us that acceleration may just be another way of saying: "We don't know what to do with this child!" In our district, we prefer to try to meet the students' needs in age-appropriate classrooms. There is an obvious danger that the child who skips grades will be out of place socially and emotionally, if not intellectually. In the past, "educators for some reason never realized that a child who could read at three and learn differential calculus at ten was no more capable of emotional self-sufficiency than anyone else" (de Villiers, 1977).

John Scott (1977), as a sixteen-year-old gifted child, expressed his feelings about skipping grades in no uncertain terms:

"I'm sorry to report that I got skipped twice. After my kindergarten performance, the first grade teacher didn't want me . . . Anyway, the principal convinced my parents I should start the next year in second grade. At first I found myself behind the others in both motor and formal skills . . . Also, the kids who had been in first grade . . . had less trouble sitting at their desks for long periods of time . . . My second skipping came after I was in fourth grade for two months. I felt the teacher wanted to get rid of her 'Ex Ch' [Exceptional Child] so she pushed me off on the fifth-grade teacher . . . I paid for it in high school . . . Absolutely, I don't recommend skipping for 'Ex Chs'. It may be an immediate solution, but it's a long-range detriment. It's no fun being 13, 14, and 15 in tenth, eleventh, and twelfth grades."

John's reaction to skipping is not atypical by any means, and we feel it is safe to say that the social problems involved in terms of emotional maturity and peer relationships make skipping a hazardous procedure at best.

A less disruptive method of accelerating gifted children is to identify and enter them into school early (that is, the children are allowed in early, but thereafter proceed through the system in normal fashion). In all honesty, we are somewhat ambivalent and uncertain about early entrance in general. In an effort to be as fair and flexible as possible, our district does, in fact, have an early entrance policy — and we have decidedly mixed feelings about it. In our province, children who will be five by December 31st enter into the system in September. In an effort to be malleable, however, we also consider children (born in January or February) who miss the deadline. If parents want their children looked at for early entrance, we set up interviews with the parents and informal "testing sessions" where we run through some things with the youngsters in question. Then, if we feel the child has the ability, we communicate with the schools (and arrange for the parents and child, to meet with the kindergarten teacher and principal) and place the child in kindergarten for a six-week trial period. If things go well, he stays in. Judging from the number of children we have placed, early entrance can work. A number of the kids have fit right in and done very well; early entrance was an opportunity for them.

Conversely, early entrance can be an incredible hassle. Since it seems that all parents out there feel they have a gifted child, we are subjected to unbelievable pressure to put in certain little ones — many of whom are definitely not ready. And when we say we are subjected to pressure, we mean it! Some parents have ignored our recommendations and attempted to "smuggle" their children into school. On more than one occasion, we have had people forge birth certificates. And in one instance, a mother stole stationery from one of our local pediatricians, wrote a letter of recommendation for her daughter, and signed his name to it. The only reason we caught on was that her handwriting — unlike any doctor's of our acquaintance — was legible. Of course, it also goes without saying that, in this age of economic hardship, many women want the schools to act as a babysitting service so that they can go out to work.

Again — getting back to the same old thing — another problem with early entrance is the testing part of it. We have serious reservations about putting four-year-old children through a testing session as if they were trying to gain admittance to graduate school. Try as we might, it is impossible not to put on pressures here — some parents even phone in trying to get advance information about the tests so their child will be able to "study" the appropriate material. It is easy to understand why we are uncomfortable with this sort of thing.

You can see the dilemma. Although some of our own experiences and Reynolds' (1962) review of the literature indicate that early entrance is sometimes beneficial (in that it can help prevent bright youngsters from becoming bored with work that does not adequately challenge them), it can still be fraught with danger. In the first place, just as in the case of skipping, the bright child who is admitted early into kindergarten or grade one may lack a certain degree of social or emotional maturity. While he may cope intellectually, he can run into difficulties getting along with his peers. Secondly, it is incorrect to assume that because a youngster is above average at the age of four or five, he will remain so for the rest of his life. Ability is not static; it can change over time. It is no easy matter to assess the intellectual potential of a very young child, and too often a kid who starts off like a house on fire ends up being very average. Some children, for example, get off to an early start due to favourable home environments (they may spend a lot of time with adults and be taught how to colour, count, and read), but find the other youngsters catching up to them within a relatively short period of time. Besides, test results — especially results on young children — are not "guarantees". When all is said and done, it is remarkably easy to slip up and put a child into early entrance who does not really belong (and who cannot take the pressure). This type of misplacement can have serious and far-reaching consequences. As a result, we do not put many kids in. To our minds, we would rather prevent than lament; we avoid making early entrance placements unless we are convinced — beyond any reasonable doubt — that the child will do well. Still, if we really feel a child looks ready, we are willing to give him a chance.

Ability Grouping

Another method of dealing with the gifted is homogeneous ability grouping, essentially a subtle, partial form of segregation (which we will discuss in a moment). Putting kids into groups with others of similar ability has the definite advantage of making them easier to handle. Bearing this fact in mind, we might be tempted to voice the tantalizing thought that grouping may help the teacher far more than it does the students.

This is not to say that we believe grouping is always poor practice, only that it can be overdone. Dividing students into groups is valuable and essential upon many occasions, but it does get a trifle upsetting to find classes continually broken into groups. All too often, one sees primary children placed — somewhat arbitrarily — into one of three groups: the Beavers, the Racoons, or the Mud Turtles. To put it more honestly in terms of the teacher's perceptions and behaviour, the groups may as well be called the Smarties, the Normals, and the Dummies.

While it is not all that bad for the top group, the Mud Turtles do not usually think too highly of this system. Besides, constant grouping of this nature must be regarded as a bit artificial and confining; the children simply do not get enough opportunity to interact with and learn about each other. Obviously, students at the higher levels can help those in the lower groups. And make no mistake about it, the Beavers can also learn lessons in living from the Mud Turtles, who sometimes possess abilities and viewpoints far different from their own.

We have yet to meet a pro-grouping teacher who has not insisted that there is a great deal of mobility and flexibility built into the procedure. And we have never felt entirely comfortable with these types of assurances. Grouping sounds good as long as we keep rationalizing and telling ourselves that children have every opportunity to move up from the bottom group. In our not-so-humble opinion, however, children often do not really have all that good a chance of becoming upwardly mobile. We have seen far too many kids in the lower levels labelled, stereotyped, pigeon-holed, and forgotten.

For fear of sounding too harsh, it might be wise to repeat that we view grouping as a valuable tool — if used with care. When placed together, bright students often stimulate and encourage one another to reach greater heights. But grouping should be a technique to use part-time whenever appropriate; not a permanent abdication of responsibility. And it should be used in combination with individualization.

To those who take the attitude that it is impossible (due to curricula, personnel, and time constraints) to try to meet the individual needs of each child, we would reply "balderdash"! Good teachers always individualize (that is, they look for, respect, and try to respond to the academic and personal needs of every pupil in their class). If primary teachers in our system could be sent to New Zealand for a spell — where they would find that each child enters grade one on or about his fifth birthday — they would discover precisely what individualization is all about. In any case, by way of a summary statement, let us just say that grouping can be a good thing — if used cautiously and in combination with other techniques. Good grouping can and should involve individualization.

Segregation

One of the most popular methods of handling gifted students is to create segregated classrooms for them. In Cleveland, for example, they apparently have had segregated gifted classrooms which have worked very well since the 1920s, and there are many other places that have bought heavily into the segregated model. Special (major work) classes do, undeniably, have several advantages, basically because they give the children more opportunity to use educational materials, pursue personal interests, and be stimulated by intellectual equals (cf. Boslough, 1984; Trezise, 1976).

Certain gifted individuals seem to have a strong and perfectly understandable need to interact with other extra-bright people. (Mensa, an international society exclusively for persons with extremely high IQs, grew out of just this kind of need.) Putting children with special abilities and talents together can have very positive spin-offs, especially when things mesh into a chain reaction wherein the kids challenge, stimulate, and help each other.

Putting the gifted together into one classroom also has some very practical pluses: 1) it is easier to challenge and stimulate the bright kids as a group; 2) the gifted have intelligent peers to interact with; 3) children who may not be accepted in regular classes because they are "different" might be accepted in a segregated room; and 4) it is easier to provide differentiated programming in a segregated class. Further, segregation makes the gifted easier to manage. They can be bused en masse to one central location, provided with essentially one high level program, and put into the care of one highly trained teacher who takes it from there. At first glance, segregation looks simple and effective. If something is done to handle the problem of elitism, if things are not made too competitive, if the program is planned, designed, and maintained properly, and if the staff continue to have a high commitment to the program over a long term, a segregated system can work. However, that is a lot of "ifs", and, as they say in Mexico, "If my aunt had wheels, she'd be a wagon".

There are many disadvantages that cause us to have grave reservations about the worth of permanently segregated classrooms. To put it bluntly, they scare us. Here is why:

Costs

From a purely pragmatic perspective, the expense of setting up a segregated gifted program can be exorbitantly high, especially for a small district. The costs for special classrooms, equipment, programs, busing, skilled teachers, etc. may become prohibitive, forcing some areas to look to other alternatives.

Misplacement

With the best will in the world, there is no sure-fire way to maintain a perfect average with respect to identifying gifted children. Although educators often seem to assume there are foolproof techniques for identifying the gifted, we hope we have made it clear that no magic test exists — there is no perfect identification. In any setting where gifted kids are segregated, certain children who would have been legitimate candidates for the "special class" will be missed or passed over. You can't "get" them all. As educators are so fond of saying today, "Even Jesus Christ only got eleven out of twelve". Further, and perhaps more seriously, children who do not belong and cannot cope with the demands are sometimes placed in the gifted classroom.

Segregated gifted classes have a built-in inflexibility about them that we cannot endorse. Once a child who does not fit has been placed in a special class (and this happens more frequently than we care to think), an irredeemable situation has been created. Assuming they even notice the overwhelmed child's plight (a generous assumption, by the way), school authorities have the unenviable option of either watching him wilt away or yanking him out of the class. This rather traumatic latter procedure may leave the child with a permanent sense of insecurity, particularly if he has the all too common misfortune of being hounded beyond endurance by parents who have found his "failure" injurious to their self-esteem.

Pressure

Gifted children taught by gifted teachers (often self-ordained) in gifted classrooms are expected to behave in a gifted manner. The expectations we have of extra-bright children are sometimes just too high, and special classrooms have a way of magnifying this kind of "expectation setting". For one thing, kids in a gifted class naturally end up competing — and look what they are forced to compete against!

It is a very real tragedy when young children are subjected to inordinate pressure and pushed to the point where learning is no longer enjoyable. People tend to forget that there is a top and bottom even in a gifted classroom; you have your "smart gifted" and your "dumb gifted". How would you like to be one of the "dumb gifted" — kids who would have sailed along nicely near the top of their class in the regular stream, but who have to struggle desperately in the segregated setting. Misplaced students and those at the bottom of the class are particularly vulnerable to pressure, but it is notoriously easy to put too much strain on any gifted youngster. Incalculable harm — including the "loss" of much of what is fun in childhood — is sometimes the unhappy result.

A Cop-out

A rule of thumb of many educators seems to be: "When confronted with troublesome gifted students, stick them in a special class". Although such dreamers may have tranquil visions of an idyllic, "gifted paradise" of a classroom, things just do not work that way in real life.

Teachers in segregated rooms oftentimes assume that all extra-bright children are equally capable in all areas, and consequently attempt to design one generalized gifted program for the entire class. When one remembers that each gifted child possesses unique skills and abilities ("is in a class by himself", in a manner of speaking), such an approach appears careless, flimsy, and naive. Since children placed in a gifted classroom do not — contrary to widespread belief — form a homogeneous group but an "assembly of unalikes" (Hauck & Freehill, 1972), segregated classes will always have their share of problems. Because of their very uniqueness, giving an entire class of gifted students the same special work to do simply is not enough. Teachers must individualize, especially in a gifted classroom. And in a gifted class, it is terribly easy not to. In many ways, then, setting up a segregated program may simply be taking the easy way out. It is good for P.R. purposes, because administrators can take people on tours and show them a beautiful segregated class with beautiful segregated kids. Lovely work products and samples are easy to show and "sell". Unfortunately, however, a lot of this P.R. is just that — often there is P.R. without real substance.

Another difficulty is that often nobody is really involved with the gifted program other than "the" one teacher in the one class. (The same problem often holds true of gifted programs involving partial pull-out.) If parents ask another staff member in the school what is happening with their child, the answer is often: "I don't know anything about that. You'll have to ask Mrs. Jones down the hall". This sort of thing is not at all healthy; a sense of staff unity or solidarity does not develop and there is little overall attitude change or snowballing of ideas. While a segregated classroom often looks good at first, it is hard to maintain momentum — not enough people are involved.

The "Ivory Tower" Effect

Despite assertions to the contrary, a segregated class must still be regarded as somewhat unnatural — an ivory tower of sorts. Quite simply, gifted children placed in special classrooms may not get sufficient opportunity to interact with and respond sympathetically to other students' needs. They should; when they finish their schooling, the gifted must surface and make a place for themselves in the real world (where not everybody is extra-bright).

To be more precise, placing gifted children in segregated classrooms limits their experiences in a sense. While gifted students can undeniably be stimulated by other bright individuals, they can also learn from "normals" and even from "retarded" students. The gifted should have an opportunity to see the world as it is, and this includes interacting with individuals from all intellectual levels. The standard counterargument — that the gifted do not have to fit in or learn to communicate with others since they are going to end up apart in universities, research centres, or whatever — in untenable. One of the major problems facing education today is that universities tend to become ivory towers personified — they are having all kinds of communication problems. Many academics, forgetting that we do not live in a totally segregated world, disdain communicating with the society at large. Such a situation is clearly undesirable, potentially destructive, and, perhaps, one of the reasons universities are in the state they are in.

Futurists agree that no nation in the world today is totally self-sufficient. On the contrary, they are heavily interdependent. If the gifted are to make a contribution in a broad global sense, it would be helpful if they could learn to work with all people: the bright, the average, the slow, and those from other cultures. In some cases, the segregated model can be counter-productive in this regard; many segregated, gifted children lack skills of socialization and "interdependence" (Sirkin, 1976). And they may not be all that likely to develop these skills in a segregated classroom.

Elitism

Over time, teachers of the gifted often find, much to their chagrin, that they have created a bunch of snobs. After years of being told how smart they are and how much they are capable of, gifted kids do tend to become a bit uppity. While we obviously do not feel that special provision for the gifted is necessarily elitist, we think segregated classrooms may be.

Some gifted children develop arrogant attitudes purely as a matter of self-defense. After all, something is bound to give when they are set apart in special classes, held up as good examples to the other pupils (surely nothing could be more fatal), and labelled as "brains" or ostracized by their peers.

If a child does not see himself as special or odd when he is put into a segregated classroom, he likely will by the time he comes out. Sometimes there seems to be no apparent rhyme nor reason as to why one child is placed in a special class and given the red carpet treatment for his entire school career while another is not. Just why are gifted children considered gifted anyway? In some cases, the answer is that a gifted child is simply one who has been placed in a gifted class.

Even if they make sincere attempts to avoid it, teachers are bound to communicate subtly to students in segregated classes that they are considered something special. Undesirable side effects can result. One teacher we know had the doubtful felicity of working with segregated gifted children for a few years. In her words: "By grade ten most of the gifted students in special classes had developed a superiority attitude which made them difficult to live with, and which sometimes interfered with their performance in school". Elitism can also be a problem on staff; fellow teachers can get quite annoyed with the gifted teacher of a gifted class who gets all kinds of special privileges and attention.

In fairness, we must admit that some students thrive and blossom in a segregated setting; there is no denying that stimulating interchanges and programming can take place in a gifted classroom. However, elitism is obviously a very real danger. On staff, other educators may come to resent the "gifted teacher" who has it "so easy" with special privileges, an abundance of motivating material, and no slow learners. And with the students themselves, it is not in the least surprising that some of them start to think they are really something special — they receive special treatment all the time. Undoubtedly, it is hard for both teacher and students to be humble in a gifted class.

Torrance has said that one of the hardest tasks in gifted education is to help the extra-bright realize their potential while retaining their humility. Some gifted individuals can be a severe trial. It may be wise for us to step back and take a good look at what we are really trying to do in gifted education. Is it our aim to create individuals who are incredibly talented in one area but totally obnoxious in a social sense? All too often, pampered, gifted individuals want what they want when they want it without any concern for the thoughts and feelings of others. (For example, while one cannot help but marvel at the abilities of certain of America's spoiled "tennis brats", it can be extremely difficult to like them or respect their behaviour. They are definitely good at one thing, but other teachings have quite obviously been neglected.) It might be more meaningful to work towards the "golden mean", and attempt to give students help in many areas, including academics, athletics, and the building of social skills. Ideally, we should help our gifted children grow up to be "nice" people; "niceness" should supercede giftedness any day. To our minds, segregated classrooms can make the task of building in "niceness" doubly difficult.

It is our view that many so-called bright individuals have trouble "relating", and many of them — feeling lost and out of place in the world — seem to have the need to join "gifted clubs" such as Mensa and Supraxia Universal. To become a member of these organizations, one must distinguish oneself on certain tests of intelligence. While we may be insensitive here, we find such societies distressingly elitist; anyone who strives for membership in an organization to demonstrate how smart he is is telling you something about himself. Of course, some people join such organizations for companionship, stimulating conversation, and so on — elitism has nothing to do with it. Sometimes, however, gatherings of the "gifted" spend their time pseudo-intellectualizing, glorifying themselves at the expense of others (who supposedly are not intelligent enough to attain hallowed membership status), and looking down on those "less fortunate" than themselves. Amazingly, there are even status-seeking "gifted groupies" who follow gifted conferences from coast to coast. While we admit that we might be insensitive to the plight of these "super-intelligent" individuals and overgeneralizing in many respects, we are really quite offended by the principle underlying the very existence of these societies — that their members are somehow more intelligent than the rest of us.

Social-Emotional Factors

When all is said and done, however, our greatest objection to segregation is the psychological and sociological effects it can have on students. Perhaps the best way to illustrate this concern is to set down some comments from people who have been placed in gifted classrooms. This sort of approach involves setting up a "straw man" in many respects (it is, of course, possible to get quotes from segregated gifted students praising their classes to the sky); nevertheless, in our experience (and this experience has been backed up by several surveys), the majority of graduates from segregated rooms were, on the whole, none too pleased with their schooling. Although some liked it in their gifted rooms, many more did not enjoy what happened to them in the least.

In "On Being Gifted" (Participants, 1978) — firsthand accounts by gifted children about their educational experiences — the major emphasis is on how they tend to feel out of place. The theme running through the book is a fear of being different (and how segregation can highlight this). Other individuals have given quite dramatic accounts concerning their experiences in segregated settings. For example, Sharon Broatch, a former teacher in our district, was placed in a gifted classroom as a child, and she recalls the experience vividly:

"I was reading before I entered school. As a result I was accelerated one year in the primary grades. At the end of grade four, I was taken to a strange school for tests (IQ, I assume). I was sent on a school bus, having never been on one before. I remember going into this HUGE school with dozens of rooms and rows and rows of desks. I also remember not being able to make the pencil work as I started to do the test. I was petrified — not exactly a conducive atmosphere for testing.

I soon found myself taken to a major work class in another strange school (and I had to go on that bus again!). I got off the bus and the driver pointed me at the school. I stood outside in the yard with hundreds of other kids, amazed at the numbers of children. I didn't know what to do, where to go, or even who my teacher was supposed to be. When the bell rang, everyone lined up. I didn't know where to go, so I just stood and cried until my teacher figured out who I was and came and got me. This was a very traumatic experience for me and I still remember the feelings I had in vivid detail.

I also remember the attitude of our teachers and schoolmates. We were continually being told by our teachers that we were smarter than the other classes, that we were capable of much superior work, and so on. The other kids resented us. I don't remember ever feeling part of the school. We were always a separate class.

My years in major work were not happy ones for me. My general feelings about the experience are very negative. I cried almost every night after school. I don't feel that the program fostered the social or emotional development of the students, isolating them as it did from the rest of the school."

We have heard from a multitude of graduates of special classes who echo these sentiments. The first author himself has had personal encounters with school segregation and delights in presenting his admittedly biased account here:

"As a member of a version of the major work program described by Hersom (1962), I've had firsthand experience with this type of thing. Designated as the top five percent of the grade five population (on a group intelligence test that I now know is decidedly limited), my classmates-to-be and I were whisked from our old schools and relocated together in a new one. Even in grade five, I can recall feeling exactly like a helpless, victimized guinea pig.

Perhaps due to overcrowding (or perhaps to avoid contamination from the normal students), our major work class was housed outside the main building in a one-room country schoolhouse imported for our benefit. The following year there was a special room built for us in the basement of the main school, but we really weren't encouraged to go upstairs except to use the library.

Of course, it didn't take long for us to be summarily ostracized (i.e., labelled with the epithet "brains") by most of the other kids. In all fairness, let me say that their sentiments were entirely reciprocated: we rapidly learned to view them as 'the scum of the earth'.

Undeniably, times were different, and segregation was probably more accepted back then. And some good things happened in the major work classroom: we were well-taught, learned a lot, and certain students "blossomed" in the setting. However, others did not. Although the situation became more reasonable after the first couple of years, we went through grades five to twelve being pressured because we were the so-called bright class. By societal standards, I suppose our group was highly successful (after eight years of being told how bright we were, we really had little choice in the matter): most of us are now doctors, lawyers, systems analysts, accountants, and — most importantly — psychologists. But even today, some of us get together (no one else will have us) and wonder what price we paid for our "success." Without question, certain members of our class have, by their own admission, turned into elitist snobs and misfits (with some notable exceptions, of course).

Having rambled on in this vein for quite a spell, we rest our case. To avoid misinterpretation, however, it might be best for us to restate our position briefly. We can go along with partial segregation and grouping; a teacher who uses these techniques is at least making a move towards individualization (by recognizing that different students in her class are working at different levels). Having no quarrel with the argument that putting bright children together can stimulate them, we view grouping as an essential tool. What we react against is seeing the same kids in the same groups for all subjects all year long.

As Feldhusen (1980), Stanley (1979), and others have pointed out, segregation can be beneficial at times. One can get a lot of mileage out of partial pull-out and partial segregation. However, total segregation disturbs us. No doubt some special gifted classrooms have worked to admiration, but we still believe the whole underlying philosophy of segregation has too many basic flaws. Advocates of special classes often start up fast and then relax, thinking that once segregation is complete, the job is done. The actual segregation is only a beginning, however; the real work is in the maintenance. Over time, deficiencies in this method often come to light, sometimes opening a can of worms that can be amazingly difficult to close. Enough said! Let us go on to another alternative which we prefer immeasurably.

Integrated Approach

One of the more influential concepts in education over the last few years has been "mainstreaming". Basically, the term is synonomous with integration, and the underlying philosophy is that children's educational and individual needs are best met within the regular school program. We share the belief that the gifted can and should be dealt with in the regular stream as much as possible. In our district, then, we "play 'em where they lie"; we like to see teachers provide for gifted children in whatever setting they find them (within limits, of course). In other words, we believe there are ways of providing for the gifted in regular classrooms (cf. Treffinger, 1982), and that there can be "gifted output without pullout" (McCluskey & Walker, 1985).

Integration has several built-in advantages that are worth discussing (Henson II, 1976). These include:

Minimizing Costs

It is usually not necessary to come up with a great deal of money for integrated programs to meet the needs of the gifted. Indeed, integration in the regular classroom depends more on the teacher's ingenuity and the school's receptivity than on extravagant facilities or programs. Purchasing a few kits and materials to act as springboards and providing the necessary inservice training may be all that is necessary. And, if gifted children stay in their home schools, busing problems are, of course, eliminated. The aim is to develop an attitude and workable programs in the school, not to spend a lot of money on fancy "cookbooky" materials that look great but all too often remain on the shelves gathering dust.

Helping More Than a Few Teachers

All teachers, not just certain hand-picked ones, need and deserve to have gifted students in their classes. The gifted can provide a breath of fresh air and liven up the room. Is not every teacher entitled to have an opportunity to work with them? It would be positively unjust to try to take away all the bright kids and give them to somebody else. Taking the perspective of regular classroom teachers, we might ask, "The gifted are fun to have around; why should we have to lose them"?

Further, having to deal with gifted children forces teachers to become more aware — and this helps all the students. In other words, trying to understand and meet the needs of the gifted can increase sensitivity, improve teaching style, and help teachers help other kids. For example, becoming familiar with new questioning strategies, materials, and curriculum benefits the teacher, the gifted, and all the other kids in class.

Helping More Than a Few Children

If given the opportunity, other kids can hitchhike on the ideas of the gifted and rise to greater heights. It has even been shown that "learning disabled" students frequently turn to their gifted classmates for help and support — and there is no reason for them not to have this opportunity. Thus, there may well be another advantage to bringing a diverse group of students together in the same classroom. Mainstreaming could increase the disabled child's chances by turning the more advantaged of his classmates into a whole flock of teacher's assistants (Grossman, 1981). And, as we pointed out earlier, the gifted can learn from the other students, whatever their intellectual level.

Encouraging Schools to Take Ownership for Their Programs

Perhaps the most important thing about having an integrated gifted program in school is that the staff take ownership and develop a sense of pride in their own program. An attitude develops on staff — everyone is involved and ideas merge and get translated into action. In fact, many teachers who are opposed to special help for the gifted change their attitude and begin to get involved. In short, you do not have one special staff member, but an entire "gifted staff".

All this takes a lot of work, planning, organization, and just plain stick-to-itiveness. It is certainly not as simple as collecting a bunch of kids and segregating them. Even though it is difficult to establish, however, there can be great pay-offs from a well-planned integrated program for the gifted. As Jim Croce says: "Nobody's ever had a rainbow . . . until he's had the rain".

Longevity

Many times, a segregated class or other gifted program is the brain-child of one or two individuals. If they leave the district for any reason, the program dies. However, if one opts for an integrated model where each school runs and takes ownership for its own gifted program, that program takes on a life of its own — it will remain intact even if the originators leave the scene. Even though we may have provided some of the initial impetus for gifted education in our district, many schools now have their own programs — they forget we were ever involved. And that is as it should be; they are doing most of the work and it is their program. If we leave or — God forbid — are fired, things will still go on.

The Built-In Safety Factor

Quite simply, integrated gifted programs are less likely to do harm than segregated ones. Naturally, we feel that most of the programs we have set up have been helpful, but every now and again we fail dismally. Very importantly, however, when we are unable to help, at least we do no harm! If a student does not make it in our integrated model, he is really no worse off than when he started. With segregation, on the other hand, kids can be hurt through misplacement, pressure, and so on. The main advantage of integration, then, is simply that it helps guard against the evils of segregation.

Of course, teachers have to be careful not to segregate gifted children (and encourage elitism) in the regular classroom. It is possible to set a child up so that he is labelled as an "apple polisher" or "teacher's pet" by the other students. Murphy (1976) gives an example from his own experience:

"It was not uncommon for me to be taken out of the classroom for special testing. On one such occasion in sixth grade, I returned to the classroom just as the teacher was announcing to the class that they had a 'genius' in their midst. If there had been questioning and wondering about me before, the teacher's lack of finesse created open dislike."

Still, we feel it is easier to avoid this kind of stupidity in the regular class than in the segregated one. If there is no special classroom set aside, at least the physical arrangement is not working against the students.

Although there are a lot of positive elements to mainstreaming the gifted, it is no panacea. Far from it! One or two extra-bright children in a regular classroom can end up having an extremely disruptive influence, to put it mildly. Some gifted children are well-adjusted angels; others are holy terrors, pure and simple. Any teacher who has had a recalcitrant, talkative, attention-seeking, child in her classroom knows precisely what we mean. It is natural for some gifted children to want to ask questions, express themselves, and get attention. One has to be careful not to let the tail wag the dog, however. Unfortunately, it is difficult for a harried educator (with all sorts of other children to contend with) to be able to give the extra-bright student the time he needs. Things sometimes degenerate to an almost warlike state, where the gifted child attempts to storm the battlements over the beleagured teacher's fallen corpse. All in all, some gifted kids in the regular stream can be quite a challenge to work with (what with their continual questioning, showing off, etc.). We can

"CURRENT" AFFAIRS IN EDUCATION

"I'll fit you into the mainstream alright!"

understand the frustrations of educators goaded beyond endurance by a gifted pupil, but we would hope that most of them control themselves better than the teacher in the preceding sketch.

In other words, we are not trying to say that integration is always the answer or that it always works. Quite the contrary, things sometimes go very badly for bright children in the mainstream. (Unfortunate incidents are occasionally bound to occur regardless of the philosophy followed or the model adopted.) We understand that integration is difficult and that it can, in effect be the tough way to go; it will always be hard to individualize and attempt to meet the needs of bright children in the regular class.

Despite the difficulties, however, we know that it is definitely possible to develop a realistic, workable, gifted program that is carried out — for the most part — in the regular classroom. Some segregation, partial pullout, special field trips, opportunities, and so on are always going to be necessary, but the overall aim — in our view — should be to work towards making things as normalized and integrated as possible. Specific techniques for doing this sort of thing are presented in Chapter 6.

Partial Pullout

It must be quite obvious by now that integration is the approach we like the best. We are really biased towards programs that can be carried out with the whole class. de Bono's CoRT (Cognitive Research Trust) program for teaching thinking strategies is one good example; why should only the gifted learn to think creatively? Everybody should get the opportunity to develop their thinking skills. MACOS (Man: A Course of Study) is another of our favourites; it presents psychological, sociological, and anthropological concepts (that have hitherto been the sole province of universities) at an intermediate and junior high level. It is good for all kids — everybody should have the opportunity to develop the observation and research skills built into this excellent social-science program. Still, while such materials are good for everybody, there is so much latitude to them that they provide the gifted with an opportunity to take things one step further. In fact, inherent in these programs is the flexibility that permits those who are interested and those who are extra-bright to go beyond the bounds of the regular curriculum.

However, integration must stop short of stupidity. Being realistic, you just cannot sweep "giftedness" under the carpet; the bright kids themselves realize they are "different" and most of their classmates also know that something is going on. Ideally, it is nice to minimize the negative effects of segregation, but nonetheless, it is sometimes necessary to give the gifted something special. Partial pullout can, in many ways, bridge the gap between integration and segregation and allow teachers to have the best of both worlds. For example, the Junior Great Books Program involves pulling a select group of the best readers from the classroom for periods of time and giving them the opportunity to develop analytical skills through reading and interpretive questioning. In an abstract sort of way, we still view this type of partial pullout as integration — it gives us some of the advantages of segregation without many of the negative effects. Besides, some schools demand this sort of approach; nothing else will work in their climate. However, we always attempt to treat this type of partial pullout in a relatively low-key fashion.

An excellent way of minimizing the negative effects of partial pullout is by using Renzulli's "Revolving Door" model. Recognizing that bright individuals are not necessarily gifted in all things or at all times, Renzulli allows students to "revolve" into a gifted program for a specific period of time (to undertake a special project, a research paper, or whatever). Upon completion of the program or task, the child in question returns to regular work and somebody else "revolves" into the enriched setting. Naturally, a child can "revolve" in and out of the program more than once (and many kids — not only the "gifted" — can be given an opportunity).

What we are saying, then, is that we prefer to work towards integration and regular classroom programming wherever possible. We like our gifted materials and programs to provide opportunities for all kids. However, the integrated approach, in our eyes, also involves making judicious use of partial pullout — most often in "revolving door" fashion. True integration requires flexibility (and it can include homogeneous grouping, partial pullout, and so on — it depends how it is done).

Summation

Long before our time, Plato, Charlemagne, Suleiman the Magnificent, and others saw the need for making special provision for the gifted and talented. The emphasis of their ancient programs was almost exclusively on the welfare of the state. Even in this century, much of the concern in setting up gifted programs has been for society at large, not the individual. For example, after Sputnik, the gifted came into prominence in North America only because they seemed to be our most effective resource for keeping pace with the Soviets. After all the excitement had died down, however, interest in the gifted again became cyclic and spasmodic. Currently though, with the help of recent national funding and the legislation of the Office of the Gifted and Talented, the gifted seem to be coming back. And humanism appears to be the order of the day.

There is no doubt that extra-bright children require "unequal education" to maximize their potential. Acceleration through skipping or early entrance is one way of handling the situation, but it often results in severe social problems. Ability grouping is another alternative; one that can be effective if used carefully (and not overdone). Segregation is perhaps the most popular method of unequal education for the gifted. Due to the high costs, the effects of misplacement, pressure, the naivete surrounding its effectiveness, and elitism (among other things), segregation is not really an ideal alternative; students in segregated gifted classes often encounter personal adjustment problems which we find singularly upsetting.

In our view, flexible integrated programming is the best way to try to meet the needs of gifted students. The major focus of this approach is directed towards program enrichment for the gifted in their homerooms. While a gifted child might be pulled out once in a while for special help or grouped occasionally with other bright students who can stimulate him, an effort is made to give him the kind of attention he needs without turning him into a freak or social isolate. Individualization, flexibility, and enrichment must be pervasive elements in any successful integrated model.

4

Teachers and Parents of the Gifted

Who Should Teach the Gifted?

Some people in contemporary education seem to feel that it is easy to work with bright youngsters; they ask, "Can't anybody teach a gifted child?" The argument is that since the gifted have so much going for them anyway, there is no need to do more — we might as well leave well enough alone. To our minds, this notion is simply part and parcel of the "lazy-unfair" attitude referred to previously. Remember that gifted children are children first, and gifted only second; they often require "special" help to develop and refine their talents and personalities.

Conversely, other individuals — those in awe of giftedness — sometimes ask, "Do you have to be intellectually gifted to teach the gifted?" We like Barbe's (1982) facetious response to this question: "Yes, you have to be gifted to teach the gifted. And you have to be average to teach the average. Who of you wants to teach the retarded?"

Obviously, we would answer both ("Can't just anybody teach the gifted?" and "Do you have to be gifted to teach the gifted?") with a resounding NO! It is unsafe and unfair to assume that a gifted child can make it on his own without being given meaningful guidance and direction along the way; specialized, well-thought-out help from "special" people can make a big difference. It may be that some gifted children have done alright by themselves, but — putting our faith in the old proverb, "Trust in Allah, but tie up your camel" — we believe it is best not to take any chances. And while teachers do not have to be intellectually gifted to work with and guide extra-bright children, they do have to possess certain strengths, abilities, and characteristics (and be "gifted" in certain ways).

Essentially, teachers in general are quite a group — they have all kinds of demands placed on them, and usually manage to do many excellent things with their students. Over the years, we have been very much impressed with the commitment, enthusiasm, caring, and sheer amount of time and energy most teachers put into their work. But teachers — like everyone else — are human. Some are amazingly dedicated and competent; others, less so. And this is not necessarily bad — it can be positive for teachers to be different. In any school, there will be strict disciplinarians, permissive types, dynamic speakers, bores, tireless workers, and relaxed loungers on staff. This sort of variety is a plus; it is good for children to be exposed to a cross section of instructors and a number of personality types. It would be a pretty boring school if all the teachers were identical.

Nonetheless, while we defend variety and the right of people to be different, there is no denying that some teachers do not work all that well with gifted students. And while it may not hurt the gifted to be exposed to a boring teacher, for example, some of the time, it would not do if they were constantly subjected to malaise or boredom. By the way, when we speak of teachers of the gifted, we are referring both to teachers of segregated classes and to the multitude of teachers who have some gifted children in their regular classrooms. Bright children — whatever the setting — can be difficult and, unfortunately, some educators are ill-equipped to handle even one gifted child per class. We all know, of course, that all teachers are supposed to have the best interests of all their pupils at heart, but if we dispense with idealistic innocence, it is plain that there will always be a few who have neither the time nor inclination to respond to the needs of bright and talented children. In fact, if truth be told, certain teachers have an unsympathetic attitude towards any "abnormal" child with special needs (including the gifted), since special needs imply extra work which is not always welcome. And others, with the best will in the world, do not know how to reach or respond to their gifted students. They sometimes seem blind and deaf (and occasionally dumb) to what is happening around them in the classroom. Listening to a teacher of this type trying to converse with a gifted child is painfully like hearing two separate monologues. The child sends out a variety of verbal and nonverbal signals, while the teacher constantly misses the point, fails to pick up on the underlying theme, and remains oblivious to the fact that she could take the student on to higher abstract levels if only she would respond with alertness and sensitivity.

As we have said earlier, giftedness often goes unrecognized. Digressing to emphasize this point, one of the greatest geniuses of antiquity was the Greek mathematician Archimedes (287–212 B.C.). His work in mechanics and pure arithmetic anticipated many discoveries of modern science, while his probings into plane and solid geometry laid the foundations for later-day mathematicians to build upon. Archimedes invented the spiral pump (a hydraulic-type device consisting of a tube spiralling around an inclined axis) for raising water from low lying areas to higher levels. As well, he proposed the "principle of Archimedes" (the law of hydrostatics), stating that an object in liquid is supported by a force equal to the weight of the liquid it displaces. According to an old and perhaps apocryphal story, Archimedes made this monumental discovery as he stepped into the bath and noticed the displaced water overflowing. Realizing the importance of his insight, Archimedes — in absentminded and unrestrained excitement — supposedly rushed about unclothed through the streets of Athens shrieking "Eureka!" ("I have found it!") at the top of his lungs.

In any case, when the Romans attacked his native Syracuse, Archimedes used his gifts to defend the city. And, apparently, it was quite a defense; his mechanical inventions caused the invaders no end of difficulty. Despite his efforts, however, Syracuse finally fell before the might of the Roman armies. Archimedes, so abstracted as to be oblivious to all that was happening around him, is said to have been drawing geometric figures in the dirt as the Roman soldiers made their way into the conquered city. One soldier stumbled onto the great man, and was told simply, "Do not disturb my diagrams". The incensed soldier, not recognizing the genius in the old sage, struck him down with his sword.

A definite parallel can be drawn between this version of the death of Archimedes and the treatment many gifted students receive at the hands of their teachers. Just as the Roman soldier failed to recognize genius when he saw it, so do some teachers misunderstand and lash out at gifted children.

Naturally, there are a few (fortunately, only a few) educators who are openly hostile towards extra-bright children. We have seen one such teacher come down hard on a gifted boy who had proudly asked him to read a poem he had written in English class. The poem was exceedingly well-done, but a trifle off topic. Instead of responding constructively to the work, the teacher grabbed it off the student's desk, crumpled it up, and — dripping venom all the while — said he would "always keep it close to his heart". The sarcasm was about as subtle as a sledge-hammer, especially since he proceeded to stuff the poem in his back pocket just as he was making his "close to the heart" remark. It is no wonder that the boy appeared to be crushed by this notoriously heavy-handed display of hostility. While a gifted student does at times have "to be put in his place", this sort of unprovoked nastiness does not do anyone any good.

It is of paramount importance that a gifted child be exposed to several "good" teachers in school; continually putting him with inflexible, uninspiring, or otherwise unsuitable individuals will only cause trouble for all parties concerned. We consider it constructive intervention for administrators occasionally to slip an extra-bright child unobtrusively into the class of the teacher they deem best for him. By discreetly fitting the child into a stimulating classroom environment, numerous potential problems are nipped in the bud. (Although "strategic placement" is one technique we ourselves have used upon occasion, parents of "regular" kids might be a trifle annoyed — justifiably — at this sort of thing, and entitled to wonder why their "average" child should be subjected to "bad" teachers while the gifted get special treatment. That is a good question. Perhaps the best answer is that all teachers should be encouraged to develop skills to help all children. Techniques that benefit the bright should be good for everyone.)

Characteristics of Successful Teachers of the Gifted

Although some teachers are definitely not suited to gifted students, there is no reason to paint a gloomy picture of the current state of affairs. There are an abundance of excellent teachers around who do a superb job with their gifted (and other) pupils, so much so that it is a decided treat to watch them in action. Mirman (1964) has listed several attributes which he feels are necessary qualifications for teaching the gifted. Other writers, such as Maker (1975), Martinson (1976), and Nelson and Cleland (1971), have proposed variations on this same theme. For our purposes here, we have modified, combined, and extended earlier work to the point where we have delineated what we feel are a number of desirable characteristics for a teacher of the gifted to possess. Of course, we cannot expect all gifted educators to possess all of the characteristics that are rather arbitrarily outlined by ourselves and others. Still, there are some characteristics that can be a real help, and it is nice when teachers of the gifted have

— or are willing to acquire — a goodly number of them. Some of these helpful characteristics, as we see them, are:

Wide Background of General Knowledge, and "Brightness"

A teacher of gifted children ought to have an ample body of general knowledge on which to call. She should share experiences with the students (in which case she must possess a reasonable amount of knowledge to share) and be willing to learn from them whenever necessary.

Really, knowledge alone is not enough; a teacher of bright students must also possess a reasonable amount of intelligence and creativity in her own right. However, we are definitely not saying that teachers of the gifted have to be gifted themselves. As we see so often in the math and science areas, truly brilliant people can be totally useless when it comes to getting their ideas across. Still, while a teacher of the gifted does not necessarily have to be gifted, it is important that she at least have her wits about her. Since a gifted child is going to be quick as a whip in many respects, a teacher should be bright enough to keep pace.

Also, it seems to us that if a teacher is relatively bright, she will be more likely to have an appreciation for the needs of the gifted. Torrance (1965) has noted that a teacher is unable to bring out the creative capacities of her pupils if her own value system does not support creativity. In some respects, the essence of teaching the gifted is the ability to develop a creative environment in the classroom. A bright person with solid general knowledge should be able to do this most effectively.

Empathy and Sensitivity

A teacher of the gifted must be able to identify and respond to special needs. Too many adults, teachers included, forget what it was like to be a child. In some senses, it may be that the best teachers are those who remember their childhoods vividly. Be that as it may, however, teachers do need to "see" and be sensitive to both the academic and social-emotional needs of their students.

Security Within Oneself

At times, it is easy to be threatened by the gifted. One teacher we know seemed to be quite upset by a young gifted student in her room. When we asked her early in the year how she felt about this particular student, she replied, "Oh, I haven't had time to hate him yet". But it was more than clear that she was gearing up for it — she was threatened by the child and not happy with the situation in general.

A teacher who is secure within herself is more likely to be willing to help gifted children grow intellectually beyond her own level. And she is less likely to be threatened by bright students. Anyone working with the gifted must be prepared to be questioned and challenged and must be willing to admit when she is wrong or does not know. In fact, it is a good idea to use the bright kids to help with the lessons, especially when dealing with an area in which one is weak. A secure teacher is also more likely to believe in individual differences, accept the fact that each child has unique needs, and react and individualize accordingly.

Specialized Training in the Area of Giftedness

One teacher in our district was, in the past, thrust into the role of teaching gifted students without any prior training or experience in this realm. In her words: "The children were shortchanged by not having an experienced teacher. They could have accomplished so much more if they had somebody who was geared towards giftedness. However, they taught the teacher a great deal and their teaching benefited the classes that followed." To put it another way, Martinson and Wiener (1968) have demonstrated that even when teachers of the gifted have been carefully selected, their performance in the classroom improves markedly (in terms of content, communication, quality of learning, and diversity of experience) following course and inservice work in the area (cf. Maker, 1975).

Although we agree that specialized training in gifted education cannot but help, we regard it neither as a necessary nor sufficient requirement for teachers working with bright kids. If hiring were totally up to us, we would go for the person first; we would be looking for a warm, caring, and bright individual to work with our gifted. If they had training, that would be an added bonus, but we believe good people will learn if given the opportunity. It should be the district's responsibility to give people an opportunity to get the relevant training if they are to be given the task of working with "special" students. If teachers do not have a terribly strong background in the area, they should be pointed towards relevant books, inservices, and training sessions.

What is most important is that as many teachers as possible have positive attitudes towards special programming for the gifted. Simply stated, a teacher must believe in what she is doing. She must have a helping attitude and, in effect, buy into the philosophy that the gifted are more likely to fulfill their potential if they get some kind of special help along the way. Mead (1964) summed it up well by stating that: "Good teachers are today concerned about how they can best meet the needs of the gifted child in school. They are deeply aware that a country's greatest national resource lies in the gifts of these children."

Willingness to Communicate and Share

A teacher should be concerned with monitoring the affective and intellectual progress of each gifted child, and passing on this information to other teachers (particularly to the receiving teacher for the upcoming year). Principals and other administrators should get involved here and facilitate this process. In certain instances (for example, when a gifted child is underachieving), the teacher may wish to call on external personnel and agencies for help with the problem.

As well, it is useful to communicate with and involve parents in the program. Using parents as volunteers is one of the best ways of keeping them active and informed.

Commitment

In all seriousness, it is common for even "good" teachers to become discouraged with some of their gifted students. Often such educators put a lot of effort into a program only to see it go awry. Not surprisingly, some become disenchanted and reluctant to try anything else (which we see as somewhat akin to throwing the baby out with the bath water). Working with the gifted is not easy; a great deal of perseverance and tenacity are necessary. A teacher has to be committed and believe in what she is doing. Teaching the gifted requires a certain dedication; there is a very real need to keep one's information current. There is no doubt that teachers will often be required to do more planning for extra-bright kids, particularly in terms of searching for background information. It would also be helpful for teachers of the gifted to have a high energy level; vitality, liveliness, and vivaciousness are definite assets. In short, a teacher of the gifted should be prepared to be run ragged and love it.

Sense of Humour

The gifted child is often quick to appreciate the humourous aspects of a situation, to play on words, or to enjoy a clever joke or pun. In our experience, we have also found that their humour is frequently dry, cynical, or incredibly sarcastic. The teacher needs to be able to join in and laugh with the kids (and at herself upon occasion). If a teacher is lacking this ingredient, she might do well to go to some pains to try to develop a sense of humour — with the gifted, she will need it!

Tolerance and Patience

There are times when gifted kids can be a real "pain" (a helpful clinical term). We have a few examples: many so-called gifted students we have encountered have been yappy, attention-seeking problems, seemingly in constant need of challenge and stimulation. Others have been so moody or quiet that you don't know they exist. And many have the capacity of getting into trouble in very creative ways. One junior high student in our district, for example, almost sabotaged a school production of "Oliver". He got a cast of students together on his own and was well underway to directing and putting on a rival production ("Grease").

In any case, it helps if teachers can put themselves in the place of the child, be sensitive to his needs, and be as kind and patient as possible (McCluskey, Niemi, & Albas, 1978).

Ability to Motivate

Any good teacher should be able to challenge, enthuse, and motivate the students (and herself). Especially in the case of the gifted, ability to motivate is perhaps the best defence against the bugaboo of boredom. As Rosenthal has shown us, people often get just what they expect. While we know there is no real point mining for diamonds when there is nothing there, it really does not hurt to be positive and exciting with all kids. There is no need to treat anyone like a "mud turtle"; exuding vitality and "style" will help make the kids want to work. When teachers show a positive attitude, all kids benefit — and the gifted may end up going a long, long way.

A Facilitator of Learning

For the gifted, it is often best for the teacher to be a facilitator rather than a director of learning. This is not to say that a traditional, directive approach is bad, only that the gifted tend to thrive in a nondirective setting. We are not recommending unstructured chaos here, but if the aim is to make gifted students think and work independently, it is necessary to allow time to work on building independent, investigative skills. There is a need to challenge the gifted with stimulating work emphasizing insight and abstraction (Martinson, 1968). A large part of lesson preparation should undoubtedly be aimed at encouraging divergent, creative thinking and developing independent work habits.

Although a solid background of general knowledge is helpful, a teacher does not have to know everything. She should be a facilitator to guide learning, not the source of all knowledge or everything to everybody. It is not necessary to memorize all material the gifted are going to be channelled into — it is often sufficient to skim it over and point them in the right direction. Again, divergent and interpretive questions — rather than relying solely on simple recall of facts — can serve to get things going. The point is, a teacher should not come across as an uppity, pompous, would-be god who has climbed the mountain and seen the tablets, but rather as a guide pointing the way.

Obviously, then, democratic classroom management is often effective with the gifted. It is important to know and respect the worth of each individual student and allow him to be himself. The good teacher will provide a classroom atmosphere that promotes self-esteem and makes safe cognitive and creative risk-taking.

Flexibility

As one teacher in our district has put it: "Gifted children should be assigned to teachers who are themselves creative and flexible. It is very hard on both the student and the teacher if the latter is very set in her ways and requires that every exercise be completed even if the child already possesses the necessary skill. Boredom for the child is the inevitable result."

We do not want to leave the impression that basic skills are not important; obviously, they are essential. We only wish to stress that to enrich, it is mandatory to work with concepts as well as with facts. Also, it is necessary to be "flexible" (there is that word again). Schools very often do not have kits for gifted students interested in unique topics, social situations, aesthetics, and languages (Grost, 1970). A lack of materials is not necessarily serious, but a lack of perception is. John Scott (1977) gives a couple of examples about teachers missing opportunities for providing him with enriching experiences:

"In the summer between second and third grades, I met a Spanish boy. That fall I asked the principal if I could learn Spanish, but he turned me down . . . I think the prospect of a seven-year-old third grader learning Spanish independently may have been too much for him to accept".

"As part of an assignment (of a few years later) I was to do a piece of original writing. I wrote a funny (to me) soap-opera skit. My plot was that Isabella and Christopher were having an affair. Ferdinand discovered it and sent Chris off on the high seas. Further, Ferdy got his revenge by using Isabella's money to finance the project. The teacher went into shock and called my parents."

It is a pity when glorious opportunities of this sort are missed. A good teacher of the gifted should be open to original ideas and willing to seize the chance to take the child further than usual. This flexible attitude to enrichment must permeate a mainstreaming program, or it has no chance of real success.

This doesn't mean that teachers should be running around hither and yon in an attempt to be flexible and meet the needs of all of the bright students. Flexibility, as we see it, might better be called "alertness". The teacher should be observant, and ready, willing, and able to make changes in teaching style and programming when the occasion demands. Naturally, structure and organization are important; one does not want confused chaos. Paradoxically, however, there is a need — especially for gifted students — to be unstructured at certain times. By setting up unstructured situations every now and again, a teacher allows creativity to emerge that might have remained hidden in a highly structured setting. The late Harry Chapin, a truly gifted musician and storyteller, poignantly demonstrates this notion in the song "Flowers are Red", where he tells how a cold, highly structured teacher literally "chokes" the creativity out of a bright child (we put this in so all you structured teachers will feel guilty). Seriously though, while we have no quarrel at all with structure, we feel teachers should be flexible, alert, and unstructured at times (and on constant lookout for creativity).

Firmness

As we have been implying, we think it is both possible and necessary for a teacher with bright students to be firm as well as flexible. Gifted kids can be disruptive at times, and will soon have a weak, wishy-washy teacher climbing the walls. If given the opportunity, gifted students will take over the teacher's job and start running the class themselves.

There are certain demands that must be made on students and certain standards that must be met (and teachers of bright kids should be as concerned with the progress of learning as with the product). Although one must allow fun-time for "creativity" to emerge, there are simply some things a child must do both with respect to behaviour and academics. It takes a strong, yet kind individual to meet the needs of the gifted while preventing chaos from breaking out.

Realistic Expectations

Teachers have to be careful; it is easy to get carried away in one's enthusiasm and push the gifted child too hard. There is a need to be demanding and challenging — without being too demanding and challenging. A teacher should recognize that a gifted child's emotional needs might — and should on occasion — limit his academic progress somewhat. Remember, a child first and gifted only second.

Organizational Skills

Any teacher should be organized and well-prepared. With the gifted, strong subject background and solid preparation are essential. In an excellent study (Fifteen Thousand Hours) undertaken in Britain, it was shown that the most reliable indicator of teacher effectiveness was preparation and organization (Rutter, Maughan, Mortimore, & Ouston, 1979). Perpetually disorganized teachers get themselves into trouble. If one prepares lessons ahead of time, decides how much material to cover in how much time, and consciously plans to incorporate different styles and materials into a lesson in an organized fashion, it is hard to get sidetracked or confused. (This does not mean that you will not allow yourself to be sidetracked occasionally, but simply that you will know what is going on when it happens and, by knowing, stay in control.)

One example of lack of planning that constantly aggravates us is the typical field trip. We often see teachers taking their classes to a museum for "enrichment". Some "enrichment" — all too often what you get is a horde of screaming kids running nonsensically from exhibit to exhibit making a general nuisance of themselves. If a teacher wanted to make it a meaningful field trip, she could go in first as an "advance scout" and look things over. She might pick a few exhibits that were directly relevant, plan how she was going to present the material and use the facilities around her, and restrict the visit to cover what she wanted to cover (rather than try to do too much). She should also be aware of relevant reference material, be prepared to give the students meaningful assignments, and be ready to provide necessary stimulation and direction. In short, careful planning is the name of the game.

Simply Be a Good Teacher

Essentially, then, the characteristics of a good teacher of the gifted are the characteristics of a good teacher. We understand, of course, that anybody who possesses all the traits we have just outlined would be a candidate for sainthood; we are asking for someone to be warm, understanding, sympathetic, concerned, dedicated, intelligent, sensitive, to remember what it was like to be a child, etc. And we are asking for all this on a regular basis. While you cannot realistically expect all these things from one person, it would be nice if all teachers would try to acquire as many of these qualities as possible. Sometimes it is best to look at the world not as it is but as it should be, and, even though it may be impossible, it is worthwhile striving towards a vision of care and excellence. If teachers endeavour to be as good and effective as they can be as often as they can be, they can teach the gifted — and they will be good for all the other kids in the class as well.

What Can Parents Do?

Caring parents should always be involved in the education and growth of their children. Because they are "different", and because they so often need extra stimulation to develop to their full potential, gifted children frequently require special kinds of parental support. As pointed out in an article in the April, 1978 issue of *Homemaker* magazine: "The very best thing a bright child can have going for him is a supportive parent, who can articulate a child's learning needs to teachers, principals, and if need be, to whole school boards". There are many guides available for parents of the gifted (for example, Brumbaugh, 1959; Coffey, Ginsberg, Lockhart, McCartney, Nathan, & Wood, 1976; Delp & Martinson, 1975; Ehrlich, 1982; Kaufmann, 1976; Pickard, 1976). On the basis of our own experience, however, we would like to discuss some ways that parents can help with gifted education in the schools:

Identification

As discussed in chapter 2, we feel it is realistic to ask parents to help identify the extra-bright who may be capable of doing more. Of course, all kinds of parents feel they have a gifted child (we have even had parents refer children as gifted when they were, in reality, extremely limited and candidates for T.M.H. classes). It is important to be realistic here and not get swept away by parental enthusiasm. Still, since parents do spend so much time with their offspring, they may be the ones in the best position to determine if there are any special abilities present. There are some things to look for: 1) did your child start to walk and talk earlier than average; 2) is he reading well above age level and did he, perhaps, teach himself to read; 3) does your child use vocabulary beyond his age level; 4) does your child show special abilities in art, music, problem-solving, or whatever; 5) does your child show advanced motor skills or is he exceptionally good at physical activities; 6) does he memorize quickly, etc. If one keeps things in perspective and does not get overly concerned, it is worth taking a look at such things. There is a need to be accepting and not desperate that your child be gifted. If he is gifted, however, it only makes sense to recognize the fact and do something about it.

Communicate and Work With the School

It is essential that parents of bright students share information with principals and teachers. If everyone works together in amicable fashion, there is more likelihood that an organized and worthwhile program can be put in place for the child. Consistency is important — it is ideal when the home and school are going in the same direction. Basically, then, parents and school personnel should work together for the good of the child.

Unfortunately, there are parents who assume the school is always at fault about something or other, and they sometimes go barging about hysterically without checking the facts. We have heard many parental diatribes that have been based totally on misinformation and innuendo. It is all too easy to fly off the handle, say things you will regret, and make veiled threats you cannot carry out anyway. One should be prepared to fight if need be, but it is much more useful to try to improve things rather than setting out to destroy or "get" somebody. An adversary relationship usually does not help either party. In short, a constructive approach is always most effective. As a consequence, we caution parents not to be too pushy. Usually there is no need to set up a confrontation or take a combative stance. Most schools and school personnel are only too happy to work with the child in a positive and productive manner.

Know Your Rights

While things theoretically should go well for gifted children in the schools, the world does not always unfold as it should. There are cases where parents who try to approach things in a positive manner end up being balked by narrow, resistant educators. Unfortunately, while we definitely do not recommend confrontation, it may occasionally be necessary for parents to intervene on behalf of their gifted children (if all else fails). Remember, parents should be the best advocates and supporters of their children; if they are not willing to go to bat for them, no one else can be expected to do so. However, when it is necessary to complain, there is an appropriate way to go about it — it is only fair that parents go through the prescribed channels in orderly fashion. If they have a complaint or simply wish for more information from a certain teacher, they should first go to her and try and sort it out at that level. If they cannot get satisfaction from the teacher, then they should look to the principal and make their concerns known. This gives him an opportunity to use resource teachers or specialists of one kind or another to help the teacher with the problem. If the principal is unable or unwilling to do anything, then it is time to go to the superintendent or, eventually, to the board. It is unfair to go outside or above the principal's head without first giving the school the opportunity to handle the issue.

The fact remains, however, that — rightly or wrongly — "gifted" children (whatever they may be) are entitled to have their educational needs met in the school system. In the U.S., public law 94:142 guarantees this right. In Canada, the legal ramifications vary from province to province, but very similar bills or laws are being considered. Whether there are legal compulsions or not, it seems morally right that special needs children, including the gifted, have the necessary educational opportunities to maximize their potential.

There is one caution we would like to put forth for systems just about to initiate some form of gifted program. Reiterating what we said earlier, the focus should be on programming rather than identification. If one starts out identifying without having a specific plan of action for programming in mind, it is likely that a very troublesome situation could develop. Parents are bound to become irate if they are told their children have special abilities but nothing more is done. If you identify gifted students, you had better do something concrete for them.

Get Involved With Your Children Yourself

We feel it is a good thing for parents to spend time and work with their own children — if they do it right. All too often, parents with gifted children harass the school and demand that educators do something, when they are not prepared to do anything themselves. At one inservice, we were pounced upon by an irate parent who stated indignantly: "I've got a gifted child; what are you going to do about it?" "Uh uh," we replied urbanely, "what are *you* going to do about it?" Any time we get into a situation like this, we try to put the onus back on the parents and get them to take partial ownership for the education of their children. In other words, we feel it is wrong for parents to abdicate responsibility and start pointing their fingers at the school. Parents should be willing to participate in the education of their extra-bright youngsters, and the school should be willing to help. Again, there is the need to work together. This is not to say that parents should not express their concerns to the school when they feel things are not going well. It is just that they should be willing to make sacrifices of their own in an effort to help with the problem. As Lincoln said: "He has a right to criticize who has a heart to help".

Of course, there is no one magic technique to maximize the potential of your gifted child. All we are really talking about here is a little common sense and a willingness to get involved, for there are a multiplicity of "little" things a parent can do. Since gifted kids often like to read and make excellent use of books, it is important to have good material on your shelves at home. You can help build in a love of reading by going down to the bookstore with your child and picking out material with him. In this way, you are showing an interest, and the whole procedure becomes an adventure and an outing. Also, it is extremely worthwhile to encourage youngsters to join a library and use it regularly. In fact, there is no reason why parents cannot help their children with learning the Dewey Decimal or Library of Congress systems and with doing a literature search and writing research papers. If parents do not know how to do these things, they can find out, or at least get somebody else to help them. Books can open an entire new world for a child; enlightened parents can get involved in this world.

It also goes without saying that parents should show an interest in their children's school work and encourage them all they can. While some schools and teachers panic at the thought of parents working with their own youngsters, we do not see why it cannot be done effectively. Naturally, it might sometimes be frustrating to work with your own kids, but if you have realistic expectations, good ideas, and the proper materials, it can be a positive experience. And the school should be able to help in designing a home program. Teaching your children how to work efficiently can have all kinds of positive spin-offs; the second author regularly has his youngsters do most of his research to save him from actually having to do the work himself (this is the first author speaking).

Another important thing is for parents to make a point of taking their kids on family outings. It can be both enjoyable and informative to go together to museums, historical sights, and other points of interest. It is also good to take trips together, and there are little educational things one can do along the way. For example, if you are traveling somewhere, it pays to take a map and show the children where they are, where they are going, and where they have been. If you are traveling out of the country, you can spend time discussing the customs and culture of other people. Even something less exotic — like going out to dinner — offers educational possibilities. There is no reason why even fairly young children cannot be taught how to dress and behave in public and how to choose and order their own meals.

It is self-evident that parents can also be a positive support in many other ways. For example, parents can encourage their children to join Cubs, Scouts, Brownies, Girl Guides, or various other organizations and clubs. This sort of "joining" can be of great importance to some gifted children who may have trouble fitting in; group activities — with a lot of parental support behind the scenes — may be necessary to help some bright youngsters develop socialization skills. Along the same lines, if a child is athletically inclined, it pays to get involved in baseball, football, swimming, track and field, etc. Hobbies, such as stamp collecting, art, and photography, should also be encouraged. And problem-solving activities such as backgammon, chess, and the various computer games can serve to build "thinking" skills. Mechanical abilities can be worked on through Lego, Mechano, and so on.

It is also good to look to music if the child is so inclined. To learn to play a musical instrument well is a tremendous and enjoyable accomplishment. But, of course, like anything else, it takes a lot of work; a real commitment is required on the part of both parent and child. It is a rare child who loves music so much that he will practice as he should without some sort of parental supervision and encouragement. In some cases, it might be necessary to apply pressure and leave the child very little choice. Of course, things should be made as enjoyable as possible, but a certain amount of "insistence" may be required. Although a child may not appreciate it at the time, he will likely be extremely grateful later in life when he has developed an enjoyable talent that can provide hour upon hour of enjoyment.

One cannot overemphasize, however, that you do not want to overwork your child or push him too hard. It is difficult for parents to work with their own children because they often expect too much. Too frequently, parents put on inordinate pressure in the hope that their children will grow up to fulfill their own frustrated ambitions. How often do fathers who never quite made it to the big time in hockey, for example, push their sons mercilessly in an attempt to live vicariously through them. Obviously, it is much better (and sometimes much more difficult) to help your child become what he can and what he wants to be, rather than turning him into "my son, the doctor" from birth. Of course, it is necessary to encourage and make some demands upon children, and it is good to have reasonably high expectations. But one has to be reasonable, and remember that childhood should be a time of fun. Parents have to be aware of how easy it is to pressure children in absurd fashion and spoil what could be the happiest time of their lives.

The underlying theme here, of course, is that nothing can take the place of spending time with your children (be they gifted or otherwise). To challenge and stimulate a gifted child takes a lot of work, and it is not fair to expect schools to do it all. Just as teachers should strive to be "good" teachers, parents — regardless of what type of children they have — should continually work to become better parents. The bottom line is that parents have to be prepared to get involved.

Summation

Whenever possible, it is helpful for teachers who are going to be dealing with gifted students to have certain traits. It goes without saying that it would be delightful if all teachers possessed all of the qualities delineated in this chapter, and it is a safe bet that most good teachers have many of them. The fact that gifted students have unique needs, however, makes it especially imperative that they, of all pupils, are helped and challenged appropriately. Teachers with gifted students should be willing, and indeed eager, to become "masters of the art", and they should actually strive to develop as many characteristics of a "good teacher" as possible. Initially, all the preparation can get to be a bit troublesome; it takes a lot of work. However, once you have experienced the rewards that come with moving an extra-bright child on to exceptional heights, the work becomes more than worthwhile.

Parents too have to be prepared to take some responsibility for the education of their children. And if their children are in fact gifted, parents should view it as obligatory to be interested, concerned, and involved with enrichment at home and at school. As we have pointed out, there are many things parents can do to enrich (and share in) a child's experiences; they should not leave it all to the schools or expect someone else to do all the work.

5

If a man does not know to what
port he is sailing no wind is
favorable.
— Socrates

Establishing a School-Based Program

Getting Things Going

When all is said and done, the proof of the pudding is in the eating. It is obvious that it pays to acquire some theoretical and philosophical background in gifted education before attempting to implement a gifted program; a thorough literature search can do much to help pave the way and save you from reinventing the wheel. And it is necessary to set up some form of identification procedure, be it loose and informal as we recommend, or more rigid and structured as others suggest. But all the theory and identification in the world are not at all useful if we do not somehow put our gifted programs into practice for the benefit of the students. Basically, there comes a time when we have to get in gear and do something.

Many districts respond by "laying on" a system-wide gifted program. It is ordained by a superintendent or co-ordinator that specific things are to happen for the gifted students in their catchment area. Of course, there can be much good that comes with a system-wide delivery system, and we have at times looked at this sort of procedure ourselves (McCluskey & Walker, 1983; Walker & McCluskey, 1981a). However, our feeling now is that a system-wide approach can oftentimes be counterproductive in the long run.

In many ways, it is very natural for zealous superintendents, psychologists, or gifted co-ordinators to get excited about a new pet project.

Having such projects justifies one's position and is a raison d'être for some individuals. Even when the enthusiasm is genuine and well-intentioned, it is terribly easy to make mistakes when a gifted program is, in fact, laid on district-wide. In the first place, the ideas coming down from the top are not always good; they are all too frequently based on hearsay, bandwagons, and only a cursory inspection of the relevant issues. Secondly, district-wide schemes often fall short in that all the details are not always communicated to all the staff members in all the schools. To us, if a school staff is expected to implement a gifted program, they should have some say as to what that program ought to be. That is, they should be involved in the planning from the outset. If this grassroots involvement does not occur, certain teachers might not be as effective as possible due to the fact that they have not embraced the plan in question. Or worse yet, a few teachers may actively oppose and subtly sabotage the program. In essence, we feel it is a wise administrator who refrains from ordering that a particular program be put into place. This is not to say that administrators cannot have a vision and a sense of direction, but only that they should lay the groundwork properly and involve the people most closely concerned with the day-to-day operation of things. It is also important not to move too quickly. All too often, eager consultants or administrators want to get something going immediately. But, on balance, it pays to take time and assess the situation. Not all schools are the same; indeed, for a variety of reasons, they can evolve quite differently. Obviously, what is good and workable in one may not be quite so applicable in another. Forcing the same gifted program on everyone does not always make sense, especially when gifted education definitely demands flexibility from all concerned. We would not dream of doing it with religions; how can we do it so indiscriminately with educational programs?

One of the copestones of our model, then, is to have schools take ownership for their own programs. Usually, of course, we recognize the need not to threaten: to build rapport and credibility over time, it is often necessary to give schools "what they want". In our heart of hearts, however, we frequently feel a yearning to give them "what they need" (or at least what we think they need). But we have discovered that what we feel certain schools need is sometimes not what they think they need. From an administrative standpoint, we have now learned to accept the fact that a school's gifted program must be precisely that — their gifted program! We might get involved and gently help to identify desirable directions, but the real responsibility for planning and implementation rests with the school. The principal, resource teacher, and all other staff members must set their direction and plan as a team. Even though this means that things may be complex and proceed slowly — different schools are going to go in somewhat different directions — we think it is the best way to implement education for the gifted. As noted previously, this sort of approach has a snowballing effect, and entire staffs tend to get involved rather than only select individuals. Implicit in this philosophy is freedom. It seems that everyone recommends that students in gifted programs be allowed to diverge at times, think creatively, and move in their own directions; surely, we should offer no less to teachers who ought to have the latitude to explore and do the things that work for them.

In any case, we see school-based programs as the way to go most of the time; why not allow each school to design and implement its own program? Naturally, a co-ordinator of gifted education or someone else might be in charge of organizing the effort somewhat across the district (that is, to recommend certain programs and approaches, to co-ordinate things administratively, and to facilitate the sharing of information among schools). But each individual school staff would still be largely responsible for what happens in their building.

Factors in Setting Up a School-Based Program

It goes without saying that there are a few things to keep in mind if a school-based gifted program is to work effectively. These include:

Support From the Powers That Be

It is only sensible to inform and get the blessing of individuals who can spell the success or failure for educational programs. Do not ignore the superintendents and the board.

Support From the Principal

There is very little doubt that the principal is the key; he sets the tone in the building and can provide the necessary "spark" to make things happen. He may not be the prime mover in many respects, but he must be involved.

Interested Staff Members

It is rare to find a staff where everyone has a penchant for gifted education. However, it is essential that at least a few people be enthused and provide the catalyst to get things underway.

A Good Consultant

This consultant need not be an official gifted co-ordinator, but it should be someone with a fairly good background in the area. One can always cast a within-building person, such as the resource teacher, in this role, but often it is helpful to have outside input for some things. Also, a district consultant will serve to give some continuity and general thrust to the overall initiative, as well as facilitating information exchange among schools. If no consultant is available from within, it may pay to hunt one down from without.

A Good Resource Teacher

A solid, effective resource teacher can be a tremendous plus as a focal point and an energizer of gifted education. Certainly, the resource teacher should have a major role in any school gifted program (Wood, 1983), and can be of immeasurable help in terms of literature searches, identification, program design and implementation, materials acquisition, management of resources, and in providing direction and emotional support to regular classroom teachers.

Inservicing and Professional Development Opportunities for Staff

If teachers are expected to incorporate fresh and exciting ideas and materials into their programs, they should have some time to find out about such ideas and materials in the first place. Professional development must be a high priority for any staff considering implementing a gifted program, since they are going to need exposure to new approaches and techniques.

Material Resources

Although materials should not be seen as a panacea in education, they do help (Walker & McCluskey, 1981b). When teachers make referrals they

P 204.786.9491
F 204.772.7980
E education@uwinnipeg.ca
uwinnipeg.ca/education

THE UNIVERSITY OF
WINNIPEG | Faculty of Education

Hi Don,

Here is a library-discarded copy of the book in question. Frye now publishes out of Toronto, and since this is from the dim and distant past (written, for the most part in the late '70s, published by the Lord Selkirk School Division in 1983, and finally produced in this version in 1986 – though, as I mentioned on the phone, the date of publication was missing from the first few copies produced, including this one), I will have to get permission to use my own material ... or do a quick rewrite. Keith Walker, the co-author, actually didn't write much (and is now deceased).

Of course, given the decades that have gone by, much of the book will be irrelevant today, including almost all of Chapter 6. Be that as it may, I think a lot can be salvaged, updated, and used effectively even in our present era. And given the ethos of the day, I'm thinking of also inviting Kevin Lamoureux to come on board and produce a section on enrichment in Indigenous education.

Anyway, I see many connections between some of your work and what I wrote so long ago. Let me know what you think (and if it seems reasonable for us to join forces in this endeavor).

Cheers,
Ken

like to see concrete materials; the question asked of most consultants is "What can you give me?" If materials are readily available, one has something practical to offer when the need arises. Many districts have resource or teacher centres which lend materials to the schools. However, it does not hurt for each individual school to work on building up an in-building resource centre to allow immediate and long-term access to important programs. Incidentally, after a while, teachers begin to look beyond the materials. That is, the materials serve as a springboard to generate other ideas; after teachers build their confidence and expertise working with a few kits, they become more comfortable originating, adapting, or seeking out their own materials and programs.

Human Resources

It can be time consuming to work with the gifted, and it is naturally a great advantage to be able to have extra personnel to help out. Of course, one would always like to have additional professional staff but, when they are unobtainable for any reason (such as lack of funds), paid aides or volunteers are another obvious alternative to consider. With a bit of effort, it is possible to train aides and volunteers so that they become an effective support to any gifted program. Along these lines, one concrete thing we have tried to do for schools in the past was to set up a "High School Student Aide Model". The notion was that we would select several top-notch high school students, give them a crash course in gifted education, and use them as aides in the system. What we did was give classes to the students twice a week after school for six weeks. In brief, we covered theory, philosophy, identification, and programming. Then we simply assigned our high school student aides to some of the schools throughout the district. With our input, the schools developed programs for the students to implement with the gifted youngsters in their elementary classrooms. Naturally, the programs in question varied with individual needs. The high school students worked in the classrooms (for an hour or so a day) for the balance of the semester, and they were given a credit upon completion of their "course". Grades were based on participation in their training sessions, teacher evaluation of their classroom performance, and written reaction logs which they were asked to submit.

Although all this sounds terribly formal, the entire experience was really, to put it in colloquial terms, quite "laid back" and relaxing. Without doubt, there were manifold problems: we had difficulty coordinating the schedules of our aides in the schools; we had the occasional negative reaction from some teachers; we had some high school students who did not do as they were told. One definite problem was that some staff expected too much from the high schoolers; we had to convince people that — depite the training period — our high school students were still not trained teachers. Where things worked well, the teachers took ownership for planning and directing the programs (but still worked in cooperation with the aides, letting them have some degree of input). Another difficulty was that each school seemed to want something a bit different. Activities varied from field trips, Think Labs, Reach for the Top, Research Labs, Problem Solving Kits, to writing in-depth journal-type papers. It was rewarding, but difficult, to attempt to meet all these individual needs.

Still, the overall experience was a decidedly positive one. Most teachers really felt that the added input was of great help to the bright students in their classrooms. And all the high school students were convinced that they had benefited substantially in terms of their own growth and development. To illustrate, we will quote from a few of the reaction logs. In one student's words:

"Teaching these children was an experience I'll never forget. I consider the time spent with the students very worthwhile. These children were, at first, a far cry from what I had expected gifted children to be, but now I realize that they were indeed a very talented bunch. I'm not sure who learned the most from whom, but I do know that I gained a great deal from the experience."

Another student "found that these kids have a thirst that is unquenchable; they definitely need something set up for them in the schools". Yet another of our high school aides noted:

"This course helped me to decide that I want to go into the field of special education, working with gifted children, mentally retarded people, and children with learning disabilities. I thoroughly enjoyed this course; I found it to be very informative, interesting, and challenging. Thanks for making the classes really enjoyable! I have no regrets taking extra time to tackle the course. I hope tons of people will take the opportunity to work with two really great educators who know what they are talking about."

It is evident that such a perceptive, insightful student was given an "A" in the course. (Gratifyingly, by the way, she has indeed graduated from her post-secondary program and taken up a position working with "special" individuals.)

Support to Integration

If a school opts to go with an integrated model, it is essential that teachers get some real support in their classrooms. Sometimes, we in education end up having so-called integration with nothing behind the facade. That is, we occasionally have good public relations, but no real substance to the program. Simply putting "special" students into regular classes is not integration; it is negligence. What we have to do is provide teachers with the human and material resources to make the integration work. We might be able to give some aide or volunteer time, and we can surely point teachers towards programs that can be used with all their students. Good curriculum is good for all kids, and there are programs available that motivate the lower functioning students, enthuse and stimulate the "normals", and that have latitude enough to permit the gifted to go far beyond (and pick up ideas and run with them). A variety of programs of this type are discussed in depth in the following chapter. By the way, this sort of approach does not preclude partial pullout; there are some pullout programs that are excellent (in reasonable doses). However, one must use such programs wisely to avoid the dangers of segregation and elitism.

The following model summarizes our view of integration rather succinctly. We recognize that it is sometimes necessary to have a few students spend some time in segregated classrooms. As the large circles indicate, we have some special classes in our district for T.M.H. (Trainable Mentally Handicapped) students, youngsters with behaviour problems, and our language-delayed pupils. While such students do spend time in special classes, however (unshaded area of the diagram), it is still possible to work towards some integration. The T.M.H. youngsters, then, should certainly be integrated (shaded area) for physical education, music, field trips, work experience, and the like. And, as time goes by, one finds they can be integrated much more than most people might have thought at first sight.

Take as another example the segregated classroom for youngsters who are serious behavioural problems. Since they are so disruptive that they spoil the regular setting for everyone else, they are removed and placed in a special class in another school in the district. In all our talk about "special" students, it is essential to remember that the "average" individuals have their rights too. It is wrong to continually make provisions for special students if the silent majority always get the raw end of the deal. As a consequence, when a youngster is wreaking havoc in our system to the extent that he makes it impossible for others to learn, he is

INTEGRATED MODEL

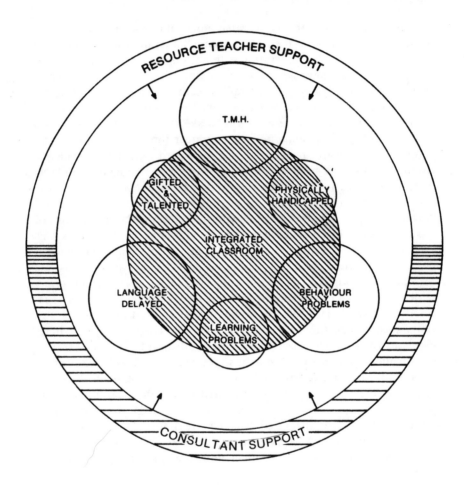

removed from the regular class. However, kids of this type are segregated with a very definite purpose in mind. Essentially, in our special class, we endeavour to provide some guidelines, structure, rules, and consistent discipline, and strive to get problem students to develop and internalize certain standards. As soon as possible, these students are integrated half days (afternoons) into regular classrooms in our special school in question. After all, if we want them to control themselves and to learn and model appropriate behaviour, they must be in a normal setting. Once this trial integration works well for a period of time, our "behaviour disordered" youngsters go back to their home schools (where, more often than not, they usually make out just fine). You see, although we may segregate for a time when absolutely necessary, the focus is nonetheless always on integration. The intent, quite simply, is to get as many children as possible back into the main stream as quickly as possible.

The same notion of integration holds for our gifted program. As indicated in the model, the gifted in our system remain, for the most part, in integrated settings. That is, most gifted programming takes place in the regular classroom. However, we must be sensible about integration; there is no doubt that gifted kids can sometimes be stimulated and gain by working with other extra-bright youngsters. One is walking a fine line here. The general aim may be to have all students together as much as possible, but there can still be a place for taking gifted students out of class for a time to work on special projects, to gain exposure to special materials, and to interact with other "sharp" individuals. It depends very much on how you do it. If done well, however, there is no reason not to make use of partial pullout in gifted education. This, to us, is part of reasonable and reasoned integration.

Appropriate Record-Keeping

With all the formal legislation in the U.S., such as Public Law 94-142 and other specific provisions for the gifted per se, it is obligatory there to keep up-to-date records on "special" students and their programs. Specifically, it is now mandatory to draw up IEPs (Individualized Education Plans) outlining both the short and long-term educational objectives for each child. Several sources (Salvia & Ysseldyke, 1985; Zigmond, Vallecorsa, & Silverman, 1983) offer a variety of information about educational assessment and programming in special education in general, and others have shown how to develop written plans for the education of gifted students in particular (Sato, Birnbaum, & LoCicero, 1974).

In Canada, the same rigid requirements are not as yet imposed by force of law and threat of litigation. And, if not abused, this freedom is positive, for it allows an open, healthy, informal, and comfortable work environment. However, legalities aside, it seems only morally proper to know where we are going with the gifted, and to have appropriate programming and record-keeping systems. While Canadian planning and records may differ from the IEPs, there ought to be something definite in place. In short, there should — in some form or other — be sensible short and long-term goals for each child receiving "enriched" programming, and an effective monitoring mechanism set up so we do not lose track of overall objectives and directions (McCluskey & Walker, 1983). Often, the resource teacher can effectively take charge of record-keeping duties at the school level.

Parent Involvement

It is only fair and sensible to consider the parents when developing any plan for a student. If our children were receiving special programming for anything whatever, we would want to know about it. However, one might decide to handle things in a low-key fashion, simply by informing parents that their child might benefit from enriched programming (and letting them know more specifically what the programming will be). This sort of low-key approach helps get around the frequent "parent-comparison syndrome" ("My child has been identified as gifted and yours hasn't. Tough luck!").

However, parents can be a tremendous support to any school's gifted program, and it is sometimes beneficial to involve them in a more formal way. One common alternative is to form parent advisory groups to input into the program, facilitate information exchange, improve home-school communications, and help insure that parents and educators work cooperatively for the good of the students.

School Gifted Committees

Perhaps the most important step in getting a successful school-based gifted program off the ground is to establish a School Gifted Committee comprised of interested teachers (and perhaps some parents and/or students). In this way, one can put a true team approach into place, and take advantage of the fact that group mind is usually superior to individual mind. (There are exceptions, which is one reason an outside consultant should be involved to some degree as well.) Having such a committee gets more staff on board, leads to total staff planning and sharing of ideas, and builds camaraderie and a gifted esprit de corps. And the Committee will have plenty to do, including arranging for professional development workshops, ordering journals, reviewing and recommending materials, discussing and planning various approaches and programs, setting directions for each year, and so on. This type of committee, then, allows a number of in-school people to take ownership for and become the driving force behind the direction of gifted education in their building. Gradually, their school will implement a true gifted program which will take on a life and a permanence of its own.

Summation

This chapter outlines some of the advantages of setting up in-school gifted programs. Although gifted models are frequently implemented system-wide, there is something to be gained by each school staff being largely responsible for its own program. For one thing, educators will feel more ownership to a program if they have had some say in its development and evolution. In any case, a variety of important factors are discussed which bear upon this issue. These include internal and external supports, human and material resources, professional development, tangible supports to integration, establishment of a School Gifted Committee, and so on.

6

Programming for the Gifted

A Schematic Working Model

An important initial step in any gifted program is to come up with some sort of working model to serve as a signpost and philosophical guide. In our district, we did at first consider using certain models developed by other investigators. For example, one always reasonable possibility is to employ Renzulli's (1977) excellent and popular Enrichment Triad Model featuring his Type I, II, and III Activities. Essentially, Renzulli advocates that all students be exposed to Type I and II Activities. In brief, Type I Activities are those which can be of general interest to all students (for example, field trips, special visitations, guest speakers, specific films, etc.). Type II Activities have more of a group training focus, and involve interested students in exercises designed to develop thinking and feeling processes (such as problem-solving programs, brainstorming, tasks involving higher level thinking skills, value clarification, etc.). However, Renzulli emphasizes the importance of Type III Activities: individual and small group investigations for a select number of gifted and talented students. At this level, students take more responsibility for their own learning and become involved in independent investigative projects. Excellent examples of good Type I, II, and III Activities can be found elsewhere (cf. Maker, 1982; Renzulli, 1977).

However, it always surprises us when districts getting involved in gifted education rush almost instinctively to implement somebody else's

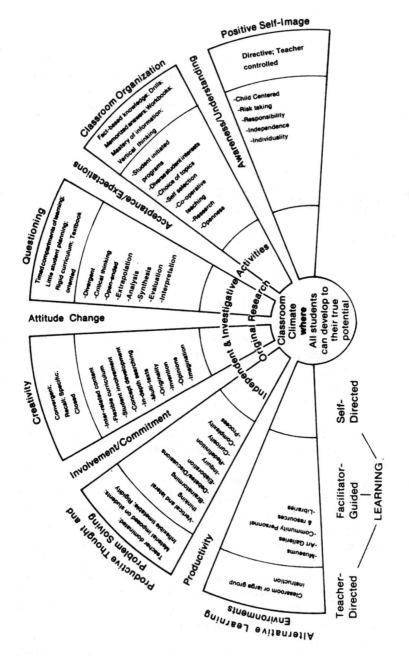

THE McCLUSKEY-WALKER INTEGRATED GIFTED MODEL

model. Since we are talking about developing creativity in kids, why not attempt to be creative and design a model of our own? After some rumination, we opted to do just that, for there was little doubt that we would have more of an emotional investment and a commitment to a creation of our own than to a plan designed by "outsiders". It goes without saying, however, that we consulted and relied heavily on much of the literature cited earlier. Many of the programs and ideas under discussion have theoretical bases in Bloom's *Taxonomy of Educational Objectives* (1956), Bruner's *Spiralling Curriculum* (1960), Feldhusen and Kolloff's *Three-Stage Model* (1979), Guilford's *Structure of the Intellect* (1967), Parnes' *Creative Problem Solving* (1966, 1977), Renzulli's *Enrichment Triad Model* (1977), Taba's *Teaching Strategies Program* (1964, 1966), Treffinger's *Self-Directed Learning* (1975), and various other theoretical "maps" too numerous to mention. A variety of other sources have also been especially helpful in the preparation of this chapter (Ashley, 1973; Callahan, 1978; Christian, 1978; Clendening & Davies, 1980; Freeman, 1979; Gallagher, 1979; Gowan & Olson, 1979; Isaacs, 1972, 1977; Jackson, 1980; Kramer, 1981; Maier, 1982; Maker, 1982; Martinson, 1976; Meredith & Landin, 1957; Ogilvie, 1973; Parnes, 1967; Passow, 1979; Renzulli, 1973; Silverman, 1982; Sisk, 1976; Swassing, 1980; Tannenbaum, 1983; Telford & Sawrey, 1981; Torrance, Torrance, Williams, & Horng, 1979; Willings, 1980). Likewise, World Conferences on Gifted and Talented Children have been of particular benefit (cf. Shore, Gagné, Larivée, Tali, & Tremblay, 1983).

From the outset, it was obvious that we needed a simple graphic to organize and narrow down ideas into some workable form, to give an overview of our philosophy as parsimoniously and effectively as possible, and to point the way and provide a concrete direction to programming for the gifted. Therefore, after considering the aforementioned sources, we put together the model on the facing page.

By way of brief explanation, we attempted to identify six main areas we would like to address in our gifted program: alternative learning environments; productive thought and problem solving; creativity; questioning; classroom organization; and positive self-image. There are also three "circles" in the model representing three different approaches to education: the outer circle emphasizing teacher-directed learning; the middle circle highlighting a facilitator-guided approach; and the innermost circle stressing the need for self-directed learning. Philosophically, we believe that the closer education can get to the inner circle, the better it will be for our gifted and talented youngsters.

This is not to say that an outer circle, teacher-directed approach is necessarily wrong; we know full well that good and innovative education can take place in some so-called "traditional" classrooms. Many children need a strong, directing hand, and in all classes there is a time for the teacher to take charge and leave no options. There are, after all, some things that students must do — period! There is nothing wrong with knowledgeable teachers getting down to direct teaching, or with them expecting their pupils to learn the information they present.

On the other hand, some teacher-directed classrooms are run as a routinized, inflexible, "tight ship", where there is little room for discussion, independent study, or individual interests. The emphasis is on facts, and questions tend to be of a closed, recall nature. Quite simply, the teacher and her reference materials are the main source of information for the students, and she becomes, in effect, "the sage on the stage". Obviously, this sort of arrangement can easily be boring, sterile, and limiting in the extreme.

Our basic argument, then, is that kids need more. A move to a facilitator-guided style — where the teacher guides and points the way rather than dictating the "truth" from on high — is more suitable for many students. For example, teachers here do not dominate the classroom, but allow pupils to have some freedom in selecting, discussing, and developing certain topics and ideas; the interests and capabilities of the children are considered and utilized in various ways. Also, in facilitator-guided classrooms, teachers tend to rely heavily on outside reference and resource materials, and to move beyond simple recall by taking a more divergent, interpretive, and open-ended approach to questioning.

Ultimately, of course, we would like to see more educators strive to reach the inner circle, where self-directed learning takes place in a classroom climate that allows all students to develop to their fullest potential. This approach features the building in of independent investigative skills; the emphasis is on learning how to learn — on process rather than content. The maxim comes to mind that education is what you have left after you have forgotten everything you learned in school. We cannot teach students everything, but we can give them the tools so that if they do not know something they usually know how to find out. And, when all is said and done, is that not what education is all about? Emphasizing invention, higher level thinking, and independent study and research will no doubt benefit many students, especially those with special abilities and talents.

It is again necessary to note that we are not suggesting a move to the facilitator-guided and self-directed approaches at the expense of teacher-directed learning. On the contrary, we feel there is a definite place and need for all three; "good" teachers are directive when the occasion demands, facilitators in some situations, and mere observers at other times. Whenever appropriate, they give their students the opportunity and skills to work on their own. Depending on their individual styles, teachers will approach things differently. Our point is simply that the needs of bright students can probably best be met if they are exposed to inner circle activities for a reasonable part of the time.

What we hope to do now is delineate — for each of the six areas in question — some materials, programs, and approaches that we have found pragmatic and useful. However, before we get underway in earnest with programming suggestions, there are a few cautions we would like to mention in passing. In the first place, we want to emphasize that the materials and programs discussed here are but a small sampling of what is available. It would be impossible to review, or indeed even list, every gifted program on the market today. As a result, we have decided to limit ourselves to materials that we have had first-hand experience with; every program we refer to has been used in at least one school in our district.

We also want to reiterate that we do not intend to give the impression that materials or certain approaches are a panacea; they are tools that are only as good as the person using them. We have found, however, that good materials can be of immense help in a direct sense, as well as serving as a springboard to generate ideas and give direction to future work. Good teachers tend to be able to go beyond their materials. Incidentally, although we describe specific programs, we are not "pushing" any particular materials or publishers — we simply hope to share some of the things that have been useful for us.

Further, we are not presumptuous enough to believe our model is the final word in programming for the gifted; it is intended only as a schematic, organizational guide. The six categories we have chosen are of course arbitrary in many ways, and often programs listed under one heading could just as easily have fit under another.

And finally, we have no desire to have this model foisted on anyone who does not want to approach things our way. Remember, giftedness is a vague intangible — in some ways, too much ado has probably been made about it already. Forcing a model on anyone is, in our view, undesirable — we would hope ours is never implemented holus-bolus on a district-wide basis. On the contrary, we would encourage other educators to create their own models to meet their own individual needs. Perhaps ours might be used simply as a gentle reminder and guide to those who are looking for some initial direction and focus. It is designed not for system-wide implementation, but to give one possible philosophical direction and some concrete, practical ideas and tools to those who are interested.

With that, however, enough has been said; let us move on to our six categories. Referring back to the model (page 106) every now and again should help to keep things in focus.

Alternative Learning Environments

It is important for educators to keep things in perspective and realize that all learning does not take place in school. Indeed, it can pay great dividends to explore and tap "outside" resources; sometimes schools are not able to motivate certain youngsters, but exposure to relevant people, projects, or materials from without can do the trick.

For example, Thomas Edison had only a few months of formal schooling, after which he was tutored by his mother. Ernest Hemingway's father had him model the style of other authors in a formal writing program. Albert Einstein, a classic "learning disabled" dropout, was guided in his studies over the years by a sympathetic uncle. John Dewey, after completing a seemingly rigid, uninspiring education, was greatly influenced by an ethics professor who helped shape his thinking (in a direction quite opposite to that which he had been taught previously). And Winston Churchill, after failing at Harrow, came under the tutelage of his parents who influenced his writing and speaking ability rather profoundly. How many others — astronomers, chemists, musicians, computer experts, or whatever — have learned more out of school than in.

Good educators, of course, can pick up on out-of-school resources, and use outside experts and alternative learning environments to expand and supplement their own programs. Naturally, there are a number of ways we can look beyond the school walls to enhance the quality of education:

Field Trips

One of the most obvious and widely used techniques to enrich the curriculum and motivate students is to go out on field trips and visitations. Taking students out of school on these excursions can naturally be a meaningful learning experience — but, in order to get the most from such "outings" and "happenings", things have to be done right.

As mentioned earlier, first-rate teachers really plan their field trips; they often go in on their own and investigate the offerings before taking the class; they tie in their visit (be it to a paper mill, post office, mint, or museum) with the curriculum; they limit what they are going to attempt to see rather than running helter-skelter all over the place; they make sure students have access to relevant resource material for relevant assignments; and they control their young charges during the visit itself.

Further, teachers should take time to show the children how to use available resources. Bright and interested students ought to be given the skills to enable them to work independently and make future visits on their own. In our case, many of our classes travel in to the Manitoba Museum of Man and Nature which offers a multiplicity of exhibits and services. The Manitoba Planetarium also has special showings, clubs, and a host of attractions for students (who can be encouraged and guided into exploring individual interests independently).

We are also fortunate to be located close to Lower Fort Garry, a historical site that contains a veritable wealth of information about our early history. Costumed hosts and hostesses show students how to make candles, churn butter, shoe horses, etc. It would be a great mistake not to take advantage of such excellent facilities so close at hand.

We realize that some schools are not situated close to major historical landmarks, but there is always something worth seeing if one looks hard enough. It is a rare community that does not have a museum, a factory of one kind or another, or a building or site just bursting with historical significance or local colour that teachers can tap into.

Museum Education

Museums can be so important to education in general that it is worth discussing their role in more depth. If museums are to have the impact they should on children and the general public, educational institutions must begin to look upon them as major resource centres which give youngsters opportunities to explore, to think, to investigate, and to wonder. Indeed, our students should see museums as being resources for learning throughout their lives.

One thing educators can do is to make direct contact with museums and cooperate in setting up useful programs. The museums too might benefit from having students and teachers helping out with projects, research, and so on. One valuable source for fostering communication and helping children get the most from museum visits is UNESCO's *Museums and Children* (Olofsson, 1979).

Importantly, professionals are available at museums who can impart to children the observational, classifying, and organizational skills of the anthropologist, the scientist, and the historian, as well as introducing the whole area of museology. What better way to make use of alternative learning environments! Some museums such as the Geffrye in London allow children to dress up in replica period costumes and re-enact scenes in speciality rooms. And, as already stated, Lower Fort Garry in Manitoba has a program where university students and other costumed staff perform various jobs for the benefit of their guests. Nearby Seven Oaks House does the same sort of thing on a smaller but delightfully homey scale. Along with museum educators, teachers can work to tie the resources of museums into their daily curricula.

Schools can also get students to help set up museums of their own. Children might even be encouraged to play a part in designing and maintaining exhibits, conducting research, collecting specimens, developing programs, and guiding visitors.

Special Courses

When one starts to look for them, it is possible to find all kinds of special courses and outside programs designed specifically for our gifted and talented youth. Perhaps the most famous of these is Julian Stanley's program for mathematically precocious students at the Johns Hopkins University. However, many similar courses are offered in Canada as well. To illustrate, a fairly recent Canadian survey indicates that there is now a growing interest in gifted education; one of every three responding school boards was either planning or conducting a pilot project for their ultra-capable pupils (Borthwick, Dow, Lévesque, & Banks, 1980). And, almost universally, there was tremendous curiosity concerning the latest data in the field.

McGill, for example, offers its Summer School for Gifted and Talented Children (Ross & Shore, 1984), where bright children entering grades two to eight work about a month over the summer with master teachers and teachers-in-training. An attempt is made to employ teaching techniques tailored to the needs of these pupils, and topics covered include computers, languages, caves, pyramids, classic Japanese houses, and the like. Along the same lines, both Carleton and Ottawa offer specially designed, mini-courses — taught by professors at the universities — to school children in the area.

Representatives from many Manitoba school divisions/districts, along with the Continuing Education people at the University of Winnipeg, have collaborated to put into place an Enrichment Mini-Course Program, modelled in many ways after the Carleton effort. This exciting learning experience for gifted students in grades nine through twelve takes place for one week in May, when the students attend the University of Winnipeg to take an in-depth 25-hour course. All courses are designed and taught by University of Winnipeg faculty members.

Borrowing directly from the University's informational publication, "the Enrichment Mini-Course Program has been initiated to provide a short-term program for our gifted students which could later be incorporated into an overall enrichment plan for them. The University of Winnipeg's commitment to the program stems from a belief in the importance of community involvement and a recognition of certain elements important to gifted students — freedom of course selection, flexibility in grade placement, an in-depth pursuit of learning, an opportunity to interact with other gifted students, and an exposure to a university setting."

Several objectives have been outlined for the program, including: 1) to increase the awareness among educators and in the community of the special needs of gifted students; 2) to give students from different schools and districts the opportunity to pursue individual interests; 3) to give students the opportunity to interact and learn in various cross-age groupings; 4) to give each participating student the chance to evaluate the experience in the program; and 5) to interest students in pursuing post-secondary studies.

Courses offered are designed to stimulate and broaden the horizons of the junior and senior high students. Many of the courses are extremely exciting. It is hard to imagine a gifted student in the public school system not being interested in several of the following imaginative course offerings: Anthropology in Life, Recombinant DNA, Topics in Organic Chemistry and Bio-chemistry, Classical Athens, Oral Communication Through Video, Becoming a Storyteller, Le Français Pratique, Physical Geography in Today's World, The Dispossessed in American History,

Moral Issues in the Time of Adolf Hitler, Einstein, The Many Facets of Finite Mathematics, Values and Moral Debate, Freudian Personality Theory, Neuropsychology: An Introduction, Crime and Justice in Canada, The Actor Who Listens, How the Law Works, The Birth and Life of the Universe, and so on.

To date, feedback from the program has been uniformly positive. Students have described it as "fantastic", "motivating", and "an unbelievable learning experience". And they had nothing but compliments for their instructors, who were described as being "very well informed", "obviously brilliant", "very friendly and open", and "the best I have ever had". The professors were equally pleased with the students, who they felt were "keen", "fascinated by everything", and "responsible". One professor summed it up by noting that "the students were brighter and more eager to learn than freshmen taught during the regular academic year". Despite the compliments, however, some professors reported being exhausted and emotionally drained after a week of working with such enthusiastic, ever-questioning charges.

There was another positive spin-off to this whole experience. Since the University required cover art for its program brochure, we were able to sponsor a competition among the grade twelve Commercial Art students in our district. Each and every one of these gifted students produced exceptional work, and the drawing selected as cover art for 1985 was highly original and thought-provoking.

It should be mentioned that the University of Manitoba offers a ten day summer "Mini University" program for children aged ten through fifteen. This program is run almost like a summer camp and, for a fee, parents can have their children exposed to enrichment activities in a university setting. In addition, the Manitoba Chapter of ABC (Association for Bright Children), a high-powered and effective group dedicated to meeting the needs of gifted children, offers a variety of interesting and beneficial children's programs. They also sponsor and organize conferences, attempt to interface with Ministries of Education, and provide help and suggestions for parents and educators.

Community Associates

Teachers do not always have to head out on field trips or to universities to take advantage of outside learning environments. They can invite the outside in. Bringing in actors, artists, dancers, musicians, and the like has become a common and worthwhile practice. Local people in the community, be they doctors, scientists, architects, mechanics, firemen, or butchers, can be asked to share their experiences and give some direction to the children. If scheduling is done effectively, it is possible to allow enough interactional time so that relationships can develop among students and adults who have similar interests and abilities. Clearly, there are people out in the community who have a lot to offer — schools that have ongoing programs involving community associates, volunteers, and mentors have found them to be an incredibly valuable resource.

However, programs using community associates do not just happen; a great deal of planning and maintenance have to be done if this sort of thing is to work. Any schools thinking of developing a program of this nature must be prepared to make a very real commitment to it.

It is also possible to use in-school personnel to help with certain programs. Other teachers in the building might work on special projects of interest with a certain student, even though that student may not be in their class. And, as we did with our High School Student Aide Model discussed previously, it is possible to have older students work with younger ones in an effort to provide something extra. Peer tutoring can be workable, but educators must remember that their student "tutors" are not trained teachers — they need plenty of direction and guidance.

Work Experiences

For truly bright and capable students, it can be beneficial to formalize things by setting up a work experience outside the school situation. Here students are given specific tasks and assignments to do while in the company of talented community adults. For instance, a bright student interested in astronomy may be assigned a special project working with a resident astronomer at the planetarium, or a gifted young musician might be given the opportunity to practice and do research with the local symphony orchestra. School and community personnel have to work in fairly close harmony (which is expected with the symphony) to clarify expectations, purposes, and responsibilities. Close monitoring and evaluation are essential if these experiences are to be useful and meaningful for the student, teacher, and the cooperating person. The tasks and assignments should be agreed to by all.

Independent Research

At times, able students should be given the opportunity to select an area of interest they might wish to pursue using both school and community resources. This is not to say youngsters should be haphazardly turned loose without the necessary skills or direction. Through discussion or the use of subtle inventories such as Renzulli's (1977) Interest-A-Lyzer, teachers can help identify potential interest areas and point the way. They should be sure that students know something about how to gather information and write up research findings. The Center for Humanities filmstrip-cassette packages on "How to Use Your Library and Media Center" and "The Research Paper Made Easy" are useful in this regard, and the Curriculum Associates' workbooks, such as "Thirty Lessons in Note Taking", certainly help in training young pupils in how to approach research for the first time. As well, students working on independent projects can use the "SRA Research Lab" as a starting point. In any case, these programs will be discussed in more detail somewhat later; at the moment, the point is simply that students need some background and guidance before they are sent off to do research. Once students receive the necessary grounding, independent research becomes meaningful.

Special project possibilities abound. Staff and students alike should be encouraged to contact universities or other institutions of higher learning in their community and take advantage of the material and human resources available. Professors are often willing to involve talented students in their projects, or at least spend some time discussing their areas of interest and expertise. Competitive challenges such as the "Think Bowl" and "Reach for the Top" can stimulate independent learning on the part of high school students. And, also at the senior high level, the well-known "Baccalaureate Program" — where advanced work is designed, guided, and graded by outside experts — is an alternative many schools are buying into for their gifted and talented students.

The S.S. Keenora Project

One local example that is perhaps relevant at this point, the "S.S. Keenora Project", was initiated in our district in 1973 in an attempt to meet the needs of "bright" students. In this instance, thirteen students in grades five, six, and seven were selected to participate on the basis of test results from the Canadian Test of Basic Skills (this sort of identification procedure embarrasses us a bit now, but obviously "high achievers" were required to make the project work). The students in question were given the chance to become involved in an innovative social studies program, where they were asked to do research on the vessel, the S.S. Keenora.

The S.S. Keenora was built in 1897, and underwent several structural changes — including conversion to two diesel engines — in 1960. From 1923 to 1965, she navigated the Red River and Lake Winnipeg carrying passengers and cargoes until she was abandoned in our town slough, where she lay rotting for seven years. In 1972, the boat was purchased by the Marine Museum of Manitoba and dry-docked in Selkirk Park. The intent was to restore the ship and create a museum to allow people to experience the rich heritage of marine travel in Manitoba. And things worked well; today the Keenora stands in the park open to an interested public (and a new generation of school children).

The Manitoba Museum of Man and Nature acted in an advisory capacity during the restoration period, and the school district — with the assistance of the program director — was able to become part of the project. A preliminary meeting was held between representatives of the Marine Museum, the Museum of Man and Nature, and school personnel to determine what part students could play in assisting with the restoration. After meetings with students, it was decided that a multi-media kit should be assembled on the history of the vessel. The kit was to contain a slide show with an accompanying cassette, a model of Lake Winnipeg, games based on facts about the S.S. Keenora, a display of changes made to the ship, blueprints, routes navigated, photographs, some labelled artifacts, a crew's menu, a play (an hour of the crew's day), costumes and dress of the period, video tapes of people interviewed, a cut-away of the ship complete with labels, news releases of the first and final voyages, etc. This multi-media kit was to be used for display purposes in our own and other districts to acquaint fifth and sixth graders with the unique marine history that surrounds them. A small budget ($500) was allocated to the project, so that resource people could be reimbursed and minor expenses met.

Students were first familiarized with relevant facts and nautical terms, and then allowed to select topics that were particularly meaningful to them. Since this was not to be merely an extra-curricular activity but an integral part of the social studies program, students were not to be required to make up for time missed from regular classes. One afternoon per six day cycle was devoted to the project. During the regular classes, the students were free to engage in writing, research, and in making contact with local resource people (such as teachers, history department heads, the project coordinator, former captains, and local community people). Students were asked to keep a diary of experiences related to the project. Every second week the group would meet to exchange ideas with their peers and the coordinator.

In essence, then, the intent of this project was to challenge the students, give them some notion of how to undertake research in a real-life setting, and to come up with something useful as an end product. And, for the most part, the aims were met; something worthwhile was produced, students honed their skills, and some cooperative learning and independent research took place. Of course there were some difficulties, in that people ran into the usual scheduling and organizational problems and confusions. Also, while administrators intended that students be freed from regular course work and that they be given credit for their projects, some teachers did not see it that way. This sort of attitude was singularly unfortunate, particularly in light of the fact that the students here were developing independent investigative skills, getting involved in pertinent research, and actually writing history. Are not these the skills we should be trying to develop in our pupils? Say what you will, however, the need of some educators to have students complete the "regular" work will always be a problem with certain enrichment projects and activities.

By way of summation, perhaps the best approach is to offer some comments from a few of the students themselves. When asked, "How has the Keenora Project been a learning experience for you?" one student replied: "Since I began the Keenora Project, I have learned to dig for information to help me in my work (for example, collecting information from books, arranging for interviews, writing away and obtaining literature, etc.). I have also had the experience of being lost, not knowing what to do, and being utterly confused. Because of this experience, I have learned to do what I think is best and yet do something I thoroughly enjoy during a learning experience." Clearly, this individual learned something about writing independently. Others reported that they learned "about nautical terms and parts of a ship", and "how to look up information and put it to use". Another student summed up by noting: "The Keenora Project has been a learning experience for me in that it has provided me with a means to do things I wished to do to enrich my education for this year. I will continue to gather information on Lake Winnipeg ships. With this information, I will present a nostalgic look at the Lake Winnipeg ships."

Again, it is worth remarking that there are many alternatives for educators who want their students to become involved in independent research; the S.S. Keenora is only one of many possibilities. Every school and community should have something on the local scene that is worth exploring further.

Travel and Student Exchange

Looking at other people and places is often a good place to start developing the observational and research skills of pupils at all levels. Of course, it is not always possible to travel to a new place and sample the experiences it may have to offer. However, certain kits and materials can go a long way towards making distant lands and peoples come alive. SRA's (Science Research Associates) "Countries and Cultures" program, United Learning's "How to Study Cultures" (available through Wintergreen Communications), Fitzhenry and Whiteside's "One World" packages, and various National Geographic kits are excellent starting points in this regard. And, in the social science area, "MACOS" (Man: A Course of Study) offers all kinds of possibilities for learning and independent work. We will go into more detail concerning this program shortly.

When teachers or other staff go away to another city or country, they have a glorious opportunity to bring back first-hand accounts, experiences, artifacts, currency, etc. from the place in question. The librarian in one of our schools was able to interest students so much in her recent trip to Greece that it became one of the highlights of the school year.

It is abundantly obvious, however, that there is no substitute for actually being there. When children get the opportunity to travel, they should be encouraged to think critically about the trip and share their experiences with others. If children go on a family holiday, teachers should pick up on the event and perhaps adapt some lessons and assignments accordingly.

Students, when possible, should be encouraged to travel whenever they can; there are a wealth of experiences to be had, sights to be seen, and friends to be made in other cultures. Looking at other people's customs, traditions, and lifestyles certainly serves to increase sensitivity and broaden horizons. At post-secondary institutions, many universities offer courses that involve some time in the classroom and some travelling abroad (at greatly reduced rates). The University of Manitoba, for example, has offered — among others — history courses featuring on-site lessons in Greece and Rome, and education courses examining the systems in Mexico and China.

Several school districts also encourage students (usually taking high school Social Studies) to travel as part of the course work. We will take directly from the March 23, 1983 edition of our local paper to describe the program in our high school.

"A group of 17 Grade Eleven and Twelve students . . . and a teacher escort leave . . . for the U.S.S.R. and Finland for an educational and cultural tour.

The 18-day trip is a school-approved program and provides students with an opportunity to travel and gain a first hand educational and cultural experience. All of the students are studying the Soviet Union in their history course. The trip is completely financed by the students and their families.

While in the U.S.S.R., the students will visit Moscow, Dushanbe, Samarkand, Tashkent, Tbilisi, Kiev and Leningrad. Highlighting their tour will be visits to museums, historic sites, and schools. They will also see the Kremlin, Red Square, and the Hermitage. It is the fifth time our students have visited the Soviet Union but it is the first time they have gone to Dushanbe in the Asiatic area. Similar tours have previously gone to Greece, Egypt, France, England, the Netherlands, Czechoslovakia, Hungary, and Austria.

The group . . . will return home . . . on April 9 after having been half-way round the world."

If the funds can be raised, there are actual courses available overseas for high school students. One such offering, the two week Oxford Vacation Course at Christ Church, Oxford, England, is designed to help young people discover and appreciate centuries-long cultural tradition by direct study and by actually being immersed in it. Morning classes are offered in English Literature, History, Music, Art, Architecture, and Drama. Afternoons bring excursions to stately homes, palaces, and medieval townships. Students are lodged in classical rooms at Christ Church, so they live and breathe English history and tradition. The drawback is, of course, the cost factor (for the transportation and for the course). For those who can surmount the pecuniary impediments, this sort of course is undeniably something out of the common way.

Student exchanges are another fascinating way to experience a different culture, in that they allow the travelers to live in local homes and develop bonds of camaraderie and friendship with their hosts (and to provide appropriate learning experiences and hospitality when they are hosts in turn). With French being so topical and relevant, excellent exchanges are fairly common between the Manitoba and Quebec systems, for example. In addition, our district has had some interesting student exchanges from other countries. Again, teachers must be on the alert to milk travel for all it is worth, and give exchange students the opportunity to discuss or write about their experiences.

In essence, the basic message we are endeavouring to get across is a relatively simple one — learning is not confined to school buildings or personnel. Looking to the outside — to community associates, interested professionals, museums, universities, other countries, or whatever — can have a highly positive impact on the education of all children. There are a wealth of outside resources for us to tap.

Productive Thought and Problem Solving

Most good gifted programs spend a fair amount of time trying to develop thinking and problem-solving skills. In fact, some researchers feel that productive thought and problem solving should be the crux and apex of gifted education in general. Problems again arise with respect to definition and programming — what are productive thought and problem solving, and how are we to develop them? For our part, we do not want to worry too much about complexities inherent in the various theories of cognitive processes. Needless to say, controversies and disagreements abound in the literature, and there are myriad unknowns. Besides, different investigators look at things in different ways. Our intent is simply to outline some general principles of cognition and problem solving, and alert the reader to a sampling of the practical programs on the market today.

Naturally, there are a variety of references — aside from ones we have mentioned or are about to mention later in the chapter — that feature a useful and pragmatic orientation. Some such sources give actual ideas, materials and "prescriptions" for gifted learners (cf. Alexander & Muia, 1981; Mallis, 1983; Stallard & Ingram, 1979; Sellin & Birch, 1980).

Thoughts About Thinking and Problem Solving

Gifted education is focusing more and more on two related and central areas: 1) training in higher order thinking processes, and 2) recognition of the importance of independent, investigative activities. The latter has already been alluded to (and will be discussed again shortly), but the former is worthy of direct consideration at this point in time.

In our rapidly changing world, the need for critical and creative problem solving is crucial. The question arises as to whether or not we can teach children to think creatively. Torrance, Guilford, Bloom, and others feel we can. The trick, however, is to find realistic ways to implement programs which develop thinking skills in the classroom.

Guilford's early work placed a major emphasis on designing curriculum which featured learning through inquiry, discovery, problem solving, and creative thinking. Educators started to teach problem-solving techniques which involved a definite sequence: stating the problem, gathering facts, "brainstorming" possible solutions, and forming and testing hypotheses. Pace (1961) was another investigator to study the relationship between children's understanding of basic processes and their ability to handle (arithmetic) problems. And she made some salient points about training youngsters in problem solving: 1) simply providing frequent problem-solving opportunities and situations may be the most important thing to do (that is, making problem solving and risk taking "safe" in the classroom setting is a necessity); 2) students should be encouraged to develop and use their own techniques to solve problems (many problems can be solved in a variety of ways); and 3) using discussion to help children structure and clarify their problem-solving practices is useful.

In a similar vein, Bloom and Broder (1950) hold certain views concerning principles of how problems are solved. They offer several suggestions for the problem solver, such as: 1) varying the method of attack. A learner must be prepared to modify his approaches to the problem — reflective thought is required in assessing, selecting, and evaluating possible alternatives. Haphazardly shifting from one random approach to another is of little avail; 2) considering older ideas, methods, or materials. Although a problem may seem totally baffling when immediately available resources are considered, an individual might succeed if he explores and alters older techniques; 3) redefining and/or restructuring the problem. A problem in its given form may defy solution, but — if it can be reinterpreted — different ideas and approaches can be brought to bear on the issue; 4) looking for new relationships. The solution to a problem frequently hinges on the learner's insight into a previously unperceived relationship. When such understanding of a new relationship occurs, his available repertoire of responses can often be recombined in a different manner to solve the problem; and 5) proceeding on the basis of an idea, hunch, or hypothesis. "Feelings" that a person has about how a problem might be solved are important. Persistence and flexibility are also necessary; the adequacy of hypotheses must be tested so the learner can change his behaviour when required.

In the final analysis, effective problem solving involves being able to try out new approaches in a thoughtful fashion. Frequent and systematic methods, stick-to-itiveness, and modification of strategy are all essential, which implies that the problem solver must be free to take risks and try out new ideas (even though many of them may not work out). There is an overwhelming need, then, for our students to have the freedom to explore alternatives in a classroom environment which emphasizes ingenuity and creativity, rather than merely the speed of response and "correctness" of answers.

Educators are greatly indebted to investigators such as Bloom, Bruner, Guilford, Renzulli, and others who have thought about thinking, and have endeavoured to devise practical problem-solving programs for classroom use. Another important "name" in the area, and one we have a particular affinity for, is Edward de Bono (1967, 1968, 1969, 1970, 1971, 1972, 1976). In one of his works, de Bono (1967) looks at two forms of thinking: 1) vertical thinking, which is logical, orthodox and generally unimaginative (but has a high probability of yielding answers in many situations); and 2) lateral thinking, which is novel, imaginative, but of low probability. Naturally, both modes of thinking have a place, but the notion of laterality has definite ramifications for gifted education; it has to do with creating new ideas through flexibility and openness. Thus, lateral thinking involves a search for new ways of looking at things, a relaxation from the rigidity of the vertical approach, and the use of chance. Certainly, as de Bono points out, many important discoveries have been more the result of luck than design. For example, X-rays were thought of when Roentgen forgot to remove a flourescent screen from the table where he was playing with a cathode tube; wireless waves were discovered when Hertz observed a spark from apparatus across the room from where he was working, and the image left by a silver spoon lying on an iodized metal surface led to the use of silver salts in making light-sensitive photographic paper. And, if the story related earlier has any truth to it, Archimedes got the insight for his law of hydrostatics as he stepped into the bath and caused the water to overflow. In short, we do not always get an idea when we want one — circumstances play a part.

At this point, we would like to borrow directly and use one of de Bono's entertaining anecdotes designed to illustrate the difference between vertical and lateral thinking. We have segmented and paraphrased somewhat, but the story is from de Bono. It nicely makes the point he wants it to make:

"Long ago in England, a merchant owed money to a cruel, wizened, old moneylender. Fearing foreclosure and imprisonment, the merchant was in quite a state. Eventually, the moneylender, who had designs on the merchant's daughter, confronted them both on a pebble-strewn path. He proposed this bargain: he would cancel the debt if the merchant gave him his daughter.

Of course, both the merchant and his daughter were horrified and resistant to the scheme. Accordingly, the moneylender recommended that they let Providence decide the matter, and suggested he pick up two pebbles from the path — one white and one black — and put them in an empty moneybag. The girl would then choose one. If she were to pick the white pebble, the debt would be cancelled — no strings attached. If, on the other hand, she chose the black one, the debt would again be cancelled . . . but she would have to marry the moneylender. If she refused to choose, her father would be thrown into jail.

The girl reluctantly agreed, and the moneylender proceeded to pick up two pebbles and put them in the bag. However, the girl noticed that he had graciously decided to help Providence along by picking up two black pebbles. What should she do?

[Vertical thinkers tend to suggest that she refuse to choose, expose the moneylender, or sacrifice herself to save her father. However, if she uses lateral thinking, she can look at things a different way and turn a hopeless dilemma to advantage.]

The girl took a pebble, but quickly dropped it on the path where it was lost among the other stones. After confessing to nerves and clumsiness, she exclaimed that it did not really matter anyway, for — if the moneylender looked into the bag — he would then be able to tell which pebble she chose by the colour of the one remaining. Since the pebble left was naturally black, it must be assumed that the girl had taken the white one. Thus, the debt was cancelled and she was able to remain with her father.

It goes without saying that de Bono feels that students should be encouraged to think laterally and see things and combinations in new ways. He believes that many original ideas are generated through play, brainstorming, and lateral thinking. An interesting aside here is that lateral thinking is open to everyone, since it is not dependent solely on sheer intellect. In any case, in his CoRT program (discussed in the next section), de Bono spells out some of the concrete ideas for teaching and developing cognitive skills.

Problem-Solving Programs

There are a variety of "informal" programs schools can use to emphasize the importance of problem solving. Chess — the traditional problem-solving activity for intellectuals (or would-be intellectuals) — can be highly challenging and stimulating, and chess clubs should be encouraged and legitimized. Science clubs, with proper direction, can also be used effectively.

There are also "formal" programs that have been developed specifically to teach problem solving to students. We will mention a few that we have found useful, giving special headings to those that have been employed particularly often or effectively in our schools.

The "Thinking Boxes"
The "Primary Thinking Box" (Academic Press Canada) is a multi-media program for grades K–3. It helps teachers to lead their students systematically to discover, experience, and practice the primary thinking skills of observing, comparing, classifying, imagining, hypothesizing, problem

solving, and decision making. The skills are built by focusing on five major content areas: math, science, social studies, language arts, and self-concept. Thinking Box 1 (grades 3–5) and Thinking Box 2 (grades 6–9) are also available. Again, these motivating, multi-media approaches are designed to hone vital thinking skills by providing theory and practice in decision making, building self-confidence and independence, and giving training in problem solving and logical thinking. Cassettes, filmstrips, skill development and self-help cards, and student reference books are used to teach twelve important approaches to thinking (Level 1: observing, comparing, classifying and imagining; Level 2: hypothesizing, criticizing, looking for assumptions, and collecting and organizing data; and Level 3: summarizing, coding, interpreting, and problem solving).

Thinklabs

One of the more well-known kits dealing with the thinking process is Ken Weber's "Thinklab" (SRA — Science Research Associates). Essentially, it is a reading and thinking kit for intermediate, junior, and senior high students. Thinklab has been used successfully in developmental and remedial settings, elementary classrooms, and with apathetic gifted children in many districts.

Since there are a great variety of problem-solving activities in the program, opportunities for independent, nonacademic challenges abound. The activity cards are arranged independently of each other and in progressively more difficult stages. Specifically, there are five basic types of problems — based on Bloom's Taxonomy — that are dealt with: 1) object manipulation (blue cards) — ways of dealing with given data; 2) perception (orange cards) — extrapolation beyond the data; 3) creative insight (green cards) — building abstract ideas and relations from the data; 4) perceiving image patterns (red cards) — analysis of structure and patterns; and 5) logical analysis (purple cards) — absorbing and interrelating data, testing hypotheses, and planning strategies.

The kit includes student progress cards, which are used to show achievement and gains (and thus keep motivation high). Teachers are encouraged not to provide answers for the pupils, but to guide them by relying on their own judgment. Oftentimes, there may be quite a diversity of opinions and responses — with creative thinking there is not usually only one correct response.

For young adolescents and adults, there is also a "Thinklab 2" — a similar cognitive development kit to improve thinking skills and encourage the use of imagination. Particular emphasis is placed on logic, creativity, quantitative analysis, synthesis of information, and reading. The package includes 700 cards, manipulative materials, student progress cards, an answer key, and of course a Teachers' Guide. Thinklab 2 can be used with a variety of students because it allows them all to use and develop their power of insight, reflection, and creativity.

Motivating students to want to read (rather than specifically trying to teach reading) is a major goal of the program. Using manipulative material, like discs and sticks, gives more meaning to the reading tasks. Coupled with this hands-on approach is the use of dialogue, variation of settings, and the sharing of reading experiences with a partner. Student progress cards are again used to provide visible evidence of progress.

Challenging students is what gifted education is all about. Thinklab 2 challenges pupils in logical problem solving through the use of six categories of problems (each designed to focus on a particular cognitive ability): object manipulation, creative insight, logical analysis, quantitative thinking, brainstorming (for generating and evaluating ideas), and "just for fun" (an integration of the other five areas arranged to incorporate social interaction).

A significant feature of this kit is the brainstorming component. Not only does brainstorming expand thinking, it also assists students in making judgments, in working cooperatively with others, and in applying ideas to other situations. No doubt, certain cognitive and affective growth can be developed through such an approach. The Teachers' Guide provides a good section on how to use brainstorming as an effective device in the classroom.

Possible answers are provided, but students are encouraged to read the problems and to try and solve them through tenacity, independent attack, and flexible thinking. As with Thinklab, there are likely to be a variety of creative answers generated that are just as acceptable as the "correct" one given.

Think Tank

Another innovative tool in this regard is the "Think Tank Mind-Development Program" (Edu-Media) for intermediate grades and junior/senior high levels. Its components include a Think Tank (a plastic sphere containing 13,000 words), a series of 60 Mind-Development Activities (under the headings of decision making, problem solving, creative expression, and word study), and a Teachers' Handbook (explaining the rationale behind the program, the types of learning activities included, how the tasks may be introduced, used, and extended, etc.).

Basically, the Think Tank Mind-Development Program is designed to use random words presented via the Think Tank to stimulate lateral thinking and the generation of novel ideas. It aims to make exciting things happen in the minds of students. In brief, objectives of the program include: 1) moving the mind from idea to idea through lateral thinking; 2) finding new solutions to old problems by redefinition and taking another look; 3) sparking ideas that will help in making decisions and value judgments; 4) stimulating creativity; 5) learning and applying techniques of brainstorming, round table and panel discussions, oral reporting, and cooperative evaluation; 6) building vocabulary; 7) developing a better understanding of the structure and function of language; 8) expressing ideas in a variety of written forms (that is, in stories, captions, reports, business letters, newspaper articles, advertisements, poetry, scripts, etc.); and 9) giving interested students the opportunity to invent other uses for the Think Tank (suggestions are welcomed by the publisher, and blank cards are enclosed for this purpose).

Other Approaches
"Problem Solving: Using Your Head Creatively" (Sunburst Communications) is yet another program that teaches problem solving as a skill. It consists of four audio filmstrips that deal with the problem-solving process, problem finding, idea finding, and solution finding. Students learn to attack problems from different perspectives and are asked to use their imaginations and intuition in order to find creative solutions. The program gets students involved by presenting real-life problems that they can relate to; issues relating to their own immediate problems are considered and discussed. Ideally, an individual who has worked through this kit should develop a "problem-centred" attitude which can help in facing and overcoming personal difficulties and challenges.

Sunburst also puts out "Creative Problem Solving: Planning New Worlds", a program that teaches Bloom's Taxonomy and the problem-solving process. In an entertaining fashion, it explains Bloom's six levels of thinking (knowledge, comprehension, application, analysis, synthesis, and evaluation), and then goes on to apply the knowledge to future-oriented problems revolving about travel, city planning, and food distribution. Intriguing activity cards present hypothetical futuristic problems concerning specific categories or "strands". These include time travel, cloning, space colonization, environmental terrorism, energy sources, robots, transportation systems, and the like.

This program can be used either individually or in groups. Creative students respond well to the "wild card" or "open choice" passages that stimulate original thought and effort. Questions on the back of each card serve to stimulate divergent thinking. Each of the concepts mastered in the program can be related and applied to real-life concerns of the present. Good Apple Inc. also produces interesting materials of a related nature. And D.O.K Publishers have excellent, step-by-step programs and units designed to teach creative problem solving to children (cf. Eberle & Stanish, 1980). Relatedly, there is also practical information available regarding memory, mnemonic strategies, and information transfer (Scruggs, Mastropieri, Jorgensen, & Monson, 1986).

Sunburst has other thinking programs out on the market as well. A sampling of these includes "Encounters with Tomorrow: Science Fiction and Human Values" (grades 5–9), "The Search for Extraterrestrial Life: Is Anybody Out There?" (grades 5+), "Forecasting the Future: Can We Make Tomorrow Work?" (grades 5+), "Sherlock Holmes Cliffhangers" (grades 4–8), and "Sherlock Holmes Spellbinders" (grades 5+).

In a similar spirit, the Canadian Red Cross Society has developed a resource package called "One Earth: Why Care?" Each unit here is comprised of a number of activities aimed at giving students some understanding of a multiplicity of problems. Simulation exercises follow that are intended to help students empathize with people from other parts of the world. Encounters with other students of their ages in third world countries are even made possible, and caring and enthused pupils are given the opportunity to do something about relevant problems in an activity that involves real people. There are also units to develop that involve popular misconceptions, and each has a theme poster for discussion (for example, "Why do they live like that?" "Why should we care?" etc.).

In addition, the Red Cross also has a resource package for secondary students called "Tomorrow's World". International development issues are examined through research, readings, simulation games, role playing, and surveys. In the unit on poverty, it is pointed out that "Some two billion of the world's current population of 4.5 billion people, 45% of the human race, live in poverty so overwhelming that Canadians have difficulty imagining their condition. Jobs, health services, housing, education, enough food — things we take for granted — are distant dreams to them." Discussion, statistical interpretations, and experiential learning help students become more sensitive to such issues.

Since several enrichment programs make use of simulation games, it is worthwhile to digress momentarily and deal with the topic in passing. Simulation games are certainly an entertaining and interesting way to learn, but there are some key features that should be kept in mind when setting up simulations: 1) the games must be teaching tools, and as such should focus on selected concepts and processes; 2) games should simulate a reality-based situation; 3) objectives must be stated; 4) characters and goals must be identified; 5) resources, props, and the background scenario and information should be available; and 6) the game should involve the dramatic qualities of a game, with points, winners and losers, and definite rules.

We have certainly found simulation games to be useful upon occasion for a variety of reasons. Aside from encouraging logical thinking, the games teach social values — cooperation is needed to reach the common goal. During simulations, children interact and participate to a marked degree. And perhaps best of all, the games have a tremendous motivational component; students see a very real reason to participate, learn, and succeed.

Motivating simulation games are available through Educational Services Incorporated. By way of example, "Crisis" — one of the more famous simulations — recreates the problem of an international emergency. Children are required to attempt to solve the crisis while looking out for the best interests of their own country. Similarly, in "Guns or Butter", students consider how an arms race begins, whether it is inevitable, and how to move towards world peace. As well, Engine-Uity has good programs in this regard.

Instrumental Enrichment
Instrumental Enrichment, Feuerstein's (1980) program for cognitive modifiability, is another approach that deserves mention. Although this Piagetian-based strategy was designed originally for work with retarded and low-performing adolescents, segments of it are in many ways applicable for everyone. That is, some of the step-by-step mediated learning experiences employed are flexible and general enough to be valuable even in gifted programming. After all, enrichment is enrichment. Through exercises involving organization of dots, orientation in space, analytic perception, and the like, a direct attempt is made to teach problem-solving skills and modify the child's cognitive abilities. Instrumental Enrichment materials are published by University Park Press, and avail-

able only to certified personnel who have completed the required training program. For more information about this intriguing program see Feuerstein (1980), Feuerstein and Jensen (1980), Link (1980), and Passow (1980).

Triad Prototype Series

The "Triad Prototype Series", based on Renzulli's (1977) Enrichment Triad Model, consists of excellent examples of how theory can be translated into practice. Each booklet in the "Triad Prototype Series: Curriculum Units for the Gifted and Talented" (Creative Learning Press) is developed by people who have applied the principles of the Triad Model to settings and curricula of their own. For example, in one unit on lunchroom waste, a teacher and some grade five gifted and talented youngsters examined "How Much?" food was wasted in the school cafeteria, and "How Come"? Their systematic study and recommendations led to a number of important changes. Other units in the series discuss entomology, restoration and photography, genealogy, and other topics. Definitely, these little booklets help teachers and students alike delineate questions, attack problems in a systematic manner, and stimulate them to initiate projects of their own.

The Productive Thinking Program

Covington, Crutchfield, Davies, and Olton have come up with an approach called "The Productive Thinking Program: A Course in Learning to Think" (Charles E. Merrill). Recommended especially for gifted students, the program develops problem-solving strategies and methods of inquiry in a variety of subject areas (such as math, science, social studies, language arts, and reading). The package contains Basic Lesson and Problem Set Booklets, spirit masters, and class record materials. Notably, a large wall Chart of Thinking Guides outlines the 16 guides to thinking covered in the basic lessons. It spells out, as it were, guided sequential steps to follow in thinking — when in doubt, students can look up at the chart on the wall, and then apply and practice relevant thinking skills on the problem at hand.

The intent, where possible, is that the Productive Thinking Program be adopted into the regular curriculum as a unit to supplement existing material. Certainly, the approach puts an emphasis on thinking as specific, teachable subject matter — students on the program have to think and evaluate for themselves (and assess their own progress). And the Productive Thinking Program fits in along our party lines; it is beneficial for gifted children, but it has also been shown to help many other students — including below-average ones — to make permanent gains in certain areas such as recognizing facts, seeing new combinations, asking good questions, generating high-quality ideas, evaluating problems and points of view, and achieving practical solutions.

CoRT

Perhaps the most systematic, organized, and effective approach to productive thought and problem solving has been developed by de Bono through the Cognitive Research Trust at Cambridge. Although the CoRT program (Pergamon Press Canada) is generally intended for students aged nine to sixteen, it can be used, with adaptation, across an even wider range of ages and abilities — from kindergarten children to I.B.M. executives.

In essence, CoRT treats thinking as a skill to be taught in the school curriculum. In de Bono's (1974) words, "The CoRT approach is to treat thinking as a broad practical skill that is to be used rather than just learnt. In tennis or cooking in order to develop a skill you have to practise it. And that means having something to do rather than a philosophical classification to contemplate." He endeavours to use simple formulae to provide tools for thinking: PMI reminds us to identify the plus, minus, and interesting elements; ADI tells us to delineate areas of agreement, disagreement, and irrelevance; AGO focuses on aims, goals, and objectives; and OPV means to take the other point of view. de Bono summarizes the CoRT techniques in three words: tools (the intent of the formulae is to give us a method of attack), transfer (the skills taught are general and can be applied to different situations), and trigger (referring to the fact that the material can be adjusted and used at many levels).

All in all, CoRT covers a broad spectrum of thinking-related skills. Students are taught to "scan" the whole situation rather than see only its parts; they are asked to consider consequences, alternatives, and other points of view. And a number of lessons are geared towards getting students to focus and direct their attention: OPV (taking the other point of view), Focus (pausing during thinking to consider precisely what is being dealt with at the moment), Being Wrong (looking at exaggeration and false generalization — two main sources of error in thinking), Random-Input (practicing using a random word to generate new thoughts and ideas), Values (dividing values into high and low to encourage their evaluation), and Operations (focusing on formulating a systematic plan of action).

To elaborate just a bit further, students work in groups and the teacher introduces and discusses the point of the lesson at hand. The groups then use the thinking process in question to address a variety of problems. In one exercise, for example, students are asked to do a PMI (to identify the plus, minus, and interest factors) on the statement, "By law all cars should be painted bright yellow". On the plus side, some students note that it would be cheaper to have cars painted after an accident (due to mass production of yellow and elimination of the need to blend paints). Others say it would be good in terms of removing status differentials — all cars would look more or less the same. On the other hand, some minus factors might be that things would be boring, and that it would be absolute chaos in a parking lot! All sorts of interest items emerge from most group discussions. Along the same lines, students doing an OPV (other point of view) might be asked, "A father forbids his daughter of thirteen to smoke. What is his point of view and what is hers?"

Often teachers and students — in their enthusiasm over one issue — have a tendency to want to pour over a single problem ad infinitum. However, CoRT forces quick movement from problem to problem; the intent is to provide practice in thinking, not overwork an issue. Clearly, CoRT offers a well-thought-out structural operating framework; there are six separate units or CoRTs (breadth, organization, interaction, creativity, information and feeling, and action), each comprised of ten specific lessons. And there are many practical operating devices, such as the Apple-Box Method involving the sorting of things and ideas into categories. Yes, CoRT definitely has an abundance of content, organization, and structure. Paradoxically, however, it also offers all kinds of latitude for divergence, lateral thinking, and creativity — once the basic processes have been absorbed. In short, it teaches people thinking skills through theory, practice, and use.

As de Bono freely admits, there can be difficulties implementing the CoRT approach in the school setting. In the first place, a great deal rides on the skill, enthusiasm, and commitment of the teacher; attempts to "fool around" or dabble with the program are not likely to meet with success. In addition, evaluation can be a problem — it is hard to grade thinking. Surprisingly, since "intelligence" is such a highly valued commodity to them, gifted students are often threatened by CoRT. It is very important to them to be thought of as "smart", and they sometimes resist putting their "smartness" on the line and risking failure. (However, although there can be an initial tendency to resist and keep things at a superficial level, it has been our experience that bright students really begin to enjoy the program after awhile.) Finally, perhaps the greatest difficulty for teachers using CoRT is actually to fit it into the timetable somehow. Still, we manage to teach art, music, health, languages, and so on; surely we ought to be able to fit in something as basic as thinking!

Be that as it may, however, the CoRT approach has some tremendous pluses. By looking at thinking as a separate subject, it gets the area the attention it deserves. And it encourages educators to teach process as well as fact. Most importantly, CoRT is good for kids. While many of them may balk at the outset and say they are not interested or "don't care", they tend to warm up to the program enthusiastically over time. Thinking becomes acceptable and risk taking okay. Students learn to listen to others rather than drown them out or vote them down (a common ploy). Eventually, the realization comes that there may be truth to the addage that a majority might simply mean that all the fools are on the same side. With CoRT, following blindly gradually gives way to evaluative and independent thought.

Not only is CoRT good for kids, it provides an opportunity for *all* kids. The learning disabled child who cannot read or write still has a chance to shine. And make no mistake about it, there are some very bright children with disabilities who need a chance to excel (Daniels, 1983). Also, children with rather limited ability are still given skills in problem solving and a direction for thinking — they cannot be expected to "produce ideas just from nowhere" (de Bono, 1974). And, when one stops to think about it, why should problem solving and thinking skills be taught only to the gifted? — other students may need to learn them even more. Thus, although CoRT is a powerful teaching tool for the gifted and talented (it has enough latitude to allow them to learn, grow, and evolve), a case can be made for teaching it to all students as part of the regular curriculum. We certainly feel it should be used in precisely this way.

Math Enrichment

While we do not want to discuss math enrichment in any detail (there is a wealth of information available through most Departments of Education), mathematics activities do highlight and emphasize problem solving to a great degree. Obviously, then, some comment is called for. As mentioned, Stanley's (1975, 1979) work with mathematically-talented youth is the classic program to explore further. As well, Baratta-Lorton's (1977) book presents a delightful analysis of how to teach math, thinking, and problem-solving skills in a fresh and fascinating way.

Several programs exist specifically designed for enrichment in mathematics. Two kits, "Have I Got A Problem for You!" and "Math for Math Lovers 1 and 2" (both from Sunburst Communications), endeavour to challenge gifted children in ten areas not typically covered in the everyday curriculum (for example, combinations, permutations, and number theory). Card/worksheet sets present projects that can involve students for long lengths of time. Both kits are self-directing, and prompt capable math students to engage in high level thinking tasks independently.

The "TOPS" (Techniques of Problem Solving) kits (Dale Seymour Publications), available through Sunburst or Setsco Educational Ltd., are also very useful. There are four separate Problem Decks in the program (for grades three through six), each containing 200 colour-coded cards of three levels of difficulty. Five problem-solving skills — use of resources, choice of operations, guess and test, organization of data, and use of logic — are covered.

We would also like to add a world about "Cuisenaire Rods" (Cuisenaire Company of America), available through Setsco Educational Limited. Cuisenaire Rods have been used for many years now, but over the last while their popularity has waned considerably. In fact, many teachers react downright negatively if they are even mentioned. However, if they are not misused, overused, or abused, Cuisenaire Rods can be useful in teaching arithmetic at all grade levels within the format of the curriculum. Indeed, they are good devices to help teach both fundamentals of arithmetic and inventive mathematical activities.

Problem Solving Kit

As soon as the topic of pocket calculators is mentioned, a few teachers again react negatively and deplore their use in the classroom (insisting that they make things too easy, get in the way of teaching basics, and so on). However, the world is changing, and we would be remiss if we did not take advantage of new tools properly. And the SRA "Problem Solving Kit" (Science Research Associates) helps teachers and students do just that. It features the use of calculators to speed up computation, estimate answers, develop solutions, and look at alternative ways to solve problems. As such, the program is ideal for students at various levels, particularly mathematically-inclined intermediate youngsters.

The Problem Solving Kit is made up of: 1) a Using Your Calculator workbook and Answer Key. Teachers take students through this workbook at the outset of the program to help the children understand and use their calculators properly. This sort of thing would be ideal for many adults who have never bothered to learn the ins-and-outs of calculator usage; 2) a How to Get Started Card provides instructions on how to use the kit; 3) 144 Problem Cards divided into twelve sections; 4) a Problem Card Answer Booklet that offers plans and solutions to each problem; 5) Spirit Masters containing tests to evaluate what the students have learned. Hidden hints appear when students rub the pages with a special marker; 6) Class Progress Records for record-keeping purposes; and 7) Student Record Folders for storing worksheets and tests. Problems are divided into twelve sections: five deal with basic problem-solving strategies (making models, identifying needed additional information, breaking down a problem into parts, simplifying, and researching), six contain problem-solving applications (averages, percents, combinations, finite differences, sequential ratios, and rates, ratios, and proportions), and one section provides mixed practice. All problems are sequenced from easy to very challenging, and there are pointers to help the child on the back of each problem card.

To make the kit more relevant, many everyday problems are drawn from newspapers, supermarkets, gas stations, classrooms, and other real-life situations. And the questions can be extremely thought-provoking and entertaining. To illustrate, one question from the Research section goes as follows: "A horsefly is annoying you. Can you run fast enough to get away from it?" Students have to refer to Peter Farb's book on insects to find the speed of a horsefly, have someone time them running over 50 meters to determine their own speed, convert to the same unit of measure (miles or kilometers per hour), and then use their calculator to solve the problem.

By using a highly motivating approach, the Problem Solving Kit builds skills in estimating, analyzing, and developing effective problem-solving strategies in the math area. It helps students learn to: 1) find relevant and discard extraneous information; 2) recognize and find missing information; 3) apply methods learned earlier to new problems; 4) evaluate several possible solutions before deciding which to use; and 5) accumulate facts and work towards solving problems in a systematic manner. And, of course, the program helps students learn to use calculators efficiently.

Instructional Gaming Program
The Instructional Gaming Group, headed by Layman E. Allan at the University of Michigan in Ann Arbor, has developed a number of highly innovative and intriguing programs using problem-solving games as the basis for teaching mathematical concepts. Available through Wff 'n Proof Publishers (distributed in Canada and elsewhere by Marvin

Melnyk Associates), the various instructional games are both stimulating and challenging in the extreme (and, incidentally, reasonably priced). The essential ingredients of the program as a whole are: 1) a problem-solving game; 2) a structure for classroom and school tournaments; 3) team organization; and 4) supplemental instructional materials. Most of the

Outrun a horsefly?

games are designed for two or more players aged seven to adult (though some of the more complex games are for those twelve years of age and over).

To illustrate, "On-Sets" is a 30-game package developed to teach players the facts and implications of set theory. It allows players to have a good time while learning "new math", and it teaches the concepts of intersection, union, inclusion, null and universal sets, and so on. Other math games include "The Real Numbers Game" (dealing with integers, real and natural numbers, etc.), "Configurations" (geometric concepts), and "Equations". This latter 5-game kit uses fairly basic arithmetic operations (addition, subtraction, multiplication, division, exponents, and roots), and then moves on to further operations and higher mathematics. Interestingly, the game can be as simple or as complicated as the players wish, depending on their mathematical sophistication. "Equations", by the way, is available in computer format.

Incidentally, other strategy games are available in different areas, such as "On Words" (a game of word structures to teach grammar, phonics, roots, prefixes, suffixes, etc.), "Queries 'n Theories" (a game of science and language which looks at linguistics through attempting to break the code of another player's symbolic, secret language), and "The Propoganda Game" (which develops insights into advertising, editorials, and political speeches by teaching the "brainwashing-like" techniques often used to mold public opinion through emotional and "bandwagon" appeals, professional jargon, out-of-context quotations, rationalization, etc.).

In all, the instructional gaming approach really does seem to go a long way towards developing problem-solving and higher-order thinking skills. Certainly, students we have seen on the program have been enthused, motivated, and completely engrossed in their games.

Computers

Computers are awfully topical at the moment. However, we do not intend to dwell for long in this realm, largely because others have written much more effective accounts than we could ever hope to produce. Let us just say that since a major part of education is to teach the processing of information, there is no getting away from the fact that the computer is one of the most powerful tools available. Without doubt, computers can be used effectively with gifted and other students (Bracy, 1982; Katz, 1983; Nazarro, 1981). We live in a changing world; the computer is a part and a cause of the change, and we have an obligation to expose students to it.

On the other hand, a note of caution is necessary — we have to be careful not to overdo it. Computers are wonderful, but they are not everything to education. They can never replace teachers, for the human element will always be the central ingredient of the teaching-learning process. We can prate on and on about techniques and equipment, but the essence of learning is in the people involved. Another concern is that we want to avoid creating "computer misfits". Many youngsters just love "going on" the school computer, which makes it a motivating and extremely useful device. However, if this is all they do day after day, we are losing something somewhere. An overall balanced program includes reading, writing, introspective thought, problem solving, computer-based programmed learning, and human interaction. To focus almost exclusively on any one aspect or approach is, in our view, often unhealthy. And there is a very real danger that certain kids may become virtually "obsessed" with computers, particularly since there are many "maladjusted" adults around to model who seem to live exclusively for their machines. If we see a child who is allowed to spend almost all his waking hours on a computer (sometimes playing video games ad nauseum), we get apprehensive. Computers are one of the most important and intrinsically motivating tools in our world, but we want to control the tool — not have it control us. Much of the onus in such "computer control" will fall upon us in education. Most youngsters in our district, then, have plenty of access to computers in their day-to-day programs. However, this access is not unlimited but, rather, carefully monitored. It would be a very good thing if parents were encouraged to consider similar careful monitoring of their children's computer time at home.

In a purely practical sense, educators might do well to be careful how they hop aboard the computer bandwagon. In this age of information explosion, technology is racing ahead, software is constantly improving, and the machines themselves are constantly changing. Much hardware and software is virtually obsolete immediately after one buys it. We would be well-advised to heed de Bono's advice from CoRT and focus, evaluate, and systematically take stock of the situation without undue haste. Too many computers are being misused, and too many are sitting around in schools not being used at all. There is naturally an urgent need to get on board, but one does not want to leap in too frantically and sink the ship.

Perhaps some clarification would be helpful in summing up here. We certainly do not want to be accused of being anti-computer, for we have seen some marvellous things done for our students via this route. Indeed,

Sunburst and others have programs that very successfully stimulate and challenge the gifted. All we are saying is that districts should get involved in computer education wisely, not foolishly. Having a coordinator of computer education and/or a computer committee of teachers would be a good start in evaluating alternatives, giving needed direction, and streamlining and guiding proceedings in general.

Creativity

As always, there is the problem of definition when a term such as creativity is used. And again, many of the thoughts, approaches, and programs to be mentioned in this section could just as easily have been placed elsewhere. Nevertheless, we view creativity — or striving for creativity — to be central in education for the gifted. For convenience, and due to the way our model is arranged, we generally associate creativity and the "arts" fairly closely in this portion of our discussion.

As noted earlier, it is important sometimes to allow unstructured, loose activities, to occur in the classroom. And, as implied in our review of the work on problem solving, "structured unstructuredness" can often allow creativity to emerge. We are not artists, but if pushed we could probably think of or find out about methods to develop ability and creativity in this realm. Artists in the Schools is one excellent program that comes to mind. Photography clubs should be encouraged in schools — possibilities for special projects here are almost endless. And, as stated previously, chess definitely should have a place through school clubs and tournaments. (While some educators frown on competitive programs, we view competition as part of life — a part that must be faced in schools, universities, sports, careers, and in the arts.) Special students have to be challenged; indeed, even in counselling and guidance, the creative needs of the gifted and talented must be considered (Baker, 1976; Gowan & Bruch, 1971; Ziv, 1976, 1977). And there are, in fact, procedures designed to develop the intuition and creative imagery of our gifted students (Brown & Wolf, 1986).

Music is obviously one area that should be considered and, conveniently, much can be done for the musical child at home. Still, the school should make every effort to accommodate talented young musicians by extending the music program and using outside resources. For, when children learn to sing, dance, or play an instrument, they in a sense learn a new mode of expression and language — a language that can literally transport them to another dimension. As discussed before, music and lyrics can be used to teach reading and other concepts, as in the "Hits-Pak" program (High Interest Teaching Systems). Here words and music clearly motivate some students. To get the most from the program, however, one must choose selectively from among many titles and pick a song with some depth and meaning to it. (We had an ordering mix-up once which resulted in us getting not the deep, poetic work of Paul Simon but a somewhat less profound hit by Donny and Marie!)

For teachers interested in developing the creative potential of children in a particular specialty area, eight good books are available in the "Creative Teaching in the Elementary School" series (Hickok & Smith, 1974; Piltz & Sund, 1974; Ritson & Smith, 1975; Smith, 1967a, 1967b, 1973, 1975; Westcott & Smith, 1967). Each book provides help for teachers trying to design creatively stimulating programs in a certain discipline (math, social studies, reading, science, etc.). Parnes and others also have some good ideas for developing creativity in a variety of areas.

Theatre

Theatre and drama are obvious interest areas of many talented people. Torrance (1975) has even considered sociodrama as a problem-solving approach to studying the future. School operettas and plays are an important part of every year. And other forms of drama have been used effectively for able students in some schools — Phil Baker discusses a program of this sort later in this section.

Another program we would like to highlight is a theatre production put on a few years back by junior high school students in a town to our north. The main industry in the town in question is pulp and paper, so the performance — "Papertown" — was produced as a salute to the history of the community. The project was sponsored by the paper company and the Manitoba Arts Council, a director was made available through Children's Theatre North, and artists from the Arts Council and Manitoba Theatre Centre served as set designers and video and music directors.

Essentially, the theatre people took over the school for a week to whip the 30 students into shape for the major production (which was presented before a large community audience at week's end). Twenty-six students became performers, while four — whose talents lay in a different direction — became part of a film crew. Although back-up support and guidance were plentiful, students researched the town's history, created the "Papertown" story on their own, rehearsed for 21 hours, helped with song lyrics, built the set, sang, performed the play in a dress rehearsal for other students and before the public, and recorded the whole event on film. It was a busy week!

This ambitious project meant a great deal to the students, imbuing them as it did with a sense of pride in their community. It also gave them a "behind the scenes" look at theatre, encouraged independent thinking, fostered cooperation, and served as a valuable learning experience. "Papertown" was also good for the community as a whole; participating students, other pupils, school staff, visiting artists, parents, and towns-people were on a "high" for weeks after the experience.

Language Arts

Many people, Covington, de Bono, Renzulli, Passow, and others (such as De Boer, 1963; Isaacs, 1968, 1974; Sebasta, 1976; Witty, 1974), have long argued that a large dose of creativity needs to be injected into the lan-guage arts curriculum. Certainly, ability to read analytically and synthes-ize information is a characteristic many bright individuals possess, and many gifted youngsters seem to have taught themselves to read without any apparent formal instruction. Somerset Maugham describes how, as a very young child, he was so captivated by the pictures in "One Thousand and One Nights" that he poured over the book until somehow he started to read on his own. And apparently, Dr. Bradley, editor of the Oxford Dictionary, began to read at the age of four by following his father's fingers as he poured over the family Bible. However, due to the fact his seat was opposite his father's, he learned to read upside down. Fortu-nately for all of us he was able to turn things right side up before putting together the dictionary.

"Literature has a unique capacity for revealing the truth of human experience" (Burton, 1960). It can open up new horizons, allow us men-tally to travel to places real and imaginary, and provide a refuge from occasionally mundane day-to-day existence. Most of us find reading to be an edifying experience, but gifted readers can in some way elevate it to another plane.

Gifted children need special opportunities to find a sense of fulfill-ment through reading. Because of their ability, the gifted are often more capable of focusing their attention for greater lengths of time, engaging in self-directed learning, and attacking diversified material of a high stand-ard. As such, they are entitled to reading experiences that extend their choices and move them on to greater literary challenges. Polette and

Hamlin (1980), in their useful book on the subject, explore methods of doing precisely that.

Many reading programs and activities can have utility for gifted education. The famed language experience approach, when taught well, has latitude enough to meet the needs of most children, including the gifted (cf. Allen & Halvorsen, 1961; Ashton-Warner, 1963; Hildreth, 1965; McCracken & McCracken, 1972). As Sylvia Ashton-Warner aptly puts it, a young child already has a wealth of experiences inside of him and, through proper programming and good relationships with teachers, these are able to surface. Her term "organic reading", emphasizes her belief that reading begins with what is already within the child, and the goal of most language experience people is to provide experiences to nurture and bring forth this relevant inner language. Obviously, programs with such a philosophy can have tremendous implications for individualizing and enriching the reading curriculum.

We will take just a bit of time to review quickly some of the language arts programs we have in use for enrichment purposes. By the way, most of these programs can be used in a broad way to complement the total language arts curriculum (in that they focus simultaneously on many overall skills involving reading, writing, speaking, listening, and problem solving). The Junior Great Books, which we have decided to include in the next segment on questioning, is a good one. Another is the "Language Box: An Elementary School Communications Kit" (Macmillan Co. of Canada). For grades four to six, the Language Box offers 299 Activity Cards, each zeroing in on one of the four communication skills (reading, writing, speaking, and listening). Yet another package is the "Independent Reading Skills Laboratory" (Educational Progress Corp.), also designed as an enrichment program for good intermediate readers. However, when the occasion demands, there is no reason why able younger children cannot have access to this motivating kit. As the name implies, the IRSL encourages working independently by making it possible for different students to work on different parts of the program at different times. The kit features highly stimulating reading matter (oriented to the ten subject areas of the Dewey Decimal System), an introduction to children's classics, and motivation through eight cassette tapes realistically dramatizing fifteen of the stories. Also, not to be forgotten are the various SRA Reading Labs, perhaps the first kits to emphasize an individualized approach to reading.

A much less expensive, yet effective, way of getting into language enrichment at the intermediate level is to get a hold of Dewar's (1963) professional pamphlet in the area. In this work, she concisely outlines practical enrichment activities to be used daily, weekly, occasionally, or once a term. Long-term planning activities are also discussed.

There are just a few more programs that deserve brief mention. The "Nelson Language Stimulus Program" (Nelson Canada) provides thematically organized stories, poems, pictures, and photos to supplement the language arts curriculum. Increasing in difficulty for grades two to eight, the sections cover Magic Seasons (seasonal variations in weather and people); Multiword (worlds near and far, past and future, and real and imaginary); Mediamind (language, communications, and the media); Manspace (both physical and psychological); Timescope (past, present, and future); and People Mirrors (adapting the sociological concepts of "looking-glass self" and "taking the role of the other" to help students to evaluate social values and reflections of themselves and others). Used well, the program can help students gain in self-understanding, grow through language, become sensitive to nonverbal messages, collaborate, and share experiences.

Sunburst has good kits comprised of classic children's books and activity cards in their "Newberry Award", "Fantasy", and "Good Book" kits. The Perfection Form Company (Iowa) also has some fine materials here. And we have gotten considerable mileage out of various fantasy readers and science fiction kits we have purchased from other sources or compiled ourselves. Also, we like the language arts "Explora Tapes" (Educational Progress Corp.) which provide 40 audio enrichment lessons for pupils in grades three to eight. The tapes show how oral language is central to the human state and encourage students to investigate and learn more about the way language affects our thoughts and behaviour.

In our district, we have found a need to use some programs to improve writing style and organization. Many bright students shine in reading and oral expression, but they shy away from writing — it is too much like work. It is surprising how many talented students can think profoundly yet be unable to get their ideas down on paper. In many instances, it is purely a matter of laziness. When we feel this is in fact the case, we try to get some sort of program in place to develop written expression. Unfortunately, a program of this nature is often painful; it requires not just thinking, but actual work. Too many students cannot write because they do not write. To learn, they must come up with ideas, organize their thoughts through outlines, put their thoughts down on paper, and edit and re-edit the product until it comes up to snuff. There is simply no substitute for hard work.

However, using motivating and stimulating topics and assignments can go a long way towards making the endeavour less onerous. Provincial or State Departments and Ministries of Education are possibly the best sources for comprehensive writing programs. At a more informal level, simply linking writing assignments to readings and activities is a good starting point. For example, after reading *Rascal* by Sterling North, students might be given an open-ended divergent question such as: "Aesop never got around to writing a fable about racoons. Bearing in mind the characteristics of racoons brought forth in the book, write one yourself. Feel free to gather and use more information from other sources." Knight (1974) identifies "strands" in teaching thinking and writing: listening critically, encouraging productive thinking, and translating productive thinking into creative writing. He gives activities for each strand, and shows how to move from one to another. Emphasizing our own feelings again, we believe it is important that students sometimes make the effort — through labourious polishing and editing — to produce a finished product of which they can be proud. Often, computer word-processing programs (for example, the Bank Street Writer or Magic Slate) are helpful in motivating youngsters to review, edit, and polish their written work.

Writing programs we have seen used productively include the fine cassette-filmstrip packages put out by the Center for Humanities. These programs on "How to Survive in School: Note-taking and Outlining Skills" and "In Your Own Words: Learning to Write" are extremely comprehensive, and motivated students can sit down at a listening centre and gradually work through the material on their own.

Phyllis Mindell and Dorothy Stracher, in their "Well-Read" materials, focus on a total language arts approach involving "reading, 'riting, and reason". Essentially, it is a solid overall literacy program for bright students from kindergarten to grade twelve. For older students and adults interested in improving their writing skills, we also like Karen Ogden's (1978) "Write On!" publication. Given the subject matter, the work should be well written. And it is — delightfully so. The small book really consists of a series of twelve newspaper articles designed to help people improve their writing styles. The articles were first published in the *Winnipeg Free Press*, then picked up by several other papers, and finally compiled in monograph form by the Continuing Education Division of the University of Manitoba. All sections — Writing Well is Thinking Well, Mastering the Simple Sentence, Putting Sentences

Together, Subordinating Ideas, Perfecting the Paragraph, Putting It All Together, Minding Your P's and Q's, The Style Is the Man, The Exact Word, Jargon, Gobbledegook, and Other Mumbo Jumbo, Writing Business Letters, and Ten Rules for Writing Well — provide some great little pointers.

Three Local Programs

We would like to close this section by citing three local programs utilized within our district. The first is an approach to help develop oral language and public-speaking skills, the second is simply a homemade (or, perhaps more appropriately, a schoolmade) kit focusing on language arts in general, and the third deals more globally with the generic implementation of various enrichment programs in a school and across a district. In all three cases, our intent is to show that enrichment need not involve anything earth shattering or all that profound, only a little ingenuity, organization, and commitment. In other words, we hope to demonstrate how in-house programs designed by district personnel can have an impact on students and start them using more of the creativity they possess.

Junior Parliament
One program we are especially proud of is our Junior Parliament. To us, it teaches a multiplicity of skills, such as how to present oneself and speak in public and how to organize, defend, and evaluate ideas. The Junior Parliament also provides a stimulating outlet for bright and interested children, and acknowledges their work through awards and a formal banquet. Over the last decade or so, the program has had an impact on very many youngsters, teaching them productive thinking, techniques of debating, and a host of other skills. Due to space limitations, it is not possible to describe the parliament in depth at this point; a complete discussion is available elsewhere (McCluskey & Walker, 1983).

For now, we will merely highlight the fact that youth parliaments can be highly effective teaching tools. And, even though it is the status quo in most districts, there is absolutely no reason to restrict this sort of thing to only the high school level. Elementary and junior high students can learn a great deal from the parliamentary experience, and we think it should be open to them. We are, to the best of our knowledge, the only elementary-junior high parliament which is open to each and every school in the district. When one gets the opportunity to see the diligence and enthusiasm generated among our grade five students, the wisdom of opening up such programs to younger pupils becomes abundantly clear.

Incidentally, our Junior Parliament is not run on a party basis; parliamentary rules are modified so that there is no government or opposition solidarity. Ministers are encouraged to take an extreme view in their bills to insure there is a debate. While this partly restricts the study of government per se, it does allow for the development of individual growth. In essence, we feel that the program helps students develop confidence in their ability to speak before a group, that it gives youngsters a chance to meet with others having similar interests, that it provides a role-playing opportunity to examine part of the operation of government, and that it goes a long way towards preparing students to make a positive contribution to their communities.

The Newspaper Reading Lab

Although reading programs based on newspapers are available commercially, we got some good mileage out of developing our own. The particular program in question was put together by the second author and his intermediate class in an open area setting (Walker, 1974). Relying on ideas from the International Reading Association and other sources, all students in the class were involved in developing the N.R.L. (Newspaper Reading Lab). Using daily newspapers, pupils were required to select an article, read it, and then ask at least five questions about it. The articles and questions were then posted on multi-coloured construction paper, colour coded (red — sports, blue — provincial news, black — obituaries, green — advertisements, etc.), and put together in kit form (in a box decorated by the class). The answers to every question were pasted onto the back of each card. As well, students using any card were asked to print their initials on the back. This procedure served as a useful guide as to the popularity of certain articles.

In developing the N.R.L., the class adhered to a list of "proofreading rules" (concerning spelling accuracy, writing so others could understand both questions and answers, writing legibly, and using correct grammar). The person who made the card initialed the top right-hand corner. Thus, if there was any discrepancy regarding questions or answers, the student responsible for originating them could be located.

The amount of learning which resulted from this program was tremendous. Each day, ten to twenty newspapers were brought in. Many of the so-called "non-readers" were making as many as five cards in the forty minute period. The good readers tended to select controversial articles or political cartoons. All students were encouraged to ask high level questions rather than strictly recall or factual ones.

Once the lab had been completed — over approximately a six-week period — the class used it as a regular reading program. The mere fact that the students had created their own reading materials meant that the incentive and motivation were already built in. In a very short time, they gained some practical language skills and a lot of knowledge about the content of newspapers. Pupils answering questions sometimes had to edit their responses and present them in polished written form for display. At other times they presented their own views orally to their classmates. As a result, students learned something about designing and asking questions, productive thinking and analysis, clarity in communication, proofreading, neatness, and reading with a purpose. And they learned in a highly practical and entertaining way. All in all, the project as a whole turned out to be a very successful undertaking.

After working through the program, the N.R.L. was offered to another class. However, the fun and excitement experienced in making the lab obviously were not there — it was just another assigned reading program and, as such, never really got off the ground. For this sort of lab to work most effectively, the students have to go through the whole process from inception to completion. In a way, then, it is a one-shot venture in any class, but an extremely useful and interesting one-shot venture.

From Theory to Practice
The third program we would like to refer to is the more global one. We feel there is a need to show — from a school perspective — how enrichment programs can be realistically implemented and how things can really start to happen. As a consequence, we have included an article by Phil Baker, a psychologist with our team. Since Phil has served as a regular classroom teacher, a "special ed." teacher, a resource teacher, and a principal before coming to our centre, he brings with him a unique and broad view of education and enrichment. Here he offers a smorgasbord of ideas to help gifted and talented students.

The main theme is that if people have the energy and willingness, all sorts of enriching activities can be put into place. It does not take a lot of money, just ingenuity, time, and effort. Enrichment should be an everyday part of what happens at school. Phil's article shows how a little creativity on the part of educators can elicit a great deal of creativity from the kids. Here are his thoughts on the subject as he traces the development of some enrichment programs in one school and throughout the district in his article entitled "The Road to Enrichment: A Program in Action":

"As a classroom teacher back in the early 70's, I held the traditional ideas on giftedness. To me, a gifted program was for my top students only and best accomplished through pullout. Accordingly, I selected five grade 5 students on the basis of general academic achievement and proficiency. These were the kids who always had their work done quickly and were back at my desk asking for more. They delighted in seeing my chagrin when I had to scramble to keep up to their rapid pace. A unit I had prepared to last two weeks took these kids all of three days, and then they would be back with the question, 'What do we do now?' My reaction, after stifling a scream, was to (1) run off more worksheets, (2) assign another book to be read, or (3) ask for a written report on something or other. Anything and everything I could think of was tried in a vain attempt to keep these bright children busy.

During my first year, of course, we were able to develop some effective programs, most notably introducing Electives into our elementary school. This is a program where the teachers choose an area in which they are personally interested, and the students are given choices as to which activity they elect to participate in. This program was run for one hour per week — usually the last hour on Friday afternoons. The students had various choices such as: gymnastics, yoga, outdoor sports, arts and crafts (weaving, puppetry, painting, etc.), choir, quiet games, chess, photography, drama, square dancing, model building, and more recently, electronic games. This variety of options gave all the kids in the school a chance to participate in something in which they had an interest, as well as letting the teachers partake in some of their favourite activities. Students had to choose electives either every term or after a set number of periods. The program was very successful and is continuing today.

Halfway through that first year, I managed to find one child's mother to serve as a volunteer for enrichment activities (her son was one of my "bright lights"). Together we planned a pullout program based on a unit on communications. Five students were selected using the criteria previously mentioned. They worked with the mother volunteer in the school's conference room for one hour per week exploring communication of the future. Specifically, they wrote future-based poems, listened to the actual sound tracks of the moon landing, developed their own scenarios about future travel, and generally brainstormed about the future and what it would hold for them. This project lasted for one term — Christmas till Easter — and proved to be a steppingstone for better things to come in the way of enrichment activities.

A few years later, I became the resource teacher for the school, and as such was given the go ahead to look at bright and gifted students. The job turned out to be a real challenge as I wracked my brains trying to find themes to motivate and enthuse these children. My first projects were on subjects that interested me — Eskimos, Early Exploration of North America, Space, Dinosaurs, Pollution, Problem Solving in Mathematics, Calculators, and Research Skills.

Typically, all the units followed much the same format. I thought up a theme (e.g., Dinosaurs) and then asked classroom teachers to nominate students they thought were bright enough to be sprung from their regular classes. These kids then met with me twice a week for approximately an hour and we would discuss the topic, listen to a tape, see a film, hear a guest speaker, and do an assignment (e.g., creative writing on the topic, artwork, murals, library research, etc.). Usually we would end up with some field trip (to the museum, planetarium, or elsewhere). The kids enjoyed being freed from the routines of their classrooms and were interested in the topics covered. I felt I had developed the ultimate and definitive enrichment program.

It was about this time that Ken and Keith came to the school to give one of their talks on gifted education. They stressed such points as: (1) an enrichment program could be developed by almost anyone, providing they were willing to take the time to plan and organize, (2) while pullout can be effective and useful much of the time, some thought should be given to meeting the needs of gifted students in the regular classroom as much as possible, (3) enrichment activities should be integrated with other school programs, (4) many bright and interested kids — not just the very top "gifted" ones — should be exposed to enrichment activities, (5) certain programs such as MACOS (Man: A Course of Study), the Junior Great Books, the SRA Research Lab, the Thinklabs, and other kits are excellent for stimulating curiosity and getting children to expand their thinking, and (6) through these types of programs, students could learn, meet, interact with each other, and form friendships based on shared interests and inquiry.

On the basis of their inservice, I rethought my own position regarding our enrichment program. I realized that I had put all the onus for enrichment on my own shoulders — it was I who thought up the topics, gathered the kids, decided who would do what, and picked the places we would visit. The students in the groups had little input other than to do what they were told.

Picking up on the new perspectives, I worked toward modifying the enrichment program for the school. The teachers held a mini-workshop on enrichment to clarify where we were heading (we all wanted to help the students become more divergent thinkers and independent workers). Teachers were also asked to become more involved in the identification process. We decided to base our selection on Renzulli's model with the three intersecting circles representing talent, academic achievement, and task commitment. A child could now enter the group not on the basis of grades alone, but as a result of having an interest in an area. There was a place for the child who stuck with a task to the end, did a good job, or who showed a talent in something such as art, music, dance, woodwork, or athletics. Thus, a child could be nominated by any teacher or fellow student by virtue of having a keen interest in the topic to be covered. Even a weaker student could be admitted to the group if he was "turned on" to a project and willing to do the required work.

The next major change was to shift the responsibility for running the groups from me to the groups themselves. Together, we decided on projects using brainstorming and decision-making processes. Our first major project was our own version of "Reach for the Top" (the game where high school students compete in areas of academic and general interest). We used the SRA Research Lab as our information source. Our elementary students chose their own areas of special interest. There were four students to a team, and each one picked an area (a card from the kit) that he or she was interested in. The categories included subject matter such as: Man, Animals, Plants, the Earth and Beyond, Famous People, Arts, Entertainment, and so on. Each team, then, had four different cards which they read and did research on for two days (Monday and Tuesday). The cards were then exchanged on Wednesday to the other team. The students had to negotiate among themselves to decide which card from the other team they would be responsible for. They had Wednesday and Thursday to prepare from this new card, and on Friday we had the competition. I acted as judge and questions were asked of the teams. The questions were assigned different weights based on difficulty level (factual questions were worth the least — 5 points — while interpretive questions were worth up to 20 points). There were six teams involved in all and we held a round-robin competition to select an overall winner. The areas examined were so divergent and interesting that we always had at least one class join us to observe the contests. The winning team performed in our local shopping mall for the community.

Not all projects were group oriented. Renzulli's Interest-A-Lyzer was given to nominated students, and — based on their own interests — we had kids working independently on projects such as fashion design present and past, science fiction readings and discussions, stamp collecting, and other activities. Together, the student and I would work out a contract to follow up on their interest. This required independence, commitment, and good work habits for students to complete their individual contracts. Some of the early contracts were done exceptionally well but, often as not, they fell below an acceptable standard. When their work didn't come up to par, students weren't punished directly, but they weren't included for further projects. Soon performance began to improve.

The enrichment group was by now made up of students from various grades, both primary and intermediate. The older ones were encouraged to help the younger children, which built in a sense of responsibility (we had very positive results with the peer teaching experience). Also, we integrated and fit some of our projects to coincide with what was happening in the classrooms. The primary teachers were working on a unit on Early Man and the Dinosaur Age, so the primary enrichment group did a project on the same theme (but at a higher level). More research, discussions, project work (art, clay, and murals) were undertaken, as well as a trip to the museum and a workshop on paleontology.

The intermediates were working on the theme of Crime Prevention as part of their language arts and social studies program. Accordingly, the intermediate enrichment group put on a series of five plays concerning shoplifting, employee theft, vandalism, and juvenile court. The selected students practiced on their own, had their own director, made their own sets and costumes, and performed their plays before the other intermediate pupils. All children at the intermediate level were involved somehow, either as participants or audience. And not only did students see the plays, they were given an opportunity to react by responding to the open-ended questions the plays elicited. There were no conclusions to the plays, so each individual had to decide what should happen next. With every play, we brought in a special guest speaker to talk to the students about the meaning and relevance of that particular work. Guests, including the local storekeeper, town shop manager, R.C.M.P. constables, and the Crime Prevention Co-ordinator for the province, contributed greatly. As a follow-up activity, some students came into town to see an actual trial. We then had many good discussions as to what they saw and felt about the judicial system. An unexpected topping to the unit came when the Crime Prevention Co-ordinator invited the theatre enrichment group to perform during Crime Prevention Week at the Concert Hall in Winnipeg. Their audience was made up of officers and probation officials.

Now, in my new role as psychologist, I've been able to help implement enrichment programs across the district as a whole. There are now chess clubs in all our elementary schools, as well as at the junior and senior highs. Kids play regularly in their school clubs, and twice a year the clubs come together to compete in divisional matches. The Junior Great Books Program is helping students in some of our schools learn through interpretive questions and discussions. And Spelling Football (a modification of the old spelling bees) is being played in classrooms and between neighbouring schools. Currently, fun tournaments for scrabble, backgammon, charades, and password are being planned.

"Race for the Answers", another version of "Reach for the Top", is also underway for our grade 5, 6, and 7 students, so that when they reach high school they will be accustomed and eager to compete in this sort of event. I co-ordinate schedules, make up and distribute the test, and demonstrate and judge the event at schools the first time it is played. Schools, however, select coaches to choose students and arrange for at least two practice times per month. At the end of every month (starting at the end of October), there is a formal game at each participating school. Games last 30–40 minutes, with 5 kids on each of the teams. The categories used are: (1) Spelling (based on themes, subject areas, etc.), (2) Math (quick snappers such as $7\times3+6=\_$, basic operations, geometry, metrics, averaging, estimating, problem solving, etc.), (3) Password, (4) Scrambled Spelling (where banana = abnnaa), (5) Famous People (scientists, entertainers, world leaders, etc.), (6) Current Events (news and sports), (7) A Research Content Area (selected from the SRA Research Lab), (8) Novels (focusing on the Newberry Award books), and (9) Puzzles (logic, creative thinking, etc.).

Obviously, good enrichment — be it at a pullout, classroom, school, or district level — requires a lot of work on the part of many people. But it really is possible, with some thought and effort, to make good things happen for bright students in our buildings. School can and must be a place for learning — a place where students can be pushed to reach for their limits and expand in an interesting and stimulating environment. With an effort on our parts, a number of worthwhile experiences can be provided for all children. Our job as educators is to ensure, to the best of our ability, that this sort of enrichment takes place."

To summarize, the three local approaches outlined here illustrate the fact that educators do not necessarily have to rely on commercially packaged programs. Published materials can be exceedingly helpful in working with the gifted, but good things can also happen when teachers use their own creativity to design their own programs for their own settings.

Questioning

In our view, the effectiveness of questioning in any classroom is largely dependent on the teacher's attitude and style. Particularly where bright children are involved, teachers should be encouraged to ask stimulating, analytical questions. Although all types of questions have a place, a move from simple recall of facts to a more in-depth, interpretive style of questioning can be genuinely productive. Again, the aim is to move along the continuum from content to process. For a more intensive look at classroom questioning see Sanders (1966).

Divergent Questions

Diverging from the subject matter and asking questions that challenge and extend the student in new directions should be an objective in any gifted program. For example, rather than pose a typical run-of-the-mill question about Marjorie Rawlings's "The Yearling", a teacher might ask: "If you could give Jody a different gift at the start of the book, what would you give and how would it change the story?" In other words, the student is being forced to think, not simply remember.

All sorts of divergent questions and assignments have been originated about all manner of subjects. For the uninitiated, we will quickly list some examples: "If you were invisible, where would you go and why?"; "Read Hamlet, and then compose a different ending for the play which you feel would be as logical as Shakespeare's"; "Compose a diary which you think might have been kept by Julius Caesar"; "Name three inventions which will make homes more comfortable in the next century"; and "Suppose our plane crashed on an uncharted island. How could we survive, improve the quality of life, and entertain ourselves?" The tremendously popular "Choose Your Own Adventure" science fiction series (Bantam Books) makes use of a divergent, multiple-ending approach. And kids just love such books.

Many problems posed to stimulate divergent thinking focus on the future. Here are a few of these "Futuristics": "Will we ever run out of rocks?"; Write a story dealing with how our natural resources are replaced"; "Experiment with a magnifying glass to show the concentration of the sun's rays, try to visit a building that uses solar heat, draw a glass-domed building showing solar heat at work, and write an essay predicting how solar power might be harnessed in the future"; and "Take the class for a walk around the neighbourhood, and watch for ways soil is being moved. Discuss ways in which erosion might be prevented in the future." One group of elementary students we have heard about were asked to discuss what kind of clothes we might wear in the year 2,000. This question stimulated the youngsters, and some of them even went so far as to draw and design futuristic outfits. Apparently, a number of novel ideas were proposed including disposable paper wardrobes and aerosol spray-on clothes. One chubby little guy got quite upset by the last notion, fearing there might not be enough in a can to do him all!

Bev Milam, in her ECA (Educational Consulting Associates) handbook on *Teaching the Gifted and Talented*, outlines categories of divergent questions originally drawn up by the South Suburban Area Service Center for Educators of Gifted Children (Governors State University, Illinois). These categories are: 1) Quantity Questions (for example, "How may ways can you come up with _____ ?"); 2) Reorganization Questions (such as, "Suppose _____ occurred, what would be the consequences?"); 3) Supposition Questions (for example, "Just suppose you could have all of the _____ in the world. How would you use it?"); 4) Viewpoint Questions (such as "How would this look to a _____ ?"); 5) Involvement

Questions ("How would you feel if you were a _____?"); and 6) Forced Association Questions (such as "How is _____ like _____?").

Questioning Programs

Many authors propose questions for children that take the form of short snappers and quick activities. For example, de Bono (1972), in "Children Solve Problems", gave youngsters paper and coloured pens and asked them to draw solutions to problems such as: "Show how you would stop a cat and dog from fighting"; "Design a fun machine"; and "Design a special bicycle for a postman". The children were always given a chance to explain or comment on their drawings.

Roger Taylor from ECA has an abundance of quick questions for the gifted, and Bev Milam — borrowing from Parnes (1967) and others — has compiled a number of short exercises in her ECA manual as well. In her workshops, she divides people into groups and has them work together in an attempt to come up with the meaning of unfamiliar words. "Sesquipedalian" — a user of long (foot-and-a-half length) words — was one term that generated quite a bit of discussion. "Triskaidekaphobia" was also a puzzler. Our group narrowed it down to a fear of biscuits, fear of altruism, fear of the number thirteen, fear of thirteen-wheel bikes, fear of ten tricks, and fear of plane schedules — take your pick!

In the "Breaking Mind Sets" section, Milam also includes a "Name That Film" exercise where participants are presented with the plot of a film in colloquial language and asked to identify the movie in question. All films are classics. Try one:

"An illiterate n'er-do-well from the sticks meets an actress from the city, who turns his head. He tries to convince her to stay home with him, but she and her producer friend convince him to go to New York and become a big star. In Manhatten, they decide to put on a big show. Opening night is a real disaster, but finally the sophisticated urbanites recognize the illiterate's talents and he makes a lasting impression on the city."

We have no doubt that all readers have correctly identified the film as "King Kong".

There are great numbers of commercial programs available that offer excellent questions for young kids. Merrill Harmin's "People Projects" (Addison-Wesley) at three levels (Series A for ages nine to eleven, Series B for ages ten to twelve, and Series C for ages eleven to thirteen) are highly imaginative and stimulating. For example, one question from Series A reads:

"Imagine that you could make yourself very, very tiny by saying the magic words Zinko Zoop. When you wanted to, you could make yourself life-sized again by saying Zoop Zinko. Tiny or normal, anytime you wanted. Zinko Zoop. Zoop Zinko.

   Write a story about what you might do. Show your story to someone and ask them what they think of it.

   If you are with others, perhaps try a chain story . . ."

In Series B, one card queries, "Why are schools so boring?" — quite a dangerous question to ask a gifted student.

   Other programs also provide a wealth of good questioning strategies. Good Apple has many intriguing question-oriented books, including "Future Think" (an activity book with four units about the future), "I Believe in Unicorns" (with mind-expanding fantasy exercises), and "Slanguage" (discovering how language might have begun). Sunburst Communications and Midwest Publications both carry a variety of materials as well (which are available through Kahl's Inc.). These include the "Deductive Thinking Skills: Mind Benders" and the "Classroom Quickies". Louise Kool & Son and New Dimensions of the 80's Publishers also have available a variety of resource books dealing with questioning and the gifted. And Educational Insights, in their "Mind Expanders" package, present activity cards for the gifted in math, creative writing, art, social studies, poetry and science. Finally, several creative writing programs, such as "The Writing Centre" (Holt, Rinehart & Winston of Canada), "Write On!" (McGraw-Hill Ryerson), and the "Story Sparkers" (Educational Insights), all use excellent interpretive and divergent questions to get students writing.

   We have no quarrel with employing stimulating divergent questions with bright students — in fact we feel appropriate questioning is an integral part of any gifted program. Motivating kids, getting them to think, and generating discussion are motherhood-type goals that no one can take issue with. However, there is a real danger here; educators have to know where they are going with their questions. If all a teacher does is try to excite children through clever questioning, things can become overly loose and wishy-washy. Sometimes random, unfocused questioning can degenerate into confusion and the playing of silly, purposeless games. To us, if stimulating questions are all you have, you do not have a program — just an activity.

   Clearly, then, we believe a real enrichment program must have its share of direction, purpose, and structure. With this philosophy, it is easy to see why we react so positively to programs such as CoRT. And, for developing an organized approach to reading, thinking, discussion, and questioning, we also think it is valuable to take a look at the following approach.

The Junior Great Books Program

"The Junior Great Books Reading and Discussion Program" (Great Books Foundation) is a widely cited and used questioning program for superior readers and thinkers in grades two through twelve. In some ways, it focuses on skills that other approaches to reading neglect such as teaching children to learn from what they have read and to apply this knowledge in new contexts. Reading, speaking, and listening are all emphasized. The program requires students to read outstanding literary works, confront and evaluate problems, listen and think reflectively, make inferences, and put forth, defend, and modify their ideas in a group setting. The group "shared inquiry" approach highlights the fact that "wrong" answers are a necessary part of the thinking process.

First, students are selected — primarily on the basis of reading ability (they really ought to be good readers to handle the material comfortably) — to make up the group. It is recommended in the manual that fourteen pupils be included, but we prefer to be more selective and intimate and work with smaller numbers, especially initially. After a leader gains confidence and experience, he can start thinking about working with less talented and greater numbers of children. To get underway, students are expected to read a selection from the books. Eight Series, from Series 2 for grade two through Series 9 for grades nine to twelve, comprise the program. Each Series is made up of twelve or more selections from stimulating literature of the past and present. For example, Series 2 includes the Grimms' *Rumpelstiltskin* and Uchida's *Wedding of the Mouse*; Series 4, Oscar Wilde's *The Happy Prince*, Tolstoy's *The Two Brothers*, and Kipling's *Just So Stories*; Series 8, Sophocles' *Antigone*, Plato's *Apology*, and Graham Greene's *The Destructors*; and Series 9, H.G. Wells' *The Time Machine*, Truman Capote's *Miriam*, and Dostoyevsky's *The Honest Thief*.

Now the difficult part of trying to facilitate the discussion begins. This process is involved enough that only Certified Discussion Leaders — who must complete a ten-hour Great Books Training Course — can purchase the books and Leader Aids in quantity. And a person needs to go through the training experience; there is a lot to learn about this complex questioning technique. To illustrate, there are three types of questions you can use in the group: 1) Fact — where you ask children simply to recall information (they can rely mostly on memory); 2) Evaluation — requiring pupils to agree or disagree with the author on the basis of their own experience; and 3) Interpretation — where the students are called upon to give some opinion, based on the story, of what the author is trying to say. All three categories of questions can be used in the discussion, the first to keep students on task or bring them down to earth, and the other two to help them look at the reading from different perspectives.

After the selection has been read, you follow some logical and ordered steps in beginning the discussion: 1) Making a seating chart. That is, you write the first names of the children in your group on a piece of paper and, as the discussion evolves, jot down brief notes about what they have said. This procedure is necessary in order to keep track of things; the kids often start off dogmatically holding to one idea, but then they may shift, change their minds, and begin to become more sensitive to other members' points of view. You need to have an ongoing record of how things are developing. 2) Pose and have the youngsters write down the opening question. This question, based on the selection at hand, should be interpretive. In other words, it should be specific, contain an element of doubt, and reflect a high degree of insight. Interpretive questions then, by definition, have no right or wrong answer — their function is to generate discussion. Appropriate questions can be obtained from the Leader Guides, but part of the fun and challenge is to formulate your own. Later, you can even ask the kids to help develop intriguing questions. 3) Give students a couple of minutes to write down their answers. This step forces them to analyze, reflect, and organize their response quickly. 4) Start following up on the answers. Again, do not behave as if you have the correct solution to the problem — you are there to guide and focus the discussion, not control it. Remember, there is no one right answer to an interpretive question; the leader can learn as much as the students during the exercise. 5) Initiate all questions with the child's first name. This keeps the kids on their toes and gives things a warm, personal touch.

We can say from firsthand experience that the Junior Great Books method of shared inquiry can really generate exciting and productive discussion. Students in groups we have run have certainly responded to the readings, the questions, and the whole interactive process. To make things come a bit more alive, we will take an example from when our adult group of educators was going through our first training session. Our leader began by having us read through *Jack and the Beanstalk*, a grade two selection. Our initial thought was, "Good heavens, what in the world is going on here?" After skeptically reading over the story, however, we were faced with the interpretive question, "Was Jack's success primarily the result of luck and magic, or a result of his own efforts?" Well, we debated and argued the question for 45 minutes (in fact, the second author and the district's Hearing Therapist almost came to blows) before resolving the issue to some extent. Take it from us, the entire exercise was intense, thought-provoking, and valuable. And again, the Junior Great Books discussions can have the same effect on kids, if not mismanaged or overdone. We do feel there are limits to how often and how long students should participate. But when it is used judiciously, students can learn an enormous amount from the Junior Great Books Program. Reading good literature, organizing and expressing thoughts, and listening and learning from others through shared inquiry should always be a thoroughly positive undertaking.

Classroom Organization

Most people in gifted education realize it is crucial that we individualize and differentiate the curriculum for our bright and talented students (cf. Dunn & Dunn, 1975; Feldhusen & Treffinger, 1980; Kaplan, 1974; Simpson, 1984; Wooster, 1978). Flexibility is the key; gifted youngsters need differentiated and varied learning opportunities to maximize their cognitive and affective growth. Since a major goal of education is to develop independent learners, our gifted children should be given the chance to try their hand at higher level tasks. It is this divergence — be it through questioning strategies, problem-solving programs, or other methods — that will stimulate and motivate these students. In other words, gifted pupils should have the opportunity to learn through discovery and inquiry, take some responsibility for their own learning, analyze and evaluate material, solve problems, generate new information, and transfer and apply knowledge.

Obviously, we have taken the position that differentiation of the curriculum for gifted students in the regular class is more appropriate than a separate curriculum. Where feasible, we prefer to use programs that are good for all children (and which permit them to work at different levels). As well, we look to partial pullout and independent investigative projects — for as many students as possible — whenever necessary. The intent, however, is to give all children — not just the extra-bright — the opportunity to experience enrichment. As noted earlier, however, we expect and allow gifted students to take things further.

While it is all very well to say what the gifted should have, it is hard to give it to them. It is no easy matter to differentiate and provide for our bright students without neglecting the others; lack of direction can result in chaos. Clearly, definite structure and framework are required for a diversified approach to be workable. In short, all the ideas in the world are worthless without good classroom organization.

In order to put things all together and keep ourselves organized, we attempt to work in four simple directions in our gifted programming. For fairly global enrichment to take place in a classroom, we would hope that: 1) many children have the opportunity to attempt some independent investigative activities (such as research projects); 2) some challenging small group activities and projects take place; 3) a certain amount of divergent questioning and thinking activities be done with the class as a whole; and 4) enriching curriculum be put into place for the whole class in some subject areas. Further discussion of each direction is warranted here.

Independent Investigative Activities

As Treffinger (1975, 1979) points out, good enrichment involves gradual movement from teacher-directed to self-directed learning. Giving students the chance to pursue some independent study on their own is one effective and commonly used procedure (Weber, 1977). Many classroom teachers are most comfortable asking the resource teacher to help them develop and schedule independent investigative activities for their bright pupils. And certainly, as Wood (1983) notes, resource teachers can be involved in organizing staff development activities, identifying bright students, developing and implementing programs, and timetabling to make everything "hang together". They are good people to turn to.

Setting up listening centres for bright students is one thing to consider (Cooperman, Fischle, & Hochstetter, 1976; Wooster, 1978). By way of simple example, suppose you wanted a gifted child to learn to study and attack material more effectively. One possibility might be to build a listening centre focusing on Robinson's (1970) SQ3R technique (devised late in the 1920s and used extensively ever since), and then allow the pupil to explore and learn about the method on his own (cf. Albas & Albas, 1984). An ideal program here is the sound-filmstrip package "School

Survival Skills: How to Study Effectively" (The Center for Humanities). It explains the SQ3R approach, ties it into school-related exercises, and gives the pupil an opportunity to practice and develop the technique. A student who has worked through this program on his own or under more formal supervision really does learn to study more efficiently.

Since it is such a relevant program, we will briefly run through the steps in the SQ3R approach: 1) Survey — the student quickly previews material by examining pictures, maps, or charts and by reading headings, sub-headings, and summaries. For a more inclusive survey, selected topic sentences are read. Basically, the survey builds in a readiness for study by revealing the nature of the content and the manner of its presentation; 2) Question — as he surveys, the student frames and jots down questions that need to be answered (who, what, where, why, when, and how). For example, if there is a picture of a plane landing on a deserted island on the book cover, a pupil might ask "Is the plane being hijacked?" or "Where is the island?" Many of the author's headings can usually be turned into questions. In questioning, a student should bring his previous knowledge to bear on the material, thinking always in terms of what he already knows and what he needs to know; 3) Read — the student now starts at the beginning and reads the material through, focusing on finding the answers to his questions (and looking for other relevant information he may not have anticipated). He is now reading, not in a disorganized, unfocused manner, but with a definite purpose; 4) Recite — at intervals, the student pauses and "tells himself" what he has read. He answers the questions in each distinct section. "Thinking over" the content while reading in short unified sections is a major step in the process. Incidentally, some programs (such as The Center for Humanities' kit) prefer 'Rite over Recite for the second of the three Rs. And there definitely is something to be said for having students write down the answers to the questions — they remember through writing, they have the material recorded for later use, and they can still employ recitation whenever they wish; 5) Review — after finishing the entire reading, the student reviews the material and the answers to all questions. He attempts to pull loose ends together and make a unified whole of separate segments. If some notes have been written down, he has a study sheet to use again for later review purposes.

Our favourite independent investigative activity is the research project. Essentially, engaging in research allows children to take the initiative and learn and explore on their own. Direction and supervision are required, however. All too often, youngsters are sent out to the library to do research without any preliminary guidance or instruction. What the teacher usually gets back in this situation is a plagiarized, unabridged version of a section of the *World Book Encyclopedia*. This sort of thing is not research in its purest form! It happens, however, simply because we are asking students to do something they have never been taught to do.

There is a procedure to be followed in starting youngsters off on research projects:

Select the Students to Participate
As stated before, we use Renzulli's "Revolving Door Model", where certain children revolve in to do enriching projects for a definite period of time. They then revolve out, and other youngsters take their place. We prefer if all pupils get to revolve in at least once but, as Renzulli (1982) says, it is necessary to ask if every student should do the project in question, if every student could do it, and if every student would want to do it. At times, it might be best to design more demanding and involving projects for our gifted students, while allowing others to participate in similarly-constructed, but less onerous activities.

Show Students How to Use Libraries and Resource Materials
"Information Fast" (Educational Insights, Inc.) teaches important skills in this regard via activity cards, and the cassette-filmstrip packages "Your Library and Media Center: How to Get the Most from Them" (Center for Humanities) and "Books and More: Library Media Center Series" (ACI Productions) provide excellent information as well. Even sending a student down to talk to the school librarian can do the trick. The point is that a student should never be left alone in a library without knowing what to do there.

Introduce the Student to the Steps Involved in Good Research
It is central that the student be introduced to the steps involved in doing and writing up systematic research projects. We cannot expect even bright students to do good research if no one shows them how to go about it! The *World Book Encyclopedia* (1986, Vol. 22, p. 6–40) offers a very superior section on writing, speaking, and research skills. The article gives basic steps involved in preparing a research report, and covers topics such as planning, choosing a subject, outlining, researching (using a variety of information sources), writing, revising, reviewing, and preparing the final report. The Center for Humanities also has another one

of their informative sound-filmstrip kits on "The Research Paper Made Easy: From Assignment to Completion".

Certain Curriculum Associates' workbooks also show teachers how to introduce research skills to youngsters and how gradually to develop their skills. For example, in Exercise 29 in "Thirty Lessons in Note Taking", children are asked to do an introductory mini-project on bees. At this early stage, however, there are clear limits placed on what they are expected to read and write. For example, the workbook has limited amounts of material on bees from five sources (an encylcopedia, an article on honey, a dictionary, a bee keeper's manual, and a book on insects). After reading this abbreviated material, the students are asked to write a short four-paragraph report dealing with bee food, where bees live, physical appearance, and a bee's year. Everything is spelled out systematically. That is, children are taught to work independently, but there is a limit as to how much they are expected to produce at first — they are not "swamped" or overwhelmed. Students are allowed to move onto more ambitious projects only after they have mastered some of the basics.

Have a Plan For Students and Get a Commitment From Them

It is also important to have management plans for individual students and to get a definite commitment from them. Renzulli's (1977) "Management Plan For Individual and Small Group Investigations" points the way for students and helps keep things organized. Contracts are also an effective way of formalizing the activity and motivating youngsters. "How to Get Out of an Egg Without Cracking the Shell: An individualized Instruction Program for Gifted Children" is a good source in this regard.

Provide Proper Reference Material

In other words, children need to have access to relevant books, articles, kits, people, and places. Good libraries and encyclopedias are a must. It is evident that there are many series which are excellent starting points for research projects. We particularly like the Usborne books (Usborne Publishing, available through Hayes Publishing). Some of their titles include Dinosaurs, Prehistoric Mammals, Early Man, The First Civilizations, Warriors and Seafarers, Knights and Castles, Monsters, Ghosts, UFOs, and the like. The "Peoples of the Past" books (Macdonald Educational Ltd., available through Macdonald, GLC Publishers), covering the Romans, Greeks, Egyptians, Vikings, Aztecs, Celts, Normans, and Incas, are also excellent references for children's research projects.

One kit especially helpful in starting intermediate students on the road to independent research is the "SRA Research Lab" (Science Research Associates). The lab builds in basic research skills through 22 colourful and motivating activity cards in each of ten content areas (Man, Animals, Plants, The Earth and Beyond, Famous People, Travel and Communication, Work and Industry, Countries of the World, The Arts and Entertainment, and Sports). There are three levels of research skills: the first requires students to cross reference from one article to another in the same content area; the second asks them to cross reference to other subject areas in the program; and the third goes beyond the kit and starts children off in the library.

One grade five girl in our district was put on the Research Lab, and she decided to attempt a project on pianos. Appropriately, she started in the school library, but there was not a wealth of material on the topic. As a consequence, she tried the town library, only to find there was not exactly an abundance of material there. Arrangements were then made to have her go into the Winnipeg Public Library, but again there was a dearth of material on the shelves at the time. Fortunately, however, a librarian took the girl under her wing and helped her call in books on inter-library loan. Soon volumes started to arrive from Vancouver, Toronto, and elsewhere. If the girl learned nothing else from the experience, she still benefited tremendously from discovering this method of accessing and acquiring information.

Expect and Insist Upon a Polished Final Product
One of the aims of research is to share and communicate findings, so the work should be presented in a lucid, meaningful, and organized form. All research projects should be edited, polished, and typed or neatly written. In this way, the reader will have an easy-to-read document, and the student will have a final product of which to be proud.

Small Group Activities and Investigations

Students should naturally be allowed to work cooperatively together in small group settings every now and again. Group work has obvious social implications revolving around learning how to listen, share, and how to help and be helped by others. And bright students can benefit greatly from bouncing ideas off their classmates. Renzulli's "Management Plan" is again helpful as an organizational guide in starting up group projects.

Many of the programs already discussed are appropriate and useful for small group work. Some of them include simulation games, divergent questions, the People Projects, The Productive Thinking Program, CoRT, research projects, and the Junior Great Books.

Questions for the Whole Class

Sometimes divergent, thought-provoking questions should be posed to the class as a whole. This procedure will get everyone involved, and encourage students to combine their talents and work together. Any of the stimulating materials mentioned in the preceding section are good sources for suitable questions. But again, an element of structure is necessary to make sure things run smoothly, especially when the entire class is participating. CoRT and other thinking programs can provide much of the required structure.

"Brainstorming" (cf. Clark, 1958; Meadow, Parnes, & Reese, 1959; Parnes & Meadow, 1959; Rapp, 1967) is another way of adding some organization to class or group discussions. Essentially, it is simply a method whereby the participants come up with as many ideas about a topic as possible. For years now, brainstorming has been used effectively by educators, businessmen, politicians, and others to give direction, generate new ideas, organize thoughts, and initiate action.

In brainstorming sessions, the members should have a chairman to remind them of the rules and a secretary to provide a written record. Usually, points are written down on a chalkboard or flip chart during the exercise, but they should also be transcribed legibly onto note paper at the end of the discussion. In this way, a permanent account is provided as a reference for later work.

There are some basic guidelines for brainstorming: 1) all ideas are acceptable, and none should be attacked or "put down". A climate of acceptance and openness encourages freedom of speech and participation. Often an idea that seems "bad" at first sight turns out to be pivotal; 2) try to generate as many ideas as possible. The more ideas people have, the better the chance of coming up with something really good; 3) encourage unusual (wild, oddball, and far-out) ideas. Points that are creative, different, and unexpected may help the group arrive at something original and useful; and 4) "hitchhike" or "piggyback" off of other ideas. If one person's idea makes the others think of something else, they should let their new thoughts be known. In other words, it is important to modify, combine, expand, and build on earlier notions.

A related technique, "webbing", has been proposed by Alexinia Baldwin (1979) as a method for developing instructional activities for the gifted. Actually, "webbing" is essentially a brainstorming-type approach featuring a unique and interesting way of recording information. Step 1 in the "webbing" process is to select a general topic (automobiles, for example) and write it down. In step 2, the teacher and class can brainstorm beginning questions for sub-topics of the general topic. For example, a question posed to one of our classes was "How would you explain what an automobile is to a hermit who had never seen one, and how would you describe the effect it has had on our lives?" Predictably, the question resulted in a number of sub-topics being mentioned (such as fuel, motor, tires, design, technology, transportation, etc.). All sub-topics suggested should be jotted down around the main topic and connected to it by a line. Step 3 involves the further expansion of each sub-topic. To illustrate, consideration of the sub-topic "fuel" in turn leads to more points being brought out (for example, drilling, pipelines, off-shore

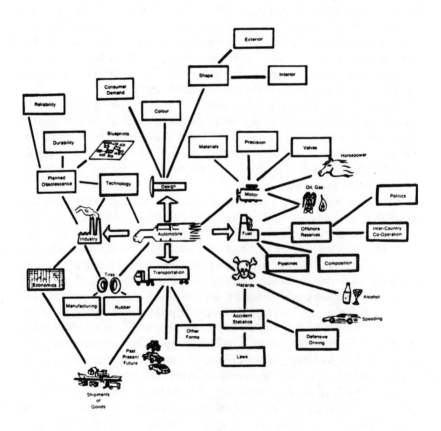

reserves, analysis of substances, differences between oil and gas, etc.). Similarly, every other sub-topic generates responses which again surround and connect to it. Some categories may be related (connected) to two sub-topics (for example, "oil" and "gas" could hook up both to "fuel" and "motor"). Gradually, a "web" is developed that increases and expands as discussion proceeds. An adapted form of the "web", produced by the class in question, is included here to illustrate the process.

In step 4, students are given the opportunity to talk about the topics in the "web" and choose an area of interest. Then, in step 5 the teacher serves as a facilitator, and points students towards taking things further through independent research projects, group work, or other activities. Thus, "webbing" acts as an organizational tool to structure, guide, stimulate, and record the discussion. Thinking, sharing, and general participation at the class level lead into more specific individual interests and projects.

Curriculum for the Whole Class

As we have said, approaches such as The Productive Thinking Program and CoRT recommend that thinking skills be taught to the whole class as part of the regular curriculum. And, at least in our province, recent attempts have been made to enrich the language arts, math, and social studies curricula for all children. For purposes of example, however, we would like to single out one social studies course to show what we mean by enrichment for the class as a whole.

Man: A Course of Study

We think MACOS (Man: A Course of Study; available through Curriculum Development Associates) is the best piece of social-science curriculum ever written (cf. Hanley, Whitla, Moo, & Walter, 1970). Essentially, it takes anthropological, sociological, psychological, and other concepts that have traditionally been the province of universities, and presents them at an intermediate or junior high level. Initially, we were told by some junior high teachers that their students could not possibly grasp the concepts involved. When the course was eventually introduced at grades five and six, however, the kids understood it just fine. (Perhaps the optimal time to implement MACOS is in grade six, where it can be run comfortably for the entire year.) The program seems to have something for everybody, from the slow learner to the gifted. Indeed, the latitude and scope of the course is simply amazing.

Through the Education Development Center (Cambridge, Massachusetts) and under grants from the National Science Foundation, MACOS was developed in the 1960s by a team of researchers headed by Jerome Bruner (1961, 1965). It reflects many of his ideas concerning curriculum design. In Bruner's (1962) own words:

"The curriculum of a subject should be determined by the most fundamental understanding that can be achieved of the underlying principles that give structure to that subject. Teaching specific topics or skills without making clear their context in the broader fundamental structure of a field of knowledge is uneconomical in several deep senses. In the first place, such teaching makes it exceedingly difficult for the student to generalize from what he has learned to what he will encounter later. In the second place, learning that has fallen short of a grasp of general principles has little reward in terms of intellectual excitement. The best way to create interest in a subject is to render it worth knowing, which means to make the knowledge gained usable in one's thinking beyond the situation in which the learning has occurred. Third, knowledge one has acquired without sufficient structure to tie it together is knowledge that is likely to be forgotten."

Many other social scientists and teachers were involved in the making of MACOS, most notably Irven DeVore, who supervised the filming of baboon troops in the Amboseli and Nairobi Game Parks, and Asen Balikci, who carried out the filmed ethnographic studies of the Netsilik Eskimo during three expeditions to the Arctic. The works of Berkowitz, Eibl-Eibesfeldt, Dewey, Rasmussen, Skinner, Tinbergen, and others are also relevant to the course.

In very brief and simplified terms, some of the goals of MACOS are: 1) to develop a thirst for and method of inquiry in children; 2) to teach research skills; 3) to help youngsters derive hypotheses and draw conclusions firsthand; 4) to make possible classroom discussions where children express themselves and listen to others; 5) to delve into open-ended and interpretive problems; 6) to encourage pupils to relate their own experience to the course content; and 7) to move towards facilitator-guided teaching and independent study. In general, the learning process is seen as being more important than simply remembering facts. However, due to the motivational component of the course, a lot of fascinating facts are learned and retained.

MACOS studies the animal kingdom, compares and contrasts various animals and man, looks at man as a species, and more or less takes stock of our role in the scheme of things. Bruner (1965) notes that there are three main questions recurring through the course: 1) "What is human about human beings?" 2) "How did they get that way?" and 3) "How can they be made more so?"

Importantly, this course cannot be implemented without first taking the prerequisite inservicing. In our district, program consultants started us off with two separate and extensive training sessions. One needs the inservicing just to become familiar with the voluminous amounts of materials that comprise MACOS: nine teacher's guides with background information and lesson plans; 30 booklets on topics such as Life Cycle, Animal Adaptation, Natural Selection, Structure and Function, Innate and Learned Behavior, Salmon, Herring Gulls, The Baboon Troop, Baboon Communication, The Observer's Handbook, The Field Notes of Irven DeVore, The Arctic, Songs and Stories of the Netsilik Eskimos; 16 films — The Life Cycle of the Salmon, Animals in Amboseli, Miss Goodall and the Wild Chimpanzees, Life on the Tundra, At the Caribou Crossing Place, for example; and various records, filmstrips, maps, posters, and educational games.

There is a clear effort to make things as lifelike and relevant as possible. Students even work directly from Irven DeVore's anthropological field notes. They have an Observer's Handbook to help them acquire some of the data-gathering skills of the social scientist (in observing human behaviour). Eskimo legends and poetry are presented and discussed, and there are simulation games involving toolmaking and other issues. And MACOS hits home even more because it is largely film-based. The National Film Board's outstanding series of films gives pupils a real feel for life in the Arctic. Also, the film "Animals of Amboseli" is particularly good. It features only the sounds of the jungle and savannah — no narration — and shows a day in the life of a baboon troop.

Questions posed in the course really make students think. They address issues such as "Do salmon have parents?" and "Why are human babies so helpless?" Certainly, teachers have to be alert when teaching MACOS. One teacher was confronted with the following query by a young student: "Even though Rasmussen didn't seem to find any sign of heartlessness in their treatment of the aged, it has been said that Eskimos leave their elderly to die on the ice flows. However, don't we do the same thing when we put our senior citizens into old folk's homes?"

Parents too can be confronted by interesting questions. Imagine the surprise of a mother being asked the following question by her grade five son. (See page 168.)

It should be noted that there can be a degree of controversy with MACOS every now and again since it sometimes deals with topics such as infanticide, magic, myths and legends, and the like. In fact, we did have a Renaissance Group complain and attempt to have the course removed

from one of our schools. However, other parents got together at a public meeting in support of MACOS — they had never seen their children so enthused, and they wanted them to be exposed to this type of material. The course stayed.

In summary, MACOS is an exceptional program for all kids. It holds their interest by presenting facts and concepts in new and exciting ways. However, it is a particularly good course for the brighter student. With the focus on problem solving, thinking, higher level questioning, research, independent study, and motivation, it has all the content and latitude a gifted child needs.

Positive Self-Image

To preface our remarks here, we believe that certain programs aimed at building self-concept and positive self-image have sometimes been over-done in the past. Some people have put so much emphasis on making kids feel good about themselves — at the expense of discipline, organiza-tion, and course content — that they seem to have created a bunch of ignorant "boors" who feel good about themselves. Our opinion is that children need concrete structure and content in programming; if they learn to do something they could not do before, it raises self-concept and confidence almost by definition. Also, rather than focus specifically on personal growth-type programs, we prefer to see this sort of growth take place on an everyday basis simply as a result of the classroom atmosphere and milieu.

Nonetheless, there are gifted youngsters who feel "different" and out of place (sometimes because they *are* "different" and out of place). At times, it may be essential to give support, encouragement, and reassur-ance to gifted "outsiders" who do not fit in. Often, these youngsters just need a little help, direction, guidance, and someone to talk to. For many children, that "someone" is their teacher.

Self-Image Programs

It is vital then, as Glasser points out in his "Ten Steps to Discipline", to give students "the time of day". Most children respond to a bit of indi-vidual attention, and simply being a good, interested listener is one of a teacher's most important roles.

However, there are some more specific things one can do to respond to the personal needs of gifted and other children. For example, Renzul-li's (1977) subtle "Interest-A-Lyzer" can be used to help pinpoint a child's present and potential interests. Running this inventory before assigning research or other projects may identify new areas to explore, as well as add a personal touch to the proceedings. There are also many well-known programs that focus on personal growth, value clarification, listening, accepting differences, distinguishing between right and wrong, building confidence, developing interpersonal communicative skills, and so on. Some of these include "Magic Circle" and "Inner Change" (Human Development Training Institute, available through Canadian Educational and Psychological Consultants), "Hole in the Fence" (Government of Canada, Department of Health and Welfare), "Building the Pieces Together" (The Alcoholism Foundation of Manitoba), "Transition" (American Guidance Service, available through Psycan), and "Feeling Good About Yourself: How to Build Self-Confidence" (Guidance Associates).

Also, there are a number of materials available through Sunburst that address similar issues. "How Do I See Myself?" (grade 5+) discusses how self-image is developed and how it can be changed. The program uses real-life examples and episodes from the lives of famous people to show how self-image can be improved. "Developing Self-Respect" (grade 6+) focuses on gaining independence and taking responsibility for one's actions. Similarly, "Self-Concept: How I Know Who I Am" (grade 7+) uses vignettes to show how to change self-concept for the better, and "As Others See You: Creating a Reputation" (grade 7+) encourages and suggests means for students to change a reputation. Finally, "How to Like Yourself: Personality and Mental Health" (grade 7+) endeavours to help students understand, face, and cope with stress.

Bibliotherapy

Griffin (cf. Carner, 1966) defines "bibliotherapy" as "the scientific application of literature toward a therapeutic goal". In education, it involves using books to help children understand, adjust to, and perhaps solve their problems (Moody & Limper, 1971; Rudman, 1976; Schultheis, 1972). Providing students with the right book at the right time is an art that takes empathy, tact, and knowledge. It requires sensitivity to know when a child is facing a personal crisis. And if you feel a book might help, it is still frequently inappropriate just to give it to the youngster and say, "Here, read this". Often a much more subtle approach is called for. Also, if you want to help students through books, it is necessary to have a wide and thorough knowledge of children's literature. (A few important general categories are divorce and separation, sibling rivalry, poverty, death, drugs, and adolescence.) As a general rule, it is good practice not to recommend a book to a child unless you have read it yourself.

Because some bright children are very sensitive, they sometimes over-analyze and bog themselves down with all kinds of problems. Also, there are many highly intelligent children who are shy and not at all forthcoming. Bibliotherapy is ideal for these sorts of youngsters. And, due to the fact that extra-bright kids can often read and interpret higher level material, there are a wealth of sources to refer them to. Obviously, however, if care is taken to match the book to the reading level, bibliotherapy can be used with all children.

An excellent source here is Sharon Spredemann Dreyer's (1977) *The Bookfinder*, written for parents, teachers, psychologists, psychiatrists, pediatricians, and others who are interested in using books to help children aged two to fifteen. It lists and abstracts a multitude of children's books in a variety of psychological, physical, developmental, and behavioural areas. The indices, categories, and listings are amazingly detailed. For example, if a child's cat died, you could look up "Death of Pets" in the index and find appropriate books for various ages. All in all, *The Bookfinder* is an invaluable reference work — there should be a copy in every school.

For Low-Functioning Students

Due to motivational, social-emotional, and other factors, some bright youngsters do not get a good start in school. In fact, we have seen many highly intelligent young children who have trouble learning to read. Most of the time, the problems of gifted nonreaders centre around motivation — if you can get them enthused about reading, they will remediate themselves. With the young ones, then, we often put them on enjoyable materials such as "The Monster Books" (Bowmar, available through The Resource Centre), the Bill Martin *Instant Readers* (Holt, Rinehart & Winston), and the attractive "Rights of Children" series (John Wiley & Sons) based on the United Nations' declaration regarding the ten rights of a child.

As mentioned previously, there are some "learning disabled" gifted children (Daniels, 1983). In the case of "disability", the basic approach and programming procedures are different. However, since motivation is again important, we still like to use some entertaining materials whenever appropriate. As a consequence, we rely heavily on high interest/low vocabulary programs such as the "Sea Wolf Mysteries", "Face-Off", "Men and Women Behind the Bright Lights", "Really Me", and other book-cassette packages put out by EMC Corporation (also available through Marvin Melnyk Associates). Another good series is the "Pacemakers" (Fearon-Pitman, available as "Pacesetters" from Children's Press). These excellent short novels are interesting even for adults, but the vocabulary is controlled at an intermediate level. Each book is accompanied by an exciting cassette. Of course, the kids often use the cassette as a crutch, and merely listen rather than read. To combat this tendency, the insidious cassette — after "hooking" the student — abruptly discontinues at an extremely exciting point at the end of the second chapter. If the pupil wants to discover how the story finishes up, he has to read the rest of it for himself. "Galaxy 5" (Fearon-Pitman), a series of four books about space, works on the same principle.

Finally, another program that we have found useful is "Our Mysterious Universe" (Pinmoney Press). This little kit contains short booklets on twenty interesting topics such as Atlantis, the Loch Ness Monster, Sasquatch, space, time travel, and so on. For each booklet, there are a number of very good interpretive questions to act as springboards for writing assignments.

In any case, there are a veritable host of solid programs of this nature. Even when a commercial package is not readily accessible, it is possible to take a hand in making material more relevant and exciting. Say, for example, the class is reading a book by a noted contemporary children's author. After discussing the story, the teacher can divide the students into groups and have them come up with a few good questions they would like to ask the author (for example, "Why did such and such happen at that particular time?", "Was there a double meaning in chapter three?", "What research was necessary in order to write the book?"). Then, for relatively modest rates, the Telephone System can bring a phone into the classroom and set up a conference call to the author. Most writers welcome the opportunity of speaking directly to their young readers, and the kids think it is great talking to the author of "their book". It makes things come alive.

In closing, it is important to remember that many gifted youngsters do have social-emotional or academic problems. Whatever the difficulty, there is a need to build up the confidence of low-functioning gifted students. When they gain in self-assurance, they are more likely to take risks and work to potential. If "personality" and "self-concept" problems are involved, specific programs or "talking things out" with someone may be beneficial. If the difficulties are more academic in nature, motivating high interest/low vocabulary materials might be one way to start "problem" gifted children on their way.

Summation

When theoretical concerns of etiology, identification, philosophy, and the like are all said and done, it is still necessary to develop differentiated programs for the gifted. In an effort to be concrete and practical, we have proposed a model focusing on six categories of enrichment. The first category, alternative learning environments, emphasizes enriching the curriculum through the use of field trips, special courses, community associates, independent research, travel, and student exchanges. In the second area, productive thought and problem solving, the focus is on ways and means to challenge bright children and get them solving problems and thinking systematically. Many approaches, including CoRT, are dealt with in some depth. Thirdly, throughout the section on creativity, the emphasis is on developing programs designed to make youngsters think creatively in a variety of areas. Special attention is given to language arts activities and to the actual setting up of creative programs in the schools. Fourthly, the questioning portion centres on divergent questioning and the stimulating approaches and techniques that are available in this regard. Classroom organization, the fifth section, shows how bright students can be challenged through independent investigative activities, small group activities, questions for the whole class, and through enriching general curriculum. And lastly, there is some discussion concerning ways and means of developing a positive self-image in our gifted pupils.

All in all, the approach is designed to give educators the theoretical and hands-on tools they need to meet the needs of their gifted children. And again, our more covert hope is that good things will happen for *all* students as educators move from teacher-directed to facilitator-guided to self-directed learning in each of the main areas highlighted in the model.

References

Adler, M., "Cycles of interest in the gifted student". *The Clearing House*, 1967, *41*, 476–478.

Albas, D.C., and C.M. Albas, *Student life and exams: Stresses and coping strategies*. Dubuque, Iowa: Kendall/Hunt, 1984.

Alexander, P.A., and J.A. Muia, *Gifted education: A comprehensive roadmap*. Gaithersburg, Maryland: Aspen Systems Corp., 1981.

Allen, R.V., and G.C. Halvorsen, *The language experience approach to reading instruction*. Boston: Ginn, 1961.

Ashley, R.M., *Activities for motivating and teaching bright children*. West Nyack, New York: Parker, 1973.

Ashton-Warner, S., *Teacher*. London: Secker and Warburg, 1963.

Baker, L.D., "Preparing school counsellors to work with exceptional students". *The School Guidance Worker*, 1976, *32*(1), 5–9.

Baldwin, A.Y., "Webbing: A technique for developing instructional activities for the gifted". *Roeper Review*, 1979, 26–31.

Baratta-Lorton, R., *Mathematics . . . A way of thinking*. Menlo Park, California: Addison-Wesley, 1977.

Barbe, W.B., Keynote Address. Winnipeg: Manitoba Elementary Teachers' Association, 1982.

Barbe, W.B., and J.S. Renzulli (eds.), *Psychology and education of the gifted*. New York: Meredith, 1975.

Birch, J.W., "Is any identification procedure necessary?" *Gifted Child Quarterly*, 1984, *28*, 157–161.

Bish, C., "The academically talented project: Gateway to the present". *Gifted Child Quarterly*, 1975, *19*(4), 282–289.

Bixler, H.H. (ed.), *The Cullowhee story: A program for superior and gifted students.* Cullowhee, North Carolina: Western Carolina College, 1962.

Bixler, H.H., C.D. Carter, and C.D. Killian, *Enriching the curriculum: A manual for teaching bright and gifted children.* Cullowhee, North Carolina: Western Carolina College, 1959.

Bleedorn, B.B., and D. Ferris, "Humor as an indicator of giftedness". *Proceedings: National Association for Gifted Children*, 1980, October–November, 4.

Bloom, B.S., *Taxonomy of education objectives. Handbook I: Cognitive Domain.* New York: David McKay Publishing, 1956.

Bloom, B.S., and L.J. Broder, "Problem-solving process of college students: An exploratory investigation". *Supplementary Educational Monographs*, 1950, *73*.

Borthwick, B., I. Dow, D. Lévesque, and R. Banks, *The gifted and talented students in Canada: Results of a CEA survey.* Toronto: CEA, 1980.

Boslough, J., "Challenging the brightest". *Psychology Today*, 1984, *18*, 28–33.

Bracy, A.W., "Computers in education: What the research shows". *Electronic Learning*, 1982, *2*, 51–55.

Brown, G.W., and J.S. Wolf, "Development of intuition in the gifted". *Journal for the Education of the Gifted*, 1986, *9*(2), 157–164.

Brown, S.H., P.L. Nichols, and W.A. Kennedy, *Preschool I.Q.: Prenatal and early developmental correlates.* Hillsdale, New Jersey: Lawrence Erlbaum Associates, 1975.

Brumbaugh, F.N., *Your gifted child: A guide for parents.* New York: Henry Holt, 1959.

Bruner, J.S., "Act of discovery". *Harvard Educational Review*, 1961, *31*, 21–32.

——. *The process of education.* Cambridge, Massachusetts: Harvard University Press, 1962.

——. "Man: A Course of Study". Occasional paper No. 3, Cambridge, Massachusetts: The Social Studies Curriculum Program, Educational Services, Inc., 1965.

Buros, O.K. (ed.), *The Eighth Mental Measurements Yearbook.* Highland Park, New Jersey: Gryphon Press, 1978.

Burroughs, M.C., *Restraints on excellence: Our waste of gifted children.* Hingham, Massachusetts: Teaching Resources, 1977.

Burt, C., "The inheritance of mental ability". *American Psychologist*, 1958, *13*(1), 1–15.

——. *The gifted child.* New York: John Wiley and Sons, 1975.

Burton, D.L., *Literature study in the high schools.* New York: Holt, Rinehart and Winston, 1960.

Callahan, C.M. *Developing creativity in the gifted and talented*. Reston, Virginia: Council for Exceptional Children, 1978.

Carlson, E.F., "Problems in educating the highly endowed". *Journal of Exceptional Children*, 1947, *13*, 201–204.

Carner, C.R., "Reaching troubled minds through reading". *Today's Health*, 1966, *44*, 32–34.

Carroll, J.L., and L.R. Laming, "Giftedness and creativity: Recent attempts at definition: A literature review". *Gifted Child Quarterly*, 1974, *18*, 85–96.

Christian, C., *Problem solving: Using your head creatively*. Pleasantville, New York: Human Relations Media, 1978.

Clark, C.A., *Brainstorming*. New York: Doubleday, 1958.

Clendening, C.P., and R.A. Davies, *Creating programs for the gifted: A guide for teachers, librarians, and students*. New York: Bowker Co., 1980.

Coffey, K., G. Ginsberg, C. Lockhart, D. McCartney, C. Nathan, and K. Wood, *Parentspeak on gifted and talented children*. Ventura, California: Ventura County Superintendent of Schools Office, 1976.

Cooperman, B., M. Fischle, and R. Hochstetter, *Teacher let me do it: Learning centers that grow*. Buffalo: D.O.K., 1976.

Cox, C.M., *Genetic studies of genius. Vol. II*. Stanford, California: Stanford University Press, 1926.

Daniels, P.R., *Teaching the gifted/learning disabled student*. Gaithersburg, Maryland: Aspen Systems Corp., 1983.

DeBoer, J.J., "Creative reading and the gifted student". *Reading Teacher*, 1963, *16*, 435–441.

de Bono, E., *The use of lateral thinking*. Harmondsworth, England: Penguin Books, 1967.

——.*The five-day course in thinking*. Harmondsworth: Penguin Books, 1968.

——.*The mechanism of mind*. Harmondsworth: Penguin Books, 1969.

——.*Lateral thinking: A textbook of creativity*. Harmondsworth: Penguin Books, 1970.

——.*Practical thinking*. Harmondsworth: Penguin Books, 1971.

——.*Children solve problems*. Harmondsworth: Penguin Books, 1972.

——."Skilled thought". *The Times Educational Supplement*, 1974, *24*, 5.

——.*Teaching thinking*. Harmondsworth: Penguin Books, 1976.

——. Interview, *Omni*, March, 1985, 74–76, 116, 118–120.

Delp, J.L. and R.A. Martinson, *The gifted and talented: A handbook for parents*. Ventura, California: Office of the Ventura County Superintendent of Schools, 1975.

Dennis, W., and M.W. Dennis (eds.), *The intellectually gifted: An overview*. New York: Grune and Stratton, 1976.

de Villiers, M., "Brains of burden". *Weekend Magazine*, Toronto Globe and Mail, January, 1977, *27*, 4–6.

Dewar, G., *Activities for language enrichment in grades four, five, and six.* Scarborough, Ontario: W.J. Gage, 1963.

Dunn, R., and K. Dunn, *Educator's self-teaching guide to individualizing instructional programs.* West Nyack, New York: Parker, 1975.

Eberle, B., and B. Stanish, *CPS for Kids: A resource book for teaching creative problem solving to children.* Buffalo, New York: D.O.K. Publishers, 1980.

Ehrlich, V.Z., *Gifted children: A guide for parents and teachers.* Englewood Cliffs, New Jersey: Prentice-Hall, 1982.

Erlenmeyer-Kimling, L., and L.F. Jarvik, "Genetics and intelligence: A review". *Science,* 1963, *142,* 1477–1479.

Feldhusen, J., General Session. Minneapolis: National Association for Gifted Children, 1980.

Feldhusen, J., and M.B. Kolloff, "A three-stage model for gifted education". *Education Digest,* January, 1979, 15–18.

Feldhusen, J., and D. Treffinger, *Creative thinking and problem solving in gifted education.* Dubuque, Iowa: Kendall/Hunt, 1980.

Feuerstein, R., *The dynamic assessment of retarded performers: The Learning Potential Assessment Device, theory, instruments, and techniques.* Baltimore: University Park Press, 1979.

———.*Instrumental Enrichment: An intervention program for cognitive modifiability.* Baltimore: University Park Press, 1980.

Feuerstein, R., and M.R. Jensen, "Instrumental Enrichment: Theoretical basis, goals, and instruments". *The Educational Forum,* May, 1980, 401–423.

Fitzgerald, E.J., I.S. Sato, W.P. Wilson, and P. Weaver (eds.), *Presentations at the First National Conference on the Disadvantaged Gifted.* Ventura, California: Ventura County Superintendent of Schools, 1975.

Freeman, J., *Gifted children: Their identification and development in a social context.* Baltimore: University Park Press, 1979.

Gallagher, J.J., *Teaching the gifted child.* Boston: Allyn and Bacon, 1975.

———.*Gifted children: Reaching their potential.* New York: Trillium Press, 1979.

Galton, F., *Hereditary genius: An inquiry into its laws and consequences.* New York: D. Appleton, 1870.

Gardner, J.W., *Excellence.* New York: Harper and Row, 1961.

Gardner, H., *Frames of mind: The theory of multiple intelligences.* New York: Basic Books, 1983.

———.PT Conversation: "The seven frames of mind". *Psychology Today,* June 1984, 20–26.

Goertzel, V., and M.G. Goertzel, *Cradles of eminence.* Boston: Little, Brown, and Co., 1962.

Gold, M.J., *Education of the intellectually gifted.* Columbus, Ohio: Charles E. Merrill, 1965.

Goldberg, M.L., "Recent research on the talented". *Teachers College Record*, 1958, *60*, 150–163.

Gowan, J.C., and C.B. Bruch, *The academically talented student and guidance.* Boston: Houghton Mifflin, 1971.

Gowan, J.C., and M. Olson, "The society which maximizes creativity". *The Journal of Creative Behavior*, 1979, *13*, 194–210.

Gowan, J.C., and E.P. Torrance (eds.), *Educating the ablest: A book of readings on the education of gifted children.* Itasca, Illinois: F.E. Peacock Publishers, 1971.

Grossman, R.P., "Stepping into the stream". *Elementary School Journal*, 1981, *14*, 487.

Grost, A. *Genius in residence.* Englewood Cliffs, New Jersey: Prentice-Hall, 1970.

Grube, G.M.A. (trans.), *Plato: The Republic.* Indianapolis: Hackett, 1974.

Guilford, J.P., *The nature of human intelligence.* New York: McGraw-Hill, 1967.

Hanley, J.P., D.K. Whitla, E.W. Moo, and A.S. Walter, *Curiosity, competence, community. Man: A course of study. An evaluation.* Cambridge, Massachusetts: Education Development Center, 1970.

Hauck, B.B., and M.F. Freehill, *The gifted — Case studies.* Dubuque, Iowa: Wm. C. Brown, 1972.

Henson II, F.O., *Mainstreaming the gifted.* Austin, Texas: Learning Concepts, 1976.

Hersom, N.L., A follow-up study of the high school performance of students who were members of the inaugural major work classes in Winnipeg. M.Ed. thesis, University of Manitoba, 1962.

Hessler, G.L., *Use and interpretation of the Woodcock-Johnson Psycho-Educational Battery.* Hingham, Massachusetts: Teaching Resources, 1982.

Hickok, D., and J.A. Smith, *Creative teaching of music in the elementary school.* Boston: Allyn and Bacon, 1974.

Hildreth, G.H., *Educating gifted children at Hunter College Elementary School.* New York: Harper and Brothers, 1952.

——. "Experience-related reading for school beginners". *Elementary English*, 1965, *42*, 280–297.

Hollingworth, L.S., *Gifted children: Their nature and nurture.* New York: Macmillan, 1929.

Horowitz, F.D., and L.Y. Paden, "The effectiveness of environmental intervention programs", in B.M. Caldwell and H.N. Ricciuti (eds.) *Review of child development research, Vol. III. Child development and social policy.* Chicago: University of Chicago Press, 1973.

Hunter, M., "Right-brained kids in left-brained schools". *Education Digest*, November/December 1976.

Hymes, R.M., and F.O. Bullock, "Alternative schools: Answer to the gifted child's boredom". *Gifted Child Quarterly*, 1975, *19*(4), 340–345.

Isaacs, A.F., "For gifted boys' and girls' personality growth and writing skills". *Gifted Child Quarterly*, 1968, *12*, 47–49.

——."Gifted children: Everybody needs them". *Gifted Child Quarterly*, 1972, *16*.

——."Creative reading can be a balance and an anchor in guiding the gifted", in M. Labuda (ed.) *Creative reading for gifted learners: A design for excellence.* Newark, Delaware: International Reading Association, 1974.

——."A bird's eye view of the gifted child movement". *Creative Child and Adult Quarterly*, 1977, *2*.

Jackson, D.M. (ed.), *Readings in foundations of gifted education.* Guilford, Connecticut: Special Learning Corp., 1980.

Jacobs, J.C., "Effectiveness of teacher and parent identification of gifted children as a function of school level". *Psychology in the Schools*, 1971, *8*, 140–142.

Janos, P.M., H.C. Fung, and N.M. Robinson, "Self-concept, self-esteem, and peer relations among gifted children who feel 'different' ". *Gifted Child Quarterly*, 1985, *29*, 78–82.

Jersild, A.T., *Child psychology.* Englewood Cliffs, New Jersey: Prentice-Hall, 1968.

Kaiser, C.F. and D.J. Berndt, "Predictors of lonliness in the gifted adolescent". *Gifted Child Quarterly*, 1985, *29*, 74–77.

Katz, E.L., "Microcomputers: A course of study for gifted students". *Focus on Exceptional Children*, 1983, *15*(6).

Kaplan, S.N., *Providing programs for the gifted and talented: A handbook.* Ventura, California: Office of the Ventura County Superintendent of Schools, 1974.

Kaufman, A.S. *Intelligent testing with the WISC-R.* New York: John Wiley and Sons, 1979.

Kaufmann, F., *Your child and you.* Reston, Virginia: Council for Exceptional Children, 1976.

Keating, D.P. (ed.), *Intellectual talent: Research and development.* Baltimore: Johns Hopkins University Press, 1976.

Kennedy, W.A., *Child psychology.* Englewood Cliffs, New Jersey: Prentice-Hall, 1971.

Khatena, J., *The creatively gifted child: Suggestions for parents and teachers.* New York: Vantage Press, 1978.

Kirk, S.A., *Educating exceptional children.* Boston: Houghton Mifflin, 1972.

Knight, L.N., *Language arts for the exceptional: The gifted and linguistically different.* Itasca, Illinois: Peacock, 1974.

Kramer, A.H. (ed.), *Gifted children: Challenging their potential.* New York: Trillium Press, 1981.

Liddle, G., "Overlap among desirable and undesirable characteristics in gifted children". *Journal of Educational Psychology*, 1958, *49*(4), 219–223.

Link, F.R., "Instrumental Enrichment: The classroom perspective". *The Educational Forum*, May 1980, 425–428.

Lyon, H.C., "Popular myths about the gifted". Address to TAG (The Association for the Gifted), Dallas: 1973.

——."The gifted and talented in the 1980's: A national report". *Program Proceedings: National Association for Gifted Children* (Twenty-Seventh Annual Convention). Minneapolis: National Association for Gifted Children, 1980.

Maier, N. (ed.), *Teaching the gifted, challenging the average.* Toronto: Guidance Centre, University of Toronto, 1982.

Maker, C.J., *Training teachers for the gifted and talented: A comparison of models.* Reston, Virginia: Council for Exceptional Children, 1975.

——.*Curriculum development for the gifted.* Gaithersburg, Maryland: Aspen Systems Corp., 1982.

Mallis, J., *Ideas for teaching gifted students.* Austin, Texas: Multi Media Arts, 1983.

Martinson, R.A., *Curriculum enrichment: For the gifted in the primary grades.* Englewood Cliffs, New Jersey: Prentice-Hall, 1968.

——.*The identification of the gifted and talented.* Ventura, California: Office of the Ventura County Superintendent of Schools, 1974.

——.*A guide toward better teaching for the gifted.* Ventura, California: Office of the Ventura County Superintendent of Schools, 1976.

Martinson, R.A., and J. Wiener, *The improvement of teaching procedures with gifted elementary and secondary school students.* Dominquez Hills: California State College, 1968.

McCluskey, K.W., "Problems of the educational psychologist". *Education Canada*, 1976, *16*, 12–17.

McCluskey, K.W., and P.A. Baker, "EDUCATIONAL psychologist or educational PSYCHOLOGIST". *Proceedings: National Association of School Psychologists*, 1982, 305–306.

McCluskey, K.W., R.R. Niemi, and D.C. Albas, "Vocal communication of emotional meaning among normal and disturbed children". *Journal of Special Education*, 1978, *12*, 443–449.

McCluskey, K.W., and K.D. Walker, *The Lord Selkirk Gifted Model.* Selkirk, Manitoba: Lord Selkirk School Division, 1983.

——. "Gifted output without pullout". Address, Council for Exceptional Children, Winnipeg, 1985.

McCracken, R.A. and M.J. McCracken, *Reading is only the tiger's tail: A language arts program.* San Rafael, California: Leswig Press, 1972.

Mead, M., "Be glad your child is different". *Parent's Magazine*, 1964, *39*, 70–71.

Meadow, A., S.J. Parnes, and H. Reese, "Influence of brainstorming instructions and problem sequence on a creative problem solving test". *Journal of Applied Psychology*, 1959, *43*, 413–416.

Meredith, P., and L. Landin, *100 Activities for gifted children.* Belmont, California: Fearon, 1957.

Mirman, N.J., "Teacher qualifications for educating the gifted". *Gifted Child Quarterly*, 1964, *8*, 123–126.

Moody, M.T., and H.K. Limper, *Bibliotherapy: Methods and materials*. Chicago: American Library Association, 1971.

Morgan, C.T., and R.A. King, *Introduction to psychology*. New York: McGraw-Hill, 1971.

Morrill, M.B. (ed.), *Gifted children: A special class conducted in the summer of 1958*. Cullowhee, North Carolina: Western Carolina College, 1959.

Murphy, N.C., "For the gifted there are other frustrations". *New York Times*, April 1976.

National Archives of the United States. *Federal Register*, 1976, *41*(89), 18660–18673.

Nazarro, J.N. (ed.), *Computer connections: For gifted children and youth*. Reston, Virginia: Council for Exceptional Children, 1981.

Nelson, J.B., and D.L. Cleland, "The role of the teacher of gifted and creative children", in P. Witty (ed.) *Reading for the gifted and the creative student*. Newark, Delaware: International Reading Association, 1971.

Newland, T.E., *The gifted in socioeducational perspective*. Englewood Cliffs, New Jersey: Prentice-Hall, 1976.

Nichols, R.C., "The national merit twin study", in S.G. Vandenberg (ed.) *Methods and goals in human behavior genetics*. New York: Academic Press, 1965.

Ogden, K., *Write on!* Winnipeg, Manitoba: Continuing Education Division, University of Manitoba, 1978.

Ogilvie, E., *Gifted children in primary schools*. London: Macmillan Education, 1973.

Olivero, J.L., and I.S. Sato, *PAB conference report and follow-up*. Ventura, California: Office of the Ventura County Superintendent of Schools, 1974.

Olofsson, U.K., *Museums and children*. Paris: UNESCO, 1979.

Pace, A., "Understanding and the ability to solve problems". *Arithmetic Teacher*, 1961, *8*, 226–233.

Parnes, S.J., *Programming creative behavior*. Buffalo: State University of New York at Buffalo, 1966.

———.*Creative behavior workbook*. New York: Charles Scribners Sons, 1967.

———."Guiding creative action". *Gifted Child Quarterly*, 1977, *21*, 460–472.

Parnes, S.J., and A. Meadow, "Effects of 'brainstorming' instructions on creative problem solving by trained and untrained subjects". *Journal of Educational Psychology*, 1959, *50*, 171–176.

Participants, National Student Symposium on the Education of the Gifted and Talented. *On being gifted*. New York: Walker and Co., 1978.

Passow, A.H. (ed.), *The gifted and the talented: Their education and development*. Chicago: The National Society for the Study of Education, 1979.

___."Instrumental Enrichment: Redeveloping cognitive structure". *The Educational Forum*, May 1980, 393–400.

Pegnato, C.W., An evaluation of various initial methods of selecting intellectually gifted children at the junior high level. Ed.D. dissertation, Pennsylvania State University, 1955.

Pegnato, C.W., and J.W. Birch, "Locating gifted children in junior high schools: A comparison of the methods". *Exceptional Children*, 1959, *25*(7), 300–304.

Perone, V., *The abuses of standardized testing*. Bloomington, Indiana: The Phi Delta Kappa Educational Foundation, 1977.

Pickard, P.M., *If you think your child is gifted*. Hamden, Connecticut: Linnet Books, 1976.

Piltz, A., and R. Sund, *Creative teaching of science in the elementary school*. Boston: Allyn and Bacon, 1974.

Polette, N., and M. Hamlin, *Exploring books with gifted children*. Littleton: Libraries Unlimited, 1980.

Rapp, M.A., "The brainstorming attitude". In J.C. Gowan and E.P. Torrance (eds.) *Creativity: Its educational implications*. New York: Wiley, 1967.

Renzulli, J.S., *New directions in creativity: Mark 1*. New York: Harper and Row, 1973.

___. *A guidebook for evaluating programs for the gifted/talented*. Ventura, California: Office of the Ventura County Superintendent of Schools, 1975.

___. *The Enrichment Triad Model: A guide for developing defensible programs for the gifted and talented*. Wethersfield, Connecticut: Creative Learning Press, 1977.

___."What makes giftedness: Reexamining a definition". *Phi Delta Kappan*, 1978, *60*(3), 180–184, 261.

___."What makes a problem real: Stalking the illusive meaning of qualitative differences in gifted education". *Gifted Child Quarterly*, 1982, *26*(4).

Renzulli, J.S. and R.K. Hartman, "Scale for rating behavioral characteristics of superior students". *Exceptional Children*, 1971, *38*, 243–248.

Reynolds, M.C. (ed.), *Early admission for mentally advanced children*. Washington, D.C.: The Council for Exceptional Children, 1962.

Rice, J.P., *Developing total talent*. Springfield, Illinois: Charles C. Thomas, 1970.

Ritson, J.E., and J.A. Smith, *Creative teaching of art in the elementary school*. Boston: Allyn and Bacon, 1975.

Roberts, J.A.F., *An introduction to medical genetics*. London: Oxford University Press, 1967.

Robinson, F., *Effective study*. New York: Harper and Row, 1970.

Rosenthal, R., and L. Jacobson, *Pygmalion in the classroom: Teacher expectation and pupil's intellectual development*. New York: Holt, Rinehart and Winston, 1968.

Ross, L., and B.M. Shore, "The McGill-PSBGM Gifted Summer School". *Special Education in Canada*, 1984, *58*, 133–134.

Rowlands, P., *Gifted children and their problems*. London: J.M. Dent and Sons, 1974.

Rudman, M.K., *Children's literature: An issues approach*. Lexington, Massachusetts: D.C. Heath, 1976.

Rutter, M., B. Maughan, P. Mortimore, and J. Ouston, *Fifteen thousand hours: Secondary schools and their effects on children*. Cambridge, Massachusetts: Harvard University Press, 1979.

Salvia, J., and J.E. Ysseldyke, *Assessment in special and remedial education*. Boston: Houghton Mifflin, 1985.

Sanders, N.M., *Classroom questions: What kinds?* New York: Harper and Row, 1966.

Sato, I.S., M. Birnbaum, and J.E. LoCicero, *Developing a written plan for the education of gifted and talented students*. Ventura, California: Office of the Ventura County Superintendent of Schools, 1974.

Scheifele, M., *The gifted child in the regular classroom*. New York: Teacher's College, Columbia University, 1953.

Schultheis, M., *A guidebook for bibliotherapy*. Glenview, Illinois: Psychotechnics, 1972.

Scott, J., "Don't make me walk when I want to fly: An open letter from a gifted child". *Instructor*, January 1977, 68–69, 71–72.

Scruggs, T.E., M.A. Mastropieri, C. Jorgensen, and J. Monson, "Effective mnemonic strategies for gifted learners". *Journal for the Education of the Gifted*, 1986, *9*(2), 105–121.

Sebasta, S., "Language arts programs for the gifted". *Gifted Child Quarterly*, 1976, *20*(1), 18–23.

Sellin, D.F., and J.W. Birch, *Educating gifted and talented learners*. Gaithersburg, Maryland: Aspen Systems Corp., 1980.

Shields, J., *Monozygotic twins, brought up apart and brought up together*. London: Oxford University Press, 1962.

Shore, B.M., F. Gagné, S. Larivée, R.H. Tali, and R.E. Tremblay (eds.), *Face to face with giftedness*. New York: Trillium Press, 1983.

Shorr, D.N., N.E. Jackson, and H.B. Robinson, "Achievement test performance of intellectually advanced preschool children". *Exceptional Children*, 1980, *46*, 646–648.

Silverman, L., "Giftedness", in E.L. Meyen (ed.) *Exceptional children in today's schools*. Denver: Love Publishing, 1982.

Simpson, D.J., "Half a loaf can be worse than none". *Special Education in Canada*, 1984, *58*(4), 120–121.

Sirkin, A., "Living with interdependence: The decades ahead in America". *The Futurist*, 1976, *10*, 4–15.

Sisk, D., *Teaching gifted children*. Columbia: South Carolina State Department of Education, 1976.

Skeels, H.M., "Adult status of children with contrasting early life experiences". *Monographs of the Society for Research in Child Development*, 1966, *31*(3), No. 105.

Skeels, H.M., and I.E. Harms, "Children with inferior social histories: Their mental development in adoptive homes". *Journal of Genetic Psychology*, 1948, *72*(2), 283–294.

Skodak, M., and H.M. Skeels, "A final follow-up study of one hundred adopted children". *Journal of Genetic Psychology*, 1949, *75*(1), 85–125.

Smith, J.A., *Creative teaching of social studies in the elementary school*. Boston: Allyn and Bacon, 1967a.

——. *Setting conditions for creative teaching in elementary school*. Boston: Allyn and Bacon, 1967b.

——. *Creative teaching of language arts in the elementary school*. Boston: Allyn and Bacon, 1973.

——. *Creative teaching of reading in the elementary school*. Boston: Allyn and Bacon, 1975.

Spredemann Dreyer, S., *The Bookfinder: A guide to children's literature about the needs and problems of youth aged 2–15*. Circle Pines, Minnesota: American Guidance Service, 1977.

Stallard, E., and K. Ingram, *RX for gifted: A manual of prescriptive education for gifted learners*. Ontario, California: Stallard Press, 1979.

Stanley, J.C., "Intellectual precocity". *Journal of Special Education*, 1975, *9*, 29–44.

——. "On educating the gifted". Boston: National Academy of Education, October 1979.

Stanley, J.C., W.C. George, and C.H. Solano (eds.), *The gifted and the creative: A fifty-year perspective*. Baltimore: Johns Hopkins University Press, 1977.

——. *Educational programs and intellectual prodigies*. Baltimore: Johns Hopkins University Press, 1978.

Stanley, J.C., D.P. Keating, and L.H. Fox (eds.), *Mathematical talent: Discovery, description, and development*. Baltimore: Johns Hopkins University Press, 1974.

Strang, R., "Mental hygiene of gifted children", in P. Witty (ed.) *The gifted child*. Boston: D.C. Heath, 1951.

——. "Psychology of gifted children and youth", in W.M. Cruickshank (ed.) *Psychology of exceptional children*. Englewood Cliffs, New Jersey: Prentice-Hall, 1955.

Sumption, M.R., and E.M. Luecking, *Education of the gifted*. New York: Ronald Press, 1960.

Swassing, R.H., "Gifted and talented children", in W.L. Heward and M.D. Orlansky (eds.) *Exceptional children: An introductory survey to special education*. Columbus, Ohio: Charles E. Merrill, 1980.

Syphers, D.F., *Gifted and talented children: Practical programming for teachers and principals*. Arlington, Virginia: Council for Exceptional Children, 1972.

Taba, H., *Thinking in elementary school children.* (U.S.O.E. Cooperative Research Project No. 1574). San Francisco: San Francisco State College, 1964.

——.*Teaching strategies and cognitive functioning in elementary school children.* (U.S.O.E. Cooperative Research Project No. 2404). San Francisco: San Francisco State College, 1966.

Tannenbaum, A.J., *Gifted children: Psychological and educational perspectives.* New York: Macmillan Publishing Co., 1983.

Taylor, C.W., "The multiple talent approach". *Instructor*, 1968, *77*, 27, 142, 144, 146.

——."Cultivating multiple creative talents in students". *Journal for the Education of the Gifted*, 1985, *8*, 187–198.

Taylor, I.A., and J.W. Getzels (eds.), *Perspectives in creativity.* Chicago: Aldine Press, 1975.

Telford, C.W., and J.M. Sawrey, *The exceptional individual.* Englewood Cliffs, New Jersey: Prentice-Hall, 1981.

Terman, L.M., *Genetic studies of genius. Vol. I. Mental and physical traits of a thousand gifted children.* Stanford, California: Stanford University Press, 1925.

Terman, L.M., and M.H. Oden, *Genetic studies of genius. Vol. IV. The gifted child grows up.* Stanford, California: Stanford University Press, 1947.

——. *Genetic studies of genius. Vol. V. The gifted group at midlife.* Stanford, California: Stanford University Press, 1959.

Thom, D.A., and N. Newell, "Hazards of high I.Q." *Mental Hygiene*, 1945, *29*, 61–77.

Tobias. P.V.. "I.Q. and the nature-nurture controversy". *Journal of Behavioral Science*, 1974, *2*, 5–24.

Torrance, E.P., "Current research on the nature of creative talent". *Journal of Counselling Psychology*, 1959, *6*, 309–316.

——.*Guiding creative talent.* Englewood Cliffs, New Jersey: Prentice-Hall, 1962.

——."Guidelines for creative teaching". *High School Journal*, 1965, 459–464.

——.*Torrance tests of creative thinking.* Princeton, New Jersey: Personnel Press, 1966.

——."Sociodrama as a creative problem-solving approach to studying the future". *Journal of Creative Behavior*, 1975, *9*(3), 182–195.

Torrance, E.P., J.P. Torrance, S.J. Williams, and R. Horng, *Handbook for training future problem solving teams.* Athens, Georgia: University of Georgia, 1979.

Trammel, J.P., *Gifted child education: Program continuity needed.* Research Report No. 115. Frankfort, Kentucky: Legislative Research Commission, 1975.

Treffinger, D., "Teaching for self-directed learning: A priority for the gifted and talented". *Gifted Child Quarterly*, 1975, *19*, 46–59.

——.*Encouraging creative learning for the gifted and talented.* Ventura, California: Ventura County Schools, LTI Publications, 1979.

___."Gifted students, regular classrooms: Sixty ingredients for a better blend". *Elementary School Journal*, January 1982, 267–272.

Trezise, R.L., "Are the gifted coming back?" *Phi Delta Kappan*, June 1973.

___."The gifted child: Back in the limelight". *Phi Delta Kappan*, November 1976, 241–243.

Vernon, P.E., *Intelligence and cultural environment*. London: Methuen, 1965.

___.(ed.) *Creativity*. Baltimore: Penguin Books, 1970.

Vernon, P.E., G. Adamson, and D.F. Vernon, *The psychology of gifted children*. Boulder, Colorado: Westview Press, 1977.

Walker, K.D., The N.R.L. (Newspaper Reading Lab). Manuscript, Lord Selkirk School Division #11, 1974.

Walker, K.D. and K.W. McCluskey, *Giftedness: An annotated bibliography*. Selkirk, Manitoba: Human Resource Centre, 1985.

___."Gifted education: A rural service delivery model". *Proceedings: Fourth World Conference on Gifted and Talented Children*, August 1981, 33–34, (a).

___."The Human Resource Centre: How to look beyond the laminator". *Education Canada*, 1981, *21*, 33–37, (b).

Walton, G., "Identification of intellectually gifted children in the public school kindergarten". Doctoral dissertation, University of California, 1961.

Ward, V.S., *Educating the gifted*. Columbus, Ohio: Charles E. Merrill, 1961.

Weber, P., *Promote: Guide to independent study*. Buffalo: D.O.K., 1977.

Weir, J.R., Quoted in "Exceptionally exceptional". *Time*, 1956, *67*, 38.

Wellman, B.L., "Our changing concept of intelligence". *Journal of Consulting Psychology*, 1939, *2*(4), 97–106.

Westcott, A.M. and J.A. Smith, *Creative teaching of mathematics in the elementary school*. Boston: Allyn and Bacon, 1967.

Whipple, F.H., "Memorial High School's advanced placement program". *Bulletin of the National Association of Secondary-School Principals*, 1958, *42*, 24–26.

Whitmore, J.R., *Giftedness, conflict, and underachievement*. Boston: Allyn and Bacon, 1980.

Williams, C.W., "Characteristics and objectives of a program for the gifted". *In Education for the gifted. Fifty-Seventh Yearbook of the National Society for the Study of Education, Part 2*. Chicago: University of Chicago Press, 1958.

Willings, D., *The creatively gifted*. Cambridge, Great Britain: Woodhead-Faulkner, 1980.

Wilson, F.T., "Some special ability test scores of gifted children". *Journal of Genetic Psychology*, 1953, *82*(1), 59–68.

Witty, P.A., "Education programs for the gifted". *School and Society*, 1959, *87*, 167.

___."Rationale for fostering creative reading in the gifted and the creative", in M. Labuda (ed.) *Creative reading for gifted learners: A design for excellence*. Newark, Delaware: International Reading Association, 1974.

Witty, P.A., and S.W. Bloom, "The education of the superior high school student". *Bulletin of the National Association of Secondary-School Principals*, 1955, *34*, 15–22.

Wolf, J., and J. Gygi, "Learning disabled and gifted: Success or failure". *Journal for the Education of the Gifted*, 1981, *4*, 199–206.

Wood, E., "Gifted and talented: Another role for the resource teacher". *MART (Manitoba Association of Resource Teachers) Newsletter*, 1983.

Wooster, J.S., *What to do with the gifted few: A handbook of strategies for differentiating instruction for gifted/talented students*. Buffalo, New York: D.O.K., 1978.

Zigmond, N., A. Vallecorsa, and R. Silverman, *Assessment for instructional planning in special education*. Englewood Cliffs, New Jersey: Prentice-Hall, 1983.

Ziv, A., "Guidance for the gifted". *The School Guidance Worker*, 1976, *32*(1), 45–47.

___. *Counselling the intellectually gifted child*. Toronto: University of Toronto, 1977.

Name Index

Adamson, G. 8
Adler, M. 16
Albas, C.A. 158
Albas, D.C. 82, 158
Alexander, P.A. 121
Allan, L.E. 135
Allen, R.V. 142
Archimedes 77, 123
Ashley, R.M. 106
Ashton-Warner, S. 142

Baker, L.D. 139
Baker, P.A. 26, 34, 140, 147
Baldwin, A.Y. 163
Balikci, A. 166
Banks, R. 112
Baratta-Lorton, R. 133
Barbe, W.B. 8, 75
Belcher, T.L. 154
Berndt, D.J. 13
Birch, J.W. 21, 34, 36, 121
Birnbaum, M. 101
Bish, C. 51
Bixler, H.H. 51

Bleedorn, B.B. 41
Bloom, B.S. 106, 121, 122, 125, 127
Bloom, S.W. 17
Borthwick, B. 112
Boslough, J. 59
Bracy, A.W. 137
Broatch, S. 65
Broder, L.J. 122
Brown, J.W. 139
Brown, S.H. 7
Bruch, C.B. 26, 139
Brumbaugh, F.N. 86
Bruner, J.S. 106, 123, 166
Bullock, F.O. 15
Buros, O.K. 34
Burroughs, M.C. 4, 13
Burt, C. 8, 9
Burton, D.L. 141

Callahan, C.M. 106
Carlson, E.F. 10
Carner, C.R. 170
Carroll, J.L. 6
Carter, C.D. 51

Chapin, H. 84
Charlemagne 49, 72
Christian, C. 106
Clark, C.A. 163
Cleland, D.L. 78
Clendening, C.P. 106
Coffey, K. 86
Cooperman, B. 158
Cox, C.M. 5

Daniels, P.R. 133, 171
Davies, R.A. 106
DeBoer, J.J. 141
de Bono, E. 41, 71, 123, 131, 132, 133, 138, 141, 153
Delp, J.L. 52, 86
Dennis, M.W. 8
Dennis, W. 8
de Villiers, M. 55
DeVore, I. 166, 167
Dewar, G. 142
Dow, I. 112
Dunn, K. 157
Dunn, R. 157

Eberle, B. 128
Ehrlich, V.Z. 86
Erlenmeyer-Kimling, L. 9

Farb, P. 135
Feldhusen, J. 66, 106, 157
Ferris, D. 41
Feuerstein, R. 26, 27, 31, 129, 130
Fischle, M. 158
Fitzgerald, E.J. 13
Fox, L.H. 54
Freehill, M.F. 7, 10, 21, 61
Freeman, J. 8, 106
Fung, H.C. 13

Gagné, F. 106
Gallagher, J.J. 8, 52, 106
Galton, F. 8
Gardner, H. 26
Gardner, J.W. 53
George, W.C. 8
Getzels, J.W. 8
Ginsberg, G. 86

Goertzel, M.G. 8
Goertzel, V. 8
Gold, M.J. 2
Goldberg, M.L. 6, 17
Gowan, J.C. ·8, 26, 53, 106, 139
Grossman, R.P. 68
Grost, A. 83
Grube, G.M.A. 49
Guilford, J.P. 27, 106, 121, 123
Gygi, J. 13

Halvorsen, G.C. 142
Hamlin, M. 153
Hanley, J.P. 165
Harmin, M. 153
Harms, I.E. 9
Hartman, R.K. 37
Hauck, B.B. 7, 10, 21, 61
Henson II, F.O. 49, 67
Hersom, N.L. 2, 13, 16, 65
Hessler, G.L. 35
Hickok, D. 140
Hildreth, G.H. 51, 142
Hochstetter, R. 158
Hollingworth, L.S. 8
Horng, R. 106
Horowitz, F.D. 8
Hunter, M. 26
Hymes, R.M. 15

Ingram, K. 121
Isaacs, A.F. 106, 141

Jackson, D.M. 106
Jackson, N.E. 30
Jacobs, J.C. 45
Jacobson, L. 47
Janos, P.M. 13
Jarvik, L.F. 9
Jensen, M.R. 130
Jersild, A.T. 9
Jorgensen, C. 128

Kaiser, C.F. 13
Kaplan, S.N. 47, 52, 157
Katz, E.L. 137
Kaufman, A.S. 27
Kaufmann, F. 86

Keating, D.P. 8, 54
Kennedy, W.A. 7, 8, 9
Khatena, J. 8
Killian, C.D. 51
King, R.A. 5
Kirk, S.A. 49, 51
Knight, L.N. 144
Kolloff, M.B. 106
Kramer, A.H. 106

Laming, L.R. 6
Landin, L. 106
Larivée, S. 106
Lévesque, D. 112
Liddle, G. 26
Limper, H.K. 170
Link, F.R. 130
LoCicero, J.E. 101
Lockhart, C. 86
Luecking, E.M. 50
Lyon, H.C. 7, 22, 23, 51

Maier, N. 106
Maker, C.J. 8, 78, 80, 105, 106
Mallis, J. 112
Martinson, R.A. 22, 28, 36, 37, 39, 45,
    52, 78, 80, 83, 86, 106
Mastropieri, M.A. 128
Maugham, S. 141
Maughan, B. 85
McCartney, D. 86
McCluskey, K.W. 4, 8, 16, 26, 34, 67,
    82, 93, 96, 102, 145
McCracken, M.J. 142
McCracken, R.A. 142
Mead, M. 81
Meadow, A. 163
Meredith, P. 106
Milam, B. 152, 153
Mindell, P. 144
Mirman, N.J. 78
Monson, J. 128
Moo, E.W. 165
Moody, M.T. 170
Morgan, C.T. 5
Morrill, M.B. 51
Mortimore, P. 85
Muia, J.A. 121
Murphy, N.C. 69

Nathan, C. 86
Nazarro, J.N. 137
Nelson, J.B. 78
Newell, N. 13
Newland, T.E. 8
Nichols, P.L. 7
Nichols, R.C. 9
Niemi, R.R. 82

Oden, M.H. 5, 10
Ogden, K. 144
Ogilvie, E. 106
Olivero, J.L. 52
Olofsson, U.K. 112
Olson, M. 106
Ouston, J. 85

Pace, A. 121
Paden, L.Y. 8
Parnes, S.J. 106, 140, 153, 163
Passow, A.H. 8, 106, 130, 141
Pegnato, C.W. 21, 25, 36
Perone, V. 26
Pickard, P.M. 86
Piltz, A. 140
Plato 49, 72
Polette, N. 141

Rapp, M.A. 163
Reese, H. 163
Renzulli, J.S. 8, 37, 52, 72, 105, 106,
    116, 123, 130, 141, 160, 161, 169
Reynolds, M.C. 56
Rice, J.P. 2
Ritson, J.E. 140
Roberts, J.A.F. 9
Robinson, F. 158
Robinson, H.B. 30
Robinson, N.M. 13
Rosenthal, R. 47, 82
Ross, L. 112
Rowlands, P. 13
Rudman, M.K. 170
Rutter, M. 85
Salvia, J. 26, 34, 101
Sanders, N.M. 151
Sato, I.S. 2, 3, 13, 23, 52, 101
Sawrey, J.M. 106
Scheifele, M. 51

Schultheis, M. 170
Scott, J. 55, 83
Scruggs, T.E. 128
Seagoe, M.V. 10
Sebasta, S. 141
Sellin, D.F. 121
Shields, J. 9
Shore, B.M. 106, 112
Shorr, D.N. 30
Silverman, L. 106
Silverman, R. 101
Simpson, D.J. 157
Sirkin, A. 62
Sisk, D. 106
Skeels, H.M. 9, 10
Skodak, M. 9, 10
Smith, J.A. 140
Solano, C.H. 8
Spredemann Dreyer, S. 171
Stallard, E. 121
Stanish, B. 128
Stanley, J.C. 8, 54, 66, 112, 133
Stracher, D. 144
Strang, R. 9, 10, 45
Suleiman the Magnificient 49, 50, 72
Sumption, M.R. 50
Sund, R. 140
Swassing, R.H. 106
Syphers, D.F. 9, 10, 16, 53

Tali, R.H. 106
Tannenbaum, A.J. 8, 106
Taylor, C.W. 3
Taylor, I.A. 8
Taylor, R. 153
Telford, C.W. 106
Terman, L.M. 5, 7, 10
Thom, D.A. 13
Tobias, P.V. 8
Torrance, E.P. 8, 28, 53, 79, 106, 121, 140

Torrance, J.P. 106
Trammell, J.P. 52
Treffinger, D. 67, 106, 157, 158
Tremblay, R.E. 106
Trezise, R.L. 51, 52, 59

Vallecorsa, A. 101
Vernon, D.F. 8
Vernon, P.E. 8, 26

Walker, K.D. 4, 8, 67, 93, 96, 102, 145, 146
Walter, A.S. 165
Walton, G. 21, 36
Ward, V.S. 47
Weaver, P. 13
Weber, K. 125
Weber, P. 158
Weir, J.R. 16
Wellman, B.L. 9
Westcott, A.M. 140
Whipple, F.H. 2
Whitla, D.K. 165
Whitmore, J.R. 8, 13
Wiener, J. 80
Williams, C.W. 47
Williams, S.J. 106
Willings, D. 106
Wilson, F.T. 26
Wilson, W.P. 13
Witty, P.A. 2, 17, 141
Wolf, J. 13
Wolf, J.S. 139
Wood, E. 96, 158
Wood, K. 86
Wooster, J.S. 157, 158

Ysseldyke, J.E. 26, 34, 101

Zigmond, N. 101
Ziv, A. 139

Subject Index

Ability grouping 57–58
Acceleration 54–55
Achievement tests 29–30

Bibliotherapy 170–171
Black Intelligence Test of Cultural
    Homogeneity 27
Boredom 15
Brainstorming 163

Center for Humanities kits 116, 144, 159,
    160, 161
Characteristics 4–8
Community associates 114–115
Computers 137–139
Creative problem solving 106
Creativity tests 28–29
– Southern California Tests of Divergent
    Production 28
– Tests of Creative Thinking 28, 35
Curriculum Associates workbooks 116, 161

Definition 1–4
Divergent questions 151–153

Early entrance 55–57
Enrichment Mini-Course Program 112–114
Enrichment Triad Model 105, 106

Field trips 111
Futuristics 152

HitsPak 41, 140
Humour 41, 81–82

Identification 21–46
– parent nomination 45–46
– peer nomination 44
– self-nomination 45
– teacher nomination 36–37
– testing 24–36
– work products 37
Identification Checklist and Referral
    Form 38–39
Independent investigative activities 115–116,
    158–162
Intelligence testing 24–28
– group 24
– individual 25

Interest-A-Lyzer 116
Integration 67–71
– advantages for teachers and
   children 67–68
– built-in safety factor 69–71
– longevity 68–69
– program ownership 68

Junior Great Books Program 72, 142,
   155–157, 163
Junior Parliament 145–146

Keenora Project 116–118

Language arts 141–145
Learning 106–109
– facilitator guided 82–83, 106–109
– self-directed 106–109
– teacher-directed 106–109
Learning Potential Assessment Device 27
Leiter International Performance Scale 27

Man: A Course of Study 71, 119, 165–169
Math enrichment 133–139
– Cuisenaire Rods 134
– Instructional Gaming Program 135–137
– Problem Solving Kit 134–135
– Techniques of Problem Solving 134
McCluskey–Walker Integrated Gifted
   Model 107–110
Museum education 111–112

Nature-nurture controversy 8–11
Newspaper Reading Lab 146–147
Nonverbal Test of Cognitive Skills 27

Parental involvement 86–91
– home-school communication 87
Partial pullout 71–72
People Projects 153, 163
Problem-solving programs 124–132
– CoRT 71, 124, 131–133, 154, 163, 165,
   173
– Instrumental Enrichment 129–130
– others 127–129
– simulation games 129

– The Productive Thinking Program 130–
   131, 163, 165
– Thinking Boxes 124–125
– Thinklabs 125–126
– Think Tank 126–127
– Triad Prototype Series 130

Research 158–162
Revolving Door Model 72, 160

Scale for Rating Behavioral Characteristics
   of Superior Students 37
School-based gifted programs 95–103
– school gifted committees 102–103
Segregation 59–66
– elitism 62–64
– pressure 60–61
– social-emotional factors 64–66
Self-image 169–170
Small group activities and
   investigations 162–163
Spiralling Curriculum 106
SRA Research Lab 116, 162
Stanford-Binet Intelligence Scale 5, 7, 25,
   26, 28, 35, 46
Structure of the Intellect Model 27–29, 106

Taxonomy of Educational Objectives 106,
   125, 127
Teachers of the gifted 78–86
Teaching Strategies Program 106
Theatre 140–141
Thinking and problem solving 121–124
Three-Stage Model 106
Travel and student exchange 118–120
Type I, II, and III Activities 105

Webbing 163–165
Wechsler Intelligence Scale for Children -
   Revised 15, 25, 26, 28, 32–35, 46
– performance tests 26
– verbal tests 26
Woodcock-Johnson Psycho-Educational
   Battery 35
Work experiences 115